THE APOCRYPHAL DIALOGUES

The Disputed Dialogues of Plato

The Complete Works of Plato
Volume 4

PLATO

Translated by
BENJAMIN JOWETT

Translated by
GEORGE BURGES

Cover by: Filibook Covers

Published by: Fili Public

Filibooks ApS

info@filibooks.com

CVR: 37100161

Original works by Plato, Benjamin Jowett, and George Burges are in the public domain

Paperback ISBN: 978-87-93494-69-5
Ebook ISBN: 978-87-93494-70-1

Contents

Book VIII

Book IX

List of Works

LIST OF THE COMPLETE WORKS OF PLATO - VOLUME 1-4

Alphabetized List

ALPHABETIZED LIST OF THE COMPLETE WORKS OF PLATO - VOLUME 1-4

1. Alcibiades I - Book VIII - Volume 4
2. Alcibiades II - Book VIII - Volume 4
3. Apology - Book I - Volume 1
4. Charmides, or Temperance - Book I - Volume 1
5. Clitopho - Book IX - Volume 4
6. Cratylus - Book III - Volume 2
7. Critias - Book VII - Volume 3
8. Crito - Book I - Volume 1
9. Epistles / Seventh Letter - Book IX - Volume 4
10. Erastai, or Lovers - Book IX - Volume 4
11. Eryxias - Book VIII - Volume 4
12. Euthydemus - Book II - Volume 1
13. Euthyphro - Book I - Volume 1
14. Gorgias - Book II - Volume 1
15. Greater Hippias - Book VIII - Volume 4
16. Hipparchus - Book IX - Volume 4
17. Ion - Book I - Volume 1
18. Laches, or Courage - Book I - Volume 1
19. Laws - Book VII - Volume 3
20. Lesser Hippias - Book VIII - Volume 4

The Dramatic Order

THE DRAMATIC ORDER OF THE COMPLETE WORKS OF PLATO - VOLUME 1-4

1. 460-450 BCE: Laws - Book VII - Volume 3
2. 460-450 BCE: The Epinomis, or the Philosopher - Book IX - Volume 4
3. 450 BCE: Parmenides - Book V - Volume 3
4. ~434 BCE: Protagoras - Book II - Volume 1
5. 432 BCE: Alcibiades I - Book VIII - Volume 4
6. 429 BCE: Charmides, or Temperance - Book I - Volume 1
7. 429 BCE: Republic - Book IV - Volume 2
8. 429 BCE: Timaeus - Book VI - Volume 3
9. 429 BCE: Critias - Book VII - Volume 3
10. ~429 BCE: Minos - Book IX - Volume 4
11. ~424 BCE: Laches, or Courage - Book I - Volume 1
12. ~421 BCE: Lysis, or Friendship - Book I - Volume 1
13. ~420 BCE: Greater Hippias - Book VIII - Volume 4
14. ~420 BCE: Lesser Hippias - Book VIII - Volume 4
15. ~420 BCE: Eryxias - Book VIII - Volume 4
16. 416 BCE: Symposium - Book III - Volume 2
17. 415 BCE: Hipparchus - Book IX - Volume 4
18. 414 BCE: Ion - Book I - Volume 1

19. 412/ 411 BCE: Euthydemus - Book II - Volume 1
20. 412/ 411 BCE: Erastai, or Lovers - Book IX - Volume 4
21. 412/ 411 BCE: Clitopho - Book IX - Volume 4
22. 409/ 408 BCE: Theages - Book IX - Volume 4
23. 407/ 406 BCE: Alcibiades II - Book VIII - Volume 4
24. 405 BCE: Gorgias - Book II - Volume 1
25. ~404 BCE: Phaedrus - Book IV - Volume 2
26. 402 BCE: Meno - Book III - Volume 2
27. ~401 BCE: Menexenus - Book VIII - Volume 4
28. 399 BCE: Theaetetus - Book V - Volume 3
29. 399 BCE: Euthyphro - Book I - Volume 1
30. 399 BCE: Cratylus - Book III - Volume 2
31. 399 BCE: Sophist - Book VI - Volume 3
32. 399 BCE: Statesman - Book VI - Volume 3
33. 399 BCE: Apology - Book I - Volume 1
34. 399 BCE: Philebus - Book VII - Volume 3
35. 399 BCE: Crito - Book I - Volume 1
36. 399 BCE: Phaedo - Book III - Volume 2
37. 360 BCE: Epistles / Seventh Letter - Book IX -
    Volume 4

Preface

In the study of history, and indeed of philosophy, there lingers a shadow world, a frontier of sorts, where the surefooted paths of established knowledge give way to territories less mapped, less known. Such is the realm we explore in the fourth volume of this series, "The Apocryphal Dialogues."

The texts assembled here, ranging from "Alcibiades I" to the philosophical notes found in the "Epinomis," stand apart from the acknowledged canon of Plato's works. They represent a different kind of inquiry, one that ventures into the margins of authenticity and the boundaries of authorship.

These dialogues are often enigmatic, elusive, and even controversial. Scholars and historians have wrestled with questions of their origin and their place within the Platonic oeuvre. Yet, within their folds, they reveal glimpses of ideas and insights that echo the grand themes of Plato, albeit sometimes faintly, sometimes with a curious twist.

There is a quality of the unknown in these texts, a sense of standing at the threshold of something tantalizingly out of reach. Whether engaging with the ethical considerations in "Greater Hippias" or the political overtones of "Minos," we find ourselves in a terrain that is both familiar and foreign, guided by a voice that may or may not be Plato's.

The very apocryphal nature of these dialogues grants them a distinct significance. They allow us to probe deeper, to question, to reflect on the nature of authorship and the evolution of ideas. They remind us that philosophy is not a stagnant pool but a living stream, fed by many tributaries, some clear and some obscure.

Crafting this volume has been both a challenge and a revelation. These texts, shrouded in uncertainty, demand from us a unique sensitivity, a willingness to engage without preconceived notions. The process has been less about defining and more about discovering, less about certainty and more about contemplation.

In "The Apocryphal Dialogues," you are invited not just to read but to explore, to journey into the less-trodden paths of philosophical inquiry. May you find in these texts not just questions and answers but a renewed appreciation for the richness and complexity of philosophical thought.

For the philosopher, as for the historian, the shadows and the margins are not mere voids but spaces teeming with possibility. In them lies a reminder that the quest for knowledge is never complete, that there are always new horizons, new questions, new paths to be forged.

Here, in this volume, is a testament to the unending journey of the mind, a tribute to the insatiable curiosity that propels us ever forward in our pursuit of wisdom.

Introduction

The works gathered in this fourth volume, "The Apocryphal Dialogues," are enveloped in a shroud of uncertainty and debate concerning their authorship. While traditionally attributed to Plato, these dialogues have been subject to rigorous scrutiny by scholars, and many have questioned whether they were penned by the philosopher himself or his followers. Below is a brief overview of each dialogue, along with a note on the level of dispute regarding its authorship:

- **Alcibiades I** - A dialogue exploring the theme of self-knowledge and political leadership, featuring Alcibiades and Socrates. *(Authorship: Highly disputed)*
- **Alcibiades II** - A work focusing on prayer and piety, less sophisticated than its predecessor. *(Authorship: Widely considered spurious)*
- **Lesser Hippias** - Engaging with themes of inconsistency and contradiction, this dialogue has elicited controversy over its authenticity. *(Authorship: Moderately disputed)*

- **Greater Hippias** - A complex discussion on the concept of beauty, questioning its relative and absolute nature. *(Authorship: Moderately disputed)*
- **Eryxias** - A lesser-known work discussing the nature of wealth, it is one of the most questionable in terms of authorship. *(Authorship: Generally considered spurious)*
- **Menexenus** - A satirical dialogue that parodies the Athenian custom of funeral oration. *(Authorship: Some dispute)*
- **The Epinomis, or the Philosopher** - Often seen as an appendix to "Laws," this dialogue delves into the role of philosophy in education. *(Authorship: Highly disputed)*
- **Theages** - Exploring the desire for wisdom, this work has been the subject of much debate among scholars. *(Authorship: Widely considered spurious)*
- **Erastai, or Lovers** - A dialogue often omitted from collections, its authorship is highly contentious. *(Authorship: Generally considered spurious)*
- **Hipparchus** - Named after the tyrant Hipparchus, this work focuses on the love of gain. *(Authorship: Highly disputed)*
- **Minos** - An exploration of law that has been subject to scrutiny due to its style and content. *(Authorship: Widely considered spurious)*
- **Clitopho** - A short dialogue discussing the inadequacy of Socratic philosophy. *(Authorship: Some dispute)*
- **Epistles / Seventh Letter** - A collection of letters, the Seventh being the most famous, discussing Plato's philosophy and personal matters. *(Authorship: Highly disputed, especially regarding the Seventh Letter)*

This volume provides readers with a chance to explore the fringe of the Platonic corpus, engaging with works that challenge our understanding of Plato and his philosophical inheritance. The dialogues within "The Apocryphal Dialogues" allow us to question and explore the nature of authorship and the transmission of philosophical thought. By including them in this collection, we recognize the rich tapestry of ideas and influences that have shaped the Western philosophical tradition. The reader is invited to approach these works with an open mind, embracing the complexity and nuance that make them an essential part of the study of Plato's philosophy.

Book VIII

Alcibiades I

Persons of the Dialogue: Alcibiades; Socrates.

SOCRATES: I DARE SAY THAT YOU MAY BE SURPRISED TO FIND, O SON of Cleinias, that I, who am your first lover, not having spoken to you for many years, when the rest of the world were wearying you with their attentions, am the last of your lovers who still speaks to you. The cause of my silence has been that I was hindered by a power more than human, of which I will some day explain to you the nature; this impediment has now been removed; I therefore here present myself before you, and I greatly hope that no similar hindrance will again occur. Meanwhile, I have observed that your pride has been too much for the pride of your admirers; they were numerous and high-spirited, but they have all run away, overpowered by your superior force of character; not one of them remains. And I want you to understand the reason why you have been too much for them. You think that you have no need of them or of any other man, for you have great possessions and lack nothing, beginning with the body, and ending with the soul. In the first place, you say to yourself that you are the fairest and tallest of the citizens, and this every one who has eyes may see to be true; in the second place, that you are among the noblest of them, highly connected both on the father's and the mother's side, and sprung from one of the most distinguished families in your own state, which is the greatest in Hellas, and having many friends and kinsmen of the best sort, who can assist you when in need; and there is one potent relative, who is more to you than all the rest, Pericles the son of Xanthippus, whom your father left guardian of you, and of your brother, and who can do as he pleases not only in this city, but in all Hellas, and among many and mighty barbarous nations. Moreover, you are rich; but I must say that you value yourself least of all upon your possessions. And all these things have lifted you up; you have overcome your lovers, and they have acknowledged that you were too much for them. Have you not remarked their absence? And now I know that you wonder why I, unlike the rest of them, have not gone away, and what can be my motive in remaining.

Alcibiades: Perhaps, Socrates, you are not aware that I was just going to ask you the very same question—What do you want? And what is your motive in annoying me, and always, wherever I am, making a point of coming? (Compare Symp.) I do really wonder what you mean, and should greatly like to know.

Socrates: Then if, as you say, you desire to know, I suppose that you will be willing to hear, and I may consider myself to be speaking to an auditor who will remain, and will not run away?

Alcibiades: Certainly, let me hear.

Socrates: You had better be careful, for I may very likely be as unwilling to end as I have hitherto been to begin.

Alcibiades: Proceed, my good man, and I will listen.

Socrates: I will proceed; and, although no lover likes to speak with one who has no feeling of love in him (compare Symp.), I will make an effort, and tell you what I meant: My love, Alcibiades, which I hardly like to confess, would long ago have passed away, as I flatter myself, if I saw you loving your good things, or thinking that you ought to pass life in the enjoyment of them. But I shall reveal other thoughts of yours, which you keep to yourself; whereby you will know that I have always had my eye on you. Suppose that at this moment some God came to you and said: Alcibiades, will you live as you are, or die in an instant if you are forbidden to make any further acquisition?—I verily believe that you would choose death. And I will tell you the hope in which you are at present living: Before many days have elapsed, you think that you will come before the Athenian assembly, and will prove to them that you are more worthy of honour than Pericles, or any other man that ever lived, and having proved this, you will have the greatest power in the state. When you have gained the greatest power among us, you will go on to other Hellenic states, and not only to Hellenes, but to all the barbarians who inhabit the same continent with us. And if the God were then to say to you again: Here in Europe is to be your seat of empire, and you must not cross over into Asia or meddle with Asiatic affairs, I do not believe that you would choose to live upon these terms; but the world, as I may say, must be filled with your power and name—no man less than Cyrus and Xerxes is of any account with you. Such I know to be your hopes—I am not guessing only—and very likely you, who know that I am speaking the truth, will reply, Well, Socrates, but what have my hopes to do with the explanation which you promised of your unwillingness to leave me? And that is what I am now going to tell you, sweet son of Cleinias and Dinomache. The explanation is, that all these designs of yours cannot be accomplished by you without my help; so great is the power which I believe myself to have over you and your concerns; and this I conceive to be the reason why the God has hitherto forbidden me to converse with you, and I have been long expecting his permission. For, as you hope to prove your own great value to the state, and having proved it, to attain at once to absolute power, so do I indulge a hope that I shall be the supreme power over you, if I am able to prove my own great value to you, and to show you that neither guardian, nor kinsman, nor any one is able to deliver into your hands the power which you desire, but I only, God being my helper. When you were young (compare Symp.) and your hopes were not yet matured, I should have wasted my time, and therefore, as I conceive, the God forbade me to converse with you;

but now, having his permission, I will speak, for now you will listen to me.

Alcibiades: Your silence, Socrates, was always a surprise to me. I never could understand why you followed me about, and now that you have begun to speak again, I am still more amazed. Whether I think all this or not, is a matter about which you seem to have already made up your mind, and therefore my denial will have no effect upon you. But granting, if I must, that you have perfectly divined my purposes, why is your assistance necessary to the attainment of them? Can you tell me why?

Socrates: You want to know whether I can make a long speech, such as you are in the habit of hearing; but that is not my way. I think, however, that I can prove to you the truth of what I am saying, if you will grant me one little favour.

Alcibiades: Yes, if the favour which you mean be not a troublesome one.

Socrates: Will you be troubled at having questions to answer?

Alcibiades: Not at all.

Socrates: Then please to answer.

Alcibiades: Ask me.

Socrates: Have you not the intention which I attribute to you?

Alcibiades: I will grant anything you like, in the hope of hearing what more you have to say.

Socrates: You do, then, mean, as I was saying, to come forward in a little while in the character of an adviser of the Athenians? And suppose that when you are ascending the bema, I pull you by the sleeve and say, Alcibiades, you are getting up to advise the Athenians —do you know the matter about which they are going to deliberate, better than they?—How would you answer?

Alcibiades: I should reply, that I was going to advise them about a matter which I do know better than they.

Socrates: Then you are a good adviser about the things which you know?

Alcibiades: Certainly.

Socrates: And do you know anything but what you have learned of others, or found out yourself?

Alcibiades: That is all.

Socrates: And would you have ever learned or discovered anything, if you had not been willing either to learn of others or to examine yourself?

Alcibiades: I should not.

Socrates: And would you have been willing to learn or to examine what you supposed that you knew?

Alcibiades: Certainly not.

Socrates: Then there was a time when you thought that you did not know what you are now supposed to know?

Alcibiades: Certainly.

Socrates: I think that I know tolerably well the extent of your acquirements; and you must tell me if I forget any of them: according to my recollection, you learned the arts of writing, of playing on the lyre, and of wrestling; the flute you never would learn; this is the sum of your accomplishments, unless there were some which you acquired in secret; and I think that secrecy was hardly possible, as you could not have come out of your door, either by day or night, without my seeing you.

Alcibiades: Yes, that was the whole of my schooling.

Socrates: And are you going to get up in the Athenian assembly, and give them advice about writing?

Alcibiades: No, indeed.

Socrates: Or about the touch of the lyre?

Alcibiades: Certainly not.

Socrates: And they are not in the habit of deliberating about wrestling, in the assembly?

Alcibiades: Hardly.

Socrates: Then what are the deliberations in which you propose to advise them? Surely not about building?

Alcibiades: No.

Socrates: For the builder will advise better than you will about that?

Alcibiades: He will.

Socrates: Nor about divination?

Alcibiades: No.

Socrates: About that again the diviner will advise better than you will?

Alcibiades: True.

Socrates: Whether he be little or great, good or ill-looking, noble or ignoble—makes no difference.

Alcibiades: Certainly not.

Socrates: A man is a good adviser about anything, not because he has riches, but because he has knowledge?

Alcibiades: Assuredly.

Socrates: Whether their counsellor is rich or poor, is not a matter which will make any difference to the Athenians when they are deliberating about the health of the citizens; they only require that he should be a physician.

Alcibiades: Of course.

Socrates: Then what will be the subject of deliberation about which you will be justified in getting up and advising them?

Alcibiades: About their own concerns, Socrates.

Socrates: You mean about shipbuilding, for example, when the question is what sort of ships they ought to build?

Alcibiades: No, I should not advise them about that.

Socrates: I suppose, because you do not understand shipbuild-ing:—is that the reason?

Alcibiades: It is.

Socrates: Then about what concerns of theirs will you advise them?

Alcibiades: About war, Socrates, or about peace, or about any other concerns of the state.

Socrates: You mean, when they deliberate with whom they ought to make peace, and with whom they ought to go to war, and in what manner?

Alcibiades: Yes.

Socrates: And they ought to go to war with those against whom it is better to go to war?

Alcibiades: Yes.

Socrates: And when it is better?

Alcibiades: Certainly.

Socrates: And for as long a time as is better?

Alcibiades: Yes.

Socrates: But suppose the Athenians to deliberate with whom they ought to close in wrestling, and whom they should grasp by the hand, would you, or the master of gymnastics, be a better adviser of them?

Alcibiades: Clearly, the master of gymnastics.

Socrates: And can you tell me on what grounds the master of gymnastics would decide, with whom they ought or ought not to close, and when and how? To take an instance: Would he not say that they should wrestle with those against whom it is best to wrestle?

Alcibiades: Yes.

Socrates: And as much as is best?

Alcibiades: Certainly.

Socrates: And at such times as are best?

Alcibiades: Yes.

Socrates: Again; you sometimes accompany the lyre with the song and dance?

Alcibiades: Yes.

Socrates: When it is well to do so?

Alcibiades: Yes.

Socrates: And as much as is well?

Alcibiades: Just so.

Socrates: And as you speak of an excellence or art of the best in wrestling, and of an excellence in playing the lyre, I wish you would tell me what this latter is;—the excellence of wrestling I call gymnastic, and I want to know what you call the other.

Alcibiades: I do not understand you.

Socrates: Then try to do as I do; for the answer which I gave is universally right, and when I say right, I mean according to rule.

Alcibiades: Yes.

Socrates: And was not the art of which I spoke gymnastic?

Alcibiades: Certainly.

Socrates: And I called the excellence in wrestling gymnastic?

Alcibiades: You did.

Socrates: And I was right?

Alcibiades: I think that you were.

Socrates: Well, now,—for you should learn to argue prettily—let me ask you in return to tell me, first, what is that art of which playing and singing, and stepping properly in the dance, are parts,—what is the name of the whole? I think that by this time you must be able to tell.

Alcibiades: Indeed I cannot.

Socrates: Then let me put the matter in another way: what do you call the Goddesses who are the patronesses of art?

Alcibiades: The Muses do you mean, Socrates?

Socrates: Yes, I do; and what is the name of the art which is called after them?

Alcibiades: I suppose that you mean music.

Socrates: Yes, that is my meaning; and what is the excellence of the art of music, as I told you truly that the excellence of wrestling was gymnastic—what is the excellence of music—to be what?

Alcibiades: To be musical, I suppose.

Socrates: Very good; and now please to tell me what is the excellence of war and peace; as the more musical was the more excellent, or the more gymnastical was the more excellent, tell me, what name do you give to the more excellent in war and peace?

Alcibiades: But I really cannot tell you.

Socrates: But if you were offering advice to another and said to him—This food is better than that, at this time and in this quantity, and he said to you—What do you mean, Alcibiades, by the word 'better'? you would have no difficulty in replying that you meant 'more wholesome,' although you do not profess to be a physician: and when the subject is one of which you profess to have knowledge, and about which you are ready to get up and advise as if you knew, are you not ashamed, when you are asked, not to be able to answer the question? Is it not disgraceful?

Alcibiades: Very.

Socrates: Well, then, consider and try to explain what is the meaning of 'better,' in the matter of making peace and going to war with those against whom you ought to go to war? To what does the word refer?

Alcibiades: I am thinking, and I cannot tell.

Socrates: But you surely know what are the charges which we bring against one another, when we arrive at the point of making war, and what name we give them?

Alcibiades: Yes, certainly; we say that deceit or violence has been employed, or that we have been defrauded.

Socrates: And how does this happen? Will you tell me how? For there may be a difference in the manner.

Alcibiades: Do you mean by 'how,' Socrates, whether we suffered these things justly or unjustly?

Socrates: Exactly.

Alcibiades: There can be no greater difference than between just and unjust.

Socrates: And would you advise the Athenians to go to war with the just or with the unjust?

Alcibiades: That is an awkward question; for certainly, even if a person did intend to go to war with the just, he would not admit that they were just.

Socrates: He would not go to war, because it would be unlawful?

Alcibiades: Neither lawful nor honourable.

Socrates: Then you, too, would address them on principles of justice?

Alcibiades: Certainly.

Socrates: What, then, is justice but that better, of which I spoke, in going to war or not going to war with those against whom we ought or ought not, and when we ought or ought not to go to war?

Alcibiades: Clearly.

Socrates: But how is this, friend Alcibiades? Have you forgotten that you do not know this, or have you been to the schoolmaster without my knowledge, and has he taught you to discern the just from the unjust? Who is he? I wish you would tell me, that I may go and learn of him—you shall introduce me.

Alcibiades: You are mocking, Socrates.

Socrates: No, indeed; I most solemnly declare to you by Zeus, who is the God of our common friendship, and whom I never will forswear, that I am not; tell me, then, who this instructor is, if he exists.

Alcibiades: But, perhaps, he does not exist; may I not have acquired the knowledge of just and unjust in some other way?

Socrates: Yes; if you have discovered them.

Alcibiades: But do you not think that I could discover them?

Socrates: I am sure that you might, if you enquired about them.

Alcibiades: And do you not think that I would enquire?

Socrates: Yes; if you thought that you did not know them.

Alcibiades: And was there not a time when I did so think?

Socrates: Very good; and can you tell me how long it is since you thought that you did not know the nature of the just and the unjust? What do you say to a year ago? Were you then in a state of conscious ignorance and enquiry? Or did you think that you knew? And please to answer truly, that our discussion may not be in vain.

Alcibiades: Well, I thought that I knew.

Socrates: And two years ago, and three years ago, and four years ago, you knew all the same?

Alcibiades: I did.

Socrates: And more than four years ago you were a child—were you not?

Alcibiades: Yes.

Socrates: And then I am quite sure that you thought you knew.

Alcibiades: Why are you so sure?

Socrates: Because I often heard you when a child, in your teacher's house, or elsewhere, playing at dice or some other game with the boys, not hesitating at all about the nature of the just and unjust; but very confident—crying and shouting that one of the boys was a rogue and a cheat, and had been cheating. Is it not true?

Alcibiades: But what was I to do, Socrates, when anybody cheated me?

Socrates: And how can you say, 'What was I to do'? if at the time you did not know whether you were wronged or not?

Alcibiades: To be sure I knew; I was quite aware that I was being cheated.

Socrates: Then you suppose yourself even when a child to have known the nature of just and unjust?

Alcibiades: Certainly; and I did know then.

Socrates: And when did you discover them—not, surely, at the time when you thought that you knew them?

Alcibiades: Certainly not.

Socrates: And when did you think that you were ignorant—if you consider, you will find that there never was such a time?

Alcibiades: Really, Socrates, I cannot say.

Socrates: Then you did not learn them by discovering them?

Alcibiades: Clearly not.

Socrates: But just before you said that you did not know them by learning; now, if you have neither discovered nor learned them, how and whence do you come to know them?

Alcibiades: I suppose that I was mistaken in saying that I knew them through my own discovery of them; whereas, in truth, I learned them in the same way that other people learn.

Socrates: So you said before, and I must again ask, of whom? Do tell me.

Alcibiades: Of the many.

Socrates: Do you take refuge in them? I cannot say much for your teachers.

Alcibiades: Why, are they not able to teach?

Socrates: They could not teach you how to play at draughts, which you would acknowledge (would you not) to be a much smaller matter than justice?

Alcibiades: Yes.

Socrates: And can they teach the better who are unable to teach the worse?

Alcibiades: I think that they can; at any rate, they can teach many far better things than to play at draughts.

Socrates: What things?

Alcibiades: Why, for example, I learned to speak Greek of them, and I cannot say who was my teacher, or to whom I am to attribute my knowledge of Greek, if not to those good-for-nothing teachers, as you call them.

Socrates: Why, yes, my friend; and the many are good enough teachers of Greek, and some of their instructions in that line may be justly praised.

Alcibiades: Why is that?

Socrates: Why, because they have the qualities which good teachers ought to have.

Alcibiades: What qualities?

Socrates: Why, you know that knowledge is the first qualification of any teacher?

Alcibiades: Certainly.

Socrates: And if they know, they must agree together and not differ?

Alcibiades: Yes.

Socrates: And would you say that they knew the things about which they differ?

Alcibiades: No.

Socrates: Then how can they teach them?

Alcibiades: They cannot.

Socrates: Well, but do you imagine that the many would differ about the nature of wood and stone? are they not agreed if you ask them what they are? and do they not run to fetch the same thing, when they want a piece of wood or a stone? And so in similar cases, which I suspect to be pretty nearly all that you mean by speaking Greek.

Alcibiades: True.

Socrates: These, as we were saying, are matters about which they are agreed with one another and with themselves; both individuals and states use the same words about them; they do not use some one word and some another.

Alcibiades: They do not.

Socrates: Then they may be expected to be good teachers of these things?

Alcibiades: Yes.

Socrates: And if we want to instruct any one in them, we shall be right in sending him to be taught by our friends the many?

Alcibiades: Very true.

Socrates: But if we wanted further to know not only which are men and which are horses, but which men or horses have powers of running, would the many still be able to inform us?

Alcibiades: Certainly not.

Socrates: And you have a sufficient proof that they do not know these things and are not the best teachers of them, inasmuch as they are never agreed about them?

Alcibiades: Yes.

Socrates: And suppose that we wanted to know not only what men are like, but what healthy or diseased men are like—would the many be able to teach us?

Alcibiades: They would not.

Socrates: And you would have a proof that they were bad teachers of these matters, if you saw them at variance?

Alcibiades: I should.

Socrates: Well, but are the many agreed with themselves, or with one another, about the justice or injustice of men and things?

Alcibiades: Assuredly not, Socrates.

Socrates: There is no subject about which they are more at variance?

Alcibiades: None.

Socrates: I do not suppose that you ever saw or heard of men quarrelling over the principles of health and disease to such an extent as to go to war and kill one another for the sake of them?

Alcibiades: No indeed.

Socrates: But of the quarrels about justice and injustice, even if you have never seen them, you have certainly heard from many people, including Homer; for you have heard of the Iliad and Odyssey?

Alcibiades: To be sure, Socrates.

Socrates: A difference of just and unjust is the argument of those poems?

Alcibiades: True.

Socrates: Which difference caused all the wars and deaths of Trojans and Achaeans, and the deaths of the suitors of Penelope in their quarrel with Odysseus.

Alcibiades: Very true.

Socrates: And when the Athenians and Lacedaemonians and Boeotians fell at Tanagra, and afterwards in the battle of Coronea, at which your father Cleinias met his end, the question was one of justice—this was the sole cause of the battles, and of their deaths.

Alcibiades: Very true.

Socrates: But can they be said to understand that about which they are quarrelling to the death?

Alcibiades: Clearly not.

Socrates: And yet those whom you thus allow to be ignorant are the teachers to whom you are appealing.

Alcibiades: Very true.

Socrates: But how are you ever likely to know the nature of justice and injustice, about which you are so perplexed, if you have neither learned them of others nor discovered them yourself?

Alcibiades: From what you say, I suppose not.

Socrates: See, again, how inaccurately you speak, Alcibiades!

Alcibiades: In what respect?

Socrates: In saying that I say so.

Alcibiades: Why, did you not say that I know nothing of the just and unjust?

Socrates: No; I did not.

Alcibiades: Did I, then?

Socrates: Yes.

Alcibiades: How was that?

Socrates: Let me explain. Suppose I were to ask you which is the greater number, two or one; you would reply 'two'?

Alcibiades: I should.

Socrates: And by how much greater?

Alcibiades: By one.

Socrates: Which of us now says that two is more than one?

Alcibiades: I do.

Socrates: Did not I ask, and you answer the question?

Alcibiades: Yes.

Socrates: Then who is speaking? I who put the question, or you who answer me?

Alcibiades: I am.

Socrates: Or suppose that I ask and you tell me the letters which make up the name Socrates, which of us is the speaker?

Alcibiades: I am.

Socrates: Now let us put the case generally: whenever there is a question and answer, who is the speaker,—the questioner or the answerer?

Alcibiades: I should say, Socrates, that the answerer was the speaker.

Socrates: And have I not been the questioner all through?

Alcibiades: Yes.

Socrates: And you the answerer?

Alcibiades: Just so.

Socrates: Which of us, then, was the speaker?

Alcibiades: The inference is, Socrates, that I was the speaker.

Socrates: Did not some one say that Alcibiades, the fair son of Cleinias, not understanding about just and unjust, but thinking that he did understand, was going to the assembly to advise the Athenians about what he did not know? Was not that said?

Alcibiades: Very true.

Socrates: Then, Alcibiades, the result may be expressed in the language of Euripides. I think that you have heard all this 'from yourself, and not from me'; nor did I say this, which you erroneously attribute to me, but you yourself, and what you said was very true. For indeed, my dear fellow, the design which you meditate of teaching what you do not know, and have not taken any pains to learn, is downright insanity.

Alcibiades: But, Socrates, I think that the Athenians and the rest of the Hellenes do not often advise as to the more just or unjust; for they see no difficulty in them, and therefore they leave them, and consider which course of action will be most expedient; for there is a difference between justice and expediency. Many persons have done great wrong and profited by their injustice; others have done rightly and come to no good.

Socrates: Well, but granting that the just and the expedient are ever so much opposed, you surely do not imagine that you know what is expedient for mankind, or why a thing is expedient?

Alcibiades: Why not, Socrates?—But I am not going to be asked again from whom I learned, or when I made the discovery.

Socrates: What a way you have! When you make a mistake which might be refuted by a previous argument, you insist on having a new and different refutation; the old argument is a worn-our garment which you will no longer put on, but some one must produce another which is clean and new. Now I shall disregard this move of yours, and shall ask over again,—Where did you learn and how do you know the nature of the expedient, and who is your teacher? All this I comprehend in a single question, and now you will manifestly be in the old difficulty, and will not be able to show that you know the expedient, either because you learned or because you discovered it yourself. But, as I perceive that you are dainty, and dislike the taste of a stale argument, I will enquire no further into your knowledge of what is expedient or what is not expedient for the Athenian people, and simply request you to say why you do not explain whether justice and expediency are the same or different? And if you like you may examine me as I have examined you, or, if you would rather, you may carry on the discussion by yourself.

Alcibiades: But I am not certain, Socrates, whether I shall be able to discuss the matter with you.

Socrates: Then imagine, my dear fellow, that I am the demus and the ecclesia; for in the ecclesia, too, you will have to persuade men individually.

Alcibiades: Yes.

Socrates: And is not the same person able to persuade one individual singly and many individuals of the things which he knows? The grammarian, for example, can persuade one and he can persuade many about letters.

Alcibiades: True.

Socrates: And about number, will not the same person persuade one and persuade many?

Alcibiades: Yes.

Socrates: And this will be he who knows number, or the arithmetician?

Alcibiades: Quite true.

Socrates: And cannot you persuade one man about that of which you can persuade many?

Alcibiades: I suppose so.

Socrates: And that of which you can persuade either is clearly what you know?

Alcibiades: Yes.

Socrates: And the only difference between one who argues as we are doing, and the orator who is addressing an assembly, is that the one seeks to persuade a number, and the other an individual, of the same things.

Alcibiades: I suppose so.

Socrates: Well, then, since the same person who can persuade a multitude can persuade individuals, try conclusions upon me, and prove to me that the just is not always expedient.

Alcibiades: You take liberties, Socrates.

Socrates: I shall take the liberty of proving to you the opposite of that which you will not prove to me.

Alcibiades: Proceed.

Socrates: Answer my questions—that is all.

Alcibiades: Nay, I should like you to be the speaker.

Socrates: What, do you not wish to be persuaded?

Alcibiades: Certainly I do.

Socrates: And can you be persuaded better than out of your own mouth?

Alcibiades: I think not.

Socrates: Then you shall answer; and if you do not hear the words, that the just is the expedient, coming from your own lips, never believe another man again.

Alcibiades: I won't; but answer I will, for I do not see how I can come to any harm.

Socrates: A true prophecy! Let me begin then by enquiring of you whether you allow that the just is sometimes expedient and sometimes not?

Alcibiades: Yes.

Socrates: And sometimes honourable and sometimes not?

Alcibiades: What do you mean?

Socrates: I am asking if you ever knew any one who did what was dishonourable and yet just?

Alcibiades: Never.

Socrates: All just things are honourable?

Alcibiades: Yes.

Socrates: And are honourable things sometimes good and sometimes not good, or are they always good?

Alcibiades: I rather think, Socrates, that some honourable things are evil.

Socrates: And are some dishonourable things good?

Alcibiades: Yes.

Socrates: You mean in such a case as the following:—In time of war, men have been wounded or have died in rescuing a companion or kinsman, when others who have neglected the duty of rescuing them have escaped in safety?

Alcibiades: True.

Socrates: And to rescue another under such circumstances is honourable, in respect of the attempt to save those whom we ought to save; and this is courage?

Alcibiades: True.

Socrates: But evil in respect of death and wounds?

Alcibiades: Yes.

Socrates: And the courage which is shown in the rescue is one thing, and the death another?

Alcibiades: Certainly.

Socrates: Then the rescue of one's friends is honourable in one point of view, but evil in another?

Alcibiades: True.

Socrates: And if honourable, then also good: Will you consider now whether I may not be right, for you were acknowledging that the courage which is shown in the rescue is honourable? Now is this courage good or evil? Look at the matter thus: which would you rather choose, good or evil?

Alcibiades: Good.

Socrates: And the greatest goods you would be most ready to choose, and would least like to be deprived of them?

Alcibiades: Certainly.

Socrates: What would you say of courage? At what price would you be willing to be deprived of courage?

Alcibiades: I would rather die than be a coward.

Socrates: Then you think that cowardice is the worst of evils?

Alcibiades: I do.

Socrates: As bad as death, I suppose?

Alcibiades: Yes.

Socrates: And life and courage are the extreme opposites of death and cowardice?

Alcibiades: Yes.

Socrates: And they are what you would most desire to have, and their opposites you would least desire?

Alcibiades: Yes.

Socrates: Is this because you think life and courage the best, and death and cowardice the worst?

Alcibiades: Yes.

Socrates: And you would term the rescue of a friend in battle honourable, in as much as courage does a good work?

Alcibiades: I should.

Socrates: But evil because of the death which ensues?

Alcibiades: Yes.

Socrates: Might we not describe their different effects as follows: —You may call either of them evil in respect of the evil which is the result, and good in respect of the good which is the result of either of them?

Alcibiades: Yes.

Socrates: And they are honourable in so far as they are good, and dishonourable in so far as they are evil?

Alcibiades: True.

Socrates: Then when you say that the rescue of a friend in battle is honourable and yet evil, that is equivalent to saying that the rescue is good and yet evil?

Alcibiades: I believe that you are right, Socrates.

Socrates: Nothing honourable, regarded as honourable, is evil; nor anything base, regarded as base, good.

Alcibiades: Clearly not.

Socrates: Look at the matter yet once more in a further light: he who acts honourably acts well?

Alcibiades: Yes.

Socrates: And he who acts well is happy?

Alcibiades: Of course.

Socrates: And the happy are those who obtain good?

Alcibiades: True.

Socrates: And they obtain good by acting well and honourably?

Alcibiades: Yes.

Socrates: Then acting well is a good?

Alcibiades: Certainly.

Socrates: And happiness is a good?

Alcibiades: Yes.

Socrates: Then the good and the honourable are again identified.

Alcibiades: Manifestly.

Socrates: Then, if the argument holds, what we find to be honourable we shall also find to be good?

Alcibiades: Certainly.

Socrates: And is the good expedient or not?

Alcibiades: Expedient.

Socrates: Do you remember our admissions about the just?

Alcibiades: Yes; if I am not mistaken, we said that those who acted justly must also act honourably.

Socrates: And the honourable is the good?

Alcibiades: Yes.

Socrates: And the good is expedient?

Alcibiades: Yes.

Socrates: Then, Alcibiades, the just is expedient?

Alcibiades: I should infer so.

Socrates: And all this I prove out of your own mouth, for I ask and you answer?

Alcibiades: I must acknowledge it to be true.

Socrates: And having acknowledged that the just is the same as the expedient, are you not (let me ask) prepared to ridicule any one who, pretending to understand the principles of justice and injustice, gets up to advise the noble Athenians or the ignoble Peparethians, that the just may be the evil?

Alcibiades: I solemnly declare, Socrates, that I do not know what I am saying. Verily, I am in a strange state, for when you put questions to me I am of different minds in successive instants.

Socrates: And are you not aware of the nature of this perplexity, my friend?

Alcibiades: Indeed I am not.

Socrates: Do you suppose that if some one were to ask you whether you have two eyes or three, or two hands or four, or anything of that sort, you would then be of different minds in successive instants?

Alcibiades: I begin to distrust myself, but still I do not suppose that I should.

Socrates: You would feel no doubt; and for this reason—because you would know?

Alcibiades: I suppose so.

Socrates: And the reason why you involuntarily contradict yourself is clearly that you are ignorant?

Alcibiades: Very likely.

Socrates: And if you are perplexed in answering about just and unjust, honourable and dishonourable, good and evil, expedient and inexpedient, the reason is that you are ignorant of them, and therefore in perplexity. Is not that clear?

Alcibiades: I agree.

Socrates: But is this always the case, and is a man necessarily perplexed about that of which he has no knowledge?

Alcibiades: Certainly he is.

Socrates: And do you know how to ascend into heaven?

Alcibiades: Certainly not.

Socrates: And in this case, too, is your judgment perplexed?

Alcibiades: No.

Socrates: Do you see the reason why, or shall I tell you?

Alcibiades: Tell me.

Socrates: The reason is, that you not only do not know, my friend, but you do not think that you know.

Alcibiades: There again; what do you mean?

Socrates: Ask yourself; are you in any perplexity about things of which you are ignorant? You know, for example, that you know nothing about the preparation of food.

Alcibiades: Very true.

Socrates: And do you think and perplex yourself about the preparation of food: or do you leave that to some one who understands the art?

Alcibiades: The latter.

Socrates: Or if you were on a voyage, would you bewilder yourself by considering whether the rudder is to be drawn inwards or outwards, or do you leave that to the pilot, and do nothing?

Alcibiades: It would be the concern of the pilot.

Socrates: Then you are not perplexed about what you do not know, if you know that you do not know it?

Alcibiades: I imagine not.

Socrates: Do you not see, then, that mistakes in life and practice are likewise to be attributed to the ignorance which has conceit of knowledge?

Alcibiades: Once more, what do you mean?

Socrates: I suppose that we begin to act when we think that we know what we are doing?

Alcibiades: Yes.

Socrates: But when people think that they do not know, they entrust their business to others?

Alcibiades: Yes.

Socrates: And so there is a class of ignorant persons who do not make mistakes in life, because they trust others about things of which they are ignorant?

Alcibiades: True.

Socrates: Who, then, are the persons who make mistakes? They cannot, of course, be those who know?

Alcibiades: Certainly not.

Socrates: But if neither those who know, nor those who know that they do not know, make mistakes, there remain those only who do not know and think that they know.

Alcibiades: Yes, only those.

Socrates: Then this is ignorance of the disgraceful sort which is mischievous?

Alcibiades: Yes.

Socrates: And most mischievous and most disgraceful when having to do with the greatest matters?

Alcibiades: By far.

Socrates: And can there be any matters greater than the just, the honourable, the good, and the expedient?

Alcibiades: There cannot be.

Socrates: And these, as you were saying, are what perplex you?

Alcibiades: Yes.

Socrates: But if you are perplexed, then, as the previous argument has shown, you are not only ignorant of the greatest matters, but being ignorant you fancy that you know them?

Alcibiades: I fear that you are right.

Socrates: And now see what has happened to you, Alcibiades! I hardly like to speak of your evil case, but as we are alone I will: My good friend, you are wedded to ignorance of the most disgraceful kind, and of this you are convicted, not by me, but out of your own mouth and by your own argument; wherefore also you rush into politics before you are educated. Neither is your case to be deemed singular. For I might say the same of almost all our statesmen, with the exception, perhaps of your guardian, Pericles.

Alcibiades: Yes, Socrates; and Pericles is said not to have got his wisdom by the light of nature, but to have associated with several of the philosophers; with Pythocleides, for example, and with Anaxagoras, and now in advanced life with Damon, in the hope of gaining wisdom.

Socrates: Very good; but did you ever know a man wise in anything who was unable to impart his particular wisdom? For example, he who taught you letters was not only wise, but he made you and any others whom he liked wise.

Alcibiades: Yes.

Socrates: And you, whom he taught, can do the same?

Alcibiades: True.

Socrates: And in like manner the harper and gymnastic-master?

Alcibiades: Certainly.

Socrates: When a person is enabled to impart knowledge to another, he thereby gives an excellent proof of his own under-standing of any matter.

Alcibiades: I agree.

Socrates: Well, and did Pericles make any one wise; did he begin by making his sons wise?

Alcibiades: But, Socrates, if the two sons of Pericles were simpletons, what has that to do with the matter?

Socrates: Well, but did he make your brother, Cleinias, wise?

Alcibiades: Cleinias is a madman; there is no use in talking of him.

Socrates: But if Cleinias is a madman and the two sons of Peri-cles were simpletons, what reason can be given why he neglects you, and lets you be as you are?

Alcibiades: I believe that I am to blame for not listening to him.

Socrates: But did you ever hear of any other Athenian or foreigner, bond or free, who was deemed to have grown wiser in the society of Pericles,—as I might cite Pythodorus, the son of Isolochus, and Callias, the son of Calliades, who have grown wiser in the society of Zeno, for which privilege they have each of them paid him the sum of a hundred minae (about 406 pounds sterling) to the increase of their wisdom and fame.

Alcibiades: I certainly never did hear of any one.

Socrates: Well, and in reference to your own case, do you mean to remain as you are, or will you take some pains about yourself?

Alcibiades: With your aid, Socrates, I will. And indeed, when I hear you speak, the truth of what you are saying strikes home to me, and I agree with you, for our statesmen, all but a few, do appear to be quite uneducated.

Socrates: What is the inference?

Alcibiades: Why, that if they were educated they would be trained athletes, and he who means to rival them ought to have knowledge and experience when he attacks them; but now, as they have become politicians without any special training, why should I have the trouble of learning and practising? For I know well that by the light of nature I shall get the better of them.

Socrates: My dear friend, what a sentiment! And how unworthy of your noble form and your high estate!

Alcibiades: What do you mean, Socrates; why do you say so?

Socrates: I am grieved when I think of our mutual love.

Alcibiades: At what?

Socrates: At your fancying that the contest on which you are entering is with people here.

Alcibiades: Why, what others are there?

Socrates: Is that a question which a magnanimous soul should ask?

Alcibiades: Do you mean to say that the contest is not with these?

Socrates: And suppose that you were going to steer a ship into action, would you only aim at being the best pilot on board? Would you not, while acknowledging that you must possess this degree of excellence, rather look to your antagonists, and not, as you are now doing, to your fellow combatants? You ought to be so far above these latter, that they will not even dare to be your rivals; and, being regarded by you as inferiors, will do battle for you against the enemy; this is the kind of superiority which you must establish over them, if you mean to accomplish any noble action really worthy of yourself and of the state.

Alcibiades: That would certainly be my aim.

Socrates: Verily, then, you have good reason to be satisfied, if you are better than the soldiers; and you need not, when you are their superior and have your thoughts and actions fixed upon them, look away to the generals of the enemy.

Alcibiades: Of whom are you speaking, Socrates?

Socrates: Why, you surely know that our city goes to war now and then with the Lacedaemonians and with the great king?

Alcibiades: True enough.

Socrates: And if you meant to be the ruler of this city, would you not be right in considering that the Lacedaemonian and Persian king were your true rivals?

Alcibiades: I believe that you are right.

Socrates: Oh no, my friend, I am quite wrong, and I think that you ought rather to turn your attention to Midias the quail-breeder and others like him, who manage our politics; in whom, as the women would remark, you may still see the slaves' cut of hair, cropping out in their minds as well as on their pates; and they come with their barbarous lingo to flatter us and not to rule us. To these, I say, you should look, and then you need not trouble yourself about your own fitness to contend in such a noble arena: there is no reason why you should either learn what has to be learned, or practise what has to be practised, and only when thoroughly prepared enter on a political career.

Alcibiades: There, I think, Socrates, that you are right; I do not suppose, however, that the Spartan generals or the great king are really different from anybody else.

Socrates: But, my dear friend, do consider what you are saying.

Alcibiades: What am I to consider?

Socrates: In the first place, will you be more likely to take care of yourself, if you are in a wholesome fear and dread of them, or if you are not?

Alcibiades: Clearly, if I have such a fear of them.

Socrates: And do you think that you will sustain any injury if you take care of yourself?

Alcibiades: No, I shall be greatly benefited.

Socrates: And this is one very important respect in which that notion of yours is bad.

Alcibiades: True.

Socrates: In the next place, consider that what you say is probably false.

Alcibiades: How so?

Socrates: Let me ask you whether better natures are likely to be found in noble races or not in noble races?

Alcibiades: Clearly in noble races.

Socrates: Are not those who are well born and well bred most likely to be perfect in virtue?

Alcibiades: Certainly.

Socrates: Then let us compare our antecedents with those of the Lacedaemonian and Persian kings; are they inferior to us in descent? Have we not heard that the former are sprung from Heracles, and the latter from Achaemenes, and that the race of Heracles and the race of Achaemenes go back to Perseus, son of Zeus?

Alcibiades: Why, so does mine go back to Eurysaces, and he to Zeus!

Socrates: And mine, noble Alcibiades, to Daedalus, and he to Hephaestus, son of Zeus. But, for all that, we are far inferior to them. For they are descended 'from Zeus,' through a line of kings— either kings of Argos and Lacedaemon, or kings of Persia, a country which the descendants of Achaemenes have always possessed, besides being at various times sovereigns of Asia, as they now are; whereas, we and our fathers were but private persons. How ridiculous would you be thought if you were to make a display of your ancestors and of Salamis the island of Eurysaces, or of Aegina, the habitation of the still more ancient Aeacus, before Artaxerxes, son of Xerxes. You should consider how inferior we are to them both in the derivation of our birth and in other particulars. Did you never observe how great is the property of the Spartan kings? And their wives are under the guardianship of the Ephori, who are public officers and watch over them, in order to preserve as far as possible the purity of the Heracleid blood. Still greater is the difference among the Persians; for no one entertains a suspicion that the father of a prince of Persia can be any one but the king. Such is the awe which invests the person of the queen, that any other guard is needless. And when the heir of the kingdom is born, all the subjects of the king feast; and the day of his birth is for ever afterwards kept as a holiday and time of sacrifice by all Asia; whereas, when you and I were born, Alcibiades, as the comic poet says, the neighbours hardly

knew of the important event. After the birth of the royal child, he is
tended, not by a good-for-nothing woman-nurse, but by the best of
the royal eunuchs, who are charged with the care of him, and especially with the fashioning and right formation of his limbs, in order
that he may be as shapely as possible; which being their calling, they
are held in great honour. And when the young prince is seven years
old he is put upon a horse and taken to the riding-masters, and
begins to go out hunting. And at fourteen years of age he is handed
over to the royal schoolmasters, as they are termed: these are four
chosen men, reputed to be the best among the Persians of a certain
age; and one of them is the wisest, another the justest, a third the
most temperate, and a fourth the most valiant. The first instructs
him in the magianism of Zoroaster, the son of Oromasus, which is
the worship of the Gods, and teaches him also the duties of his
royal office; the second, who is the justest, teaches him always to
speak the truth; the third, or most temperate, forbids him to allow
any pleasure to be lord over him, that he may be accustomed to be a
freeman and king indeed,—lord of himself first, and not a slave; the
most valiant trains him to be bold and fearless, telling him that if he
fears he is to deem himself a slave; whereas Pericles gave you, Alcibiades, for a tutor Zopyrus the Thracian, a slave of his who was past
all other work. I might enlarge on the nurture and education of
your rivals, but that would be tedious; and what I have said is a sufficient sample of what remains to be said. I have only to remark, by
way of contrast, that no one cares about your birth or nurture or
education, or, I may say, about that of any other Athenian, unless he
has a lover who looks after him. And if you cast an eye on the
wealth, the luxury, the garments with their flowing trains, the
anointings with myrrh, the multitudes of attendants, and all the
other bravery of the Persians, you will be ashamed when you
discern your own inferiority; or if you look at the temperance and
orderliness and ease and grace and magnanimity and courage and
endurance and love of toil and desire of glory and ambition of the
Lacedaemonians—in all these respects you will see that you are but
a child in comparison of them. Even in the matter of wealth, if you
value yourself upon that, I must reveal to you how you stand; for if

you form an estimate of the wealth of the Lacedaemonians, you will see that our possessions fall far short of theirs. For no one here can compete with them either in the extent and fertility of their own and the Messenian territory, or in the number of their slaves, and especially of the Helots, or of their horses, or of the animals which feed on the Messenian pastures. But I have said enough of this: and as to gold and silver, there is more of them in Lacedaemon than in all the rest of Hellas, for during many generations gold has been always flowing in to them from the whole Hellenic world, and often from the barbarian also, and never going out, as in the fable of Aesop the fox said to the lion, 'The prints of the feet of those going in are distinct enough;' but who ever saw the trace of money going out of Lacedaemon? And therefore you may safely infer that the inhabitants are the richest of the Hellenes in gold and silver, and that their kings are the richest of them, for they have a larger share of these things, and they have also a tribute paid to them which is very considerable. Yet the Spartan wealth, though great in comparison of the wealth of the other Hellenes, is as nothing in comparison of that of the Persians and their kings. Why, I have been informed by a credible person who went up to the king (at Susa), that he passed through a large tract of excellent land, extending for nearly a day's journey, which the people of the country called the queen's girdle, and another, which they called her veil; and several other fair and fertile districts, which were reserved for the adornment of the queen, and are named after her several habiliments. Now, I cannot help thinking to myself, What if some one were to go to Amestris, the wife of Xerxes and mother of Artaxerxes, and say to her, There is a certain Dinomache, whose whole wardrobe is not worth fifty minae—and that will be more than the value—and she has a son who is possessed of a three-hundred acre patch at Erchiae, and he has a mind to go to war with your son—would she not wonder to what this Alcibiades trusts for success in the conflict? 'He must rely,' she would say to herself, 'upon his training and wisdom—these are the things which Hellenes value.' And if she heard that this Alcibiades who is making the attempt is not as yet twenty years old, and is wholly uneducated, and when his lover tells him that he ought to get education and training first, and then go and fight the king, he refuses, and says that he is well enough as he is, would she not be amazed, and ask 'On what, then, does the youth rely?' And if we replied: He relies on his beauty, and stature, and birth, and mental endowments, she would think that we were mad, Alcibiades, when she compared the advantages which you possess with those of her own people. And I believe that even Lampido, the daughter of Leotychides, the wife of Archidamus and mother of Agis, all of whom were kings, would have the same feeling; if, in your present uneducated state, you were to turn your thoughts against her son, she too would be equally astonished. But how disgraceful, that we should not have as high a notion of what is required in us as our enemies' wives and mothers have of the qualities which are required in their assailants! O my friend, be persuaded by me, and hear the Delphian inscription, 'Know thyself'—not the men whom you think, but these kings are our rivals, and we can only overcome them by pains and skill. And if you fail in the required qualities, you will fail also in becoming renowned among Hellenes and Barbarians, which you seem to desire more than any other man ever desired anything.

Alcibiades: I entirely believe you; but what are the sort of pains which are required, Socrates,—can you tell me?

Socrates: Yes, I can; but we must take counsel together concerning the manner in which both of us may be most improved. For what I am telling you of the necessity of education applies to myself as well as to you; and there is only one point in which I have an advantage over you.

Alcibiades: What is that?

Socrates: I have a guardian who is better and wiser than your guardian, Pericles.

Alcibiades: Who is he, Socrates?

Socrates: God, Alcibiades, who up to this day has not allowed me to converse with you; and he inspires in me the faith that I am especially designed to bring you to honour.

Alcibiades: You are jesting, Socrates.

Socrates: Perhaps, at any rate, I am right in saying that all men greatly need pains and care, and you and I above all men.

Alcibiades: You are not far wrong about me.

Socrates: And certainly not about myself.

Alcibiades: But what can we do?

Socrates: There must be no hesitation or cowardice, my friend.

Alcibiades: That would not become us, Socrates.

Socrates: No, indeed, and we ought to take counsel together: for do we not wish to be as good as possible?

Alcibiades: We do.

Socrates: In what sort of virtue?

Alcibiades: Plainly, in the virtue of good men.

Socrates: Who are good in what?

Alcibiades: Those, clearly, who are good in the management of affairs.

Socrates: What sort of affairs? Equestrian affairs?

Alcibiades: Certainly not.

Socrates: You mean that about them we should have recourse to horsemen?

Alcibiades: Yes.

Socrates: Well, naval affairs?

Alcibiades: No.

Socrates: You mean that we should have recourse to sailors about them?

Alcibiades: Yes.

Socrates: Then what affairs? And who do them?

Alcibiades: The affairs which occupy Athenian gentlemen.

Socrates: And when you speak of gentlemen, do you mean the wise or the unwise?

Alcibiades: The wise.

Socrates: And a man is good in respect of that in which he is wise?

Alcibiades: Yes.

Socrates: And evil in respect of that in which he is unwise?

Alcibiades: Certainly.

Socrates: The shoemaker, for example, is wise in respect of the making of shoes?

Alcibiades: Yes.

Socrates: Then he is good in that?

Alcibiades: He is.

Socrates: But in respect of the making of garments he is unwise?

Alcibiades: Yes.

Socrates: Then in that he is bad?

Alcibiades: Yes.

Socrates: Then upon this view of the matter the same man is good and also bad?

Alcibiades: True.

Socrates: But would you say that the good are the same as the bad?

Alcibiades: Certainly not.

Socrates: Then whom do you call the good?

Alcibiades: I mean by the good those who are able to rule in the city.

Socrates: Not, surely, over horses?

Alcibiades: Certainly not.

Socrates: But over men?

Alcibiades: Yes.

Socrates: When they are sick?

Alcibiades: No.

Socrates: Or on a voyage?

Alcibiades: No.

Socrates: Or reaping the harvest?

Alcibiades: No.

Socrates: When they are doing something or nothing?

Alcibiades: When they are doing something, I should say.

Socrates: I wish that you would explain to me what this something is.

Alcibiades: When they are having dealings with one another, and using one another's services, as we citizens do in our daily life.

Socrates: Those of whom you speak are ruling over men who are using the services of other men?

Alcibiades: Yes.

Socrates: Are they ruling over the signal-men who give the time to the rowers?

Alcibiades: No; they are not.

Socrates: That would be the office of the pilot?

Alcibiades: Yes.

Socrates: But, perhaps you mean that they rule over flute-players, who lead the singers and use the services of the dancers?

Alcibiades: Certainly not.

Socrates: That would be the business of the teacher of the chorus?

Alcibiades: Yes.

Socrates: Then what is the meaning of being able to rule over men who use other men?

Alcibiades: I mean that they rule over men who have common rights of citizenship, and dealings with one another.

Socrates: And what sort of an art is this? Suppose that I ask you again, as I did just now, What art makes men know how to rule over their fellow-sailors,—how would you answer?

Alcibiades: The art of the pilot.

Socrates: And, if I may recur to another old instance, what art enables them to rule over their fellow-singers?

Alcibiades: The art of the teacher of the chorus, which you were just now mentioning.

Socrates: And what do you call the art of fellow-citizens?

Alcibiades: I should say, good counsel, Socrates.

Socrates: And is the art of the pilot evil counsel?

Alcibiades: No.

Socrates: But good counsel?

Alcibiades: Yes, that is what I should say,—good counsel, of which the aim is the preservation of the voyagers.

Socrates: True. And what is the aim of that other good counsel of which you speak?

Alcibiades: The aim is the better order and preservation of the city.

Socrates: And what is that of which the absence or presence improves and preserves the order of the city? Suppose you were to ask me, what is that of which the presence or absence improves or preserves the order of the body? I should reply, the presence of health and the absence of disease. You would say the same?

Alcibiades: Yes.

Socrates: And if you were to ask me the same question about the eyes, I should reply in the same way, 'the presence of sight and the absence of blindness;' or about the ears, I should reply, that they were improved and were in better case, when deafness was absent, and hearing was present in them.

Alcibiades: True.

Socrates: And what would you say of a state? What is that by the presence or absence of which the state is improved and better managed and ordered?

Alcibiades: I should say, Socrates:—the presence of friendship and the absence of hatred and division.

Socrates: And do you mean by friendship agreement or disagreement?

Alcibiades: Agreement.

Socrates: What art makes cities agree about numbers?

Alcibiades: Arithmetic.

Socrates: And private individuals?

Alcibiades: The same.

Socrates: And what art makes each individual agree with himself?

Alcibiades: The same.

Socrates: And what art makes each of us agree with himself about the comparative length of the span and of the cubit? Does not the art of measure?

Alcibiades: Yes.

Socrates: Individuals are agreed with one another about this; and states, equally?

Alcibiades: Yes.

Socrates: And the same holds of the balance?

Alcibiades: True.

Socrates: But what is the other agreement of which you speak, and about what? what art can give that agreement? And does that which gives it to the state give it also to the individual, so as to make him consistent with himself and with another?

Alcibiades: I should suppose so.

Socrates: But what is the nature of the agreement?—answer, and faint not.

Alcibiades: I mean to say that there should be such friendship and agreement as exists between an affectionate father and mother and their son, or between brothers, or between husband and wife.

Socrates: But can a man, Alcibiades, agree with a woman about the spinning of wool, which she understands and he does not?

Alcibiades: No, truly.

Socrates: Nor has he any need, for spinning is a female accomplishment.

Alcibiades: Yes.

Socrates: And would a woman agree with a man about the science of arms, which she has never learned?

Alcibiades: Certainly not.

Socrates: I suppose that the use of arms would be regarded by you as a male accomplishment?

Alcibiades: It would.

Socrates: Then, upon your view, women and men have two sorts of knowledge?

Alcibiades: Certainly.

Socrates: Then in their knowledge there is no agreement of women and men?

Alcibiades: There is not.

Socrates: Nor can there be friendship, if friendship is agreement?

Alcibiades: Plainly not.

Socrates: Then women are not loved by men when they do their own work?

Alcibiades: I suppose not.

Socrates: Nor men by women when they do their own work?

Alcibiades: No.

Socrates: Nor are states well administered, when individuals do their own work?

Alcibiades: I should rather think, Socrates, that the reverse is the truth. (Compare Republic.)

Socrates: What! do you mean to say that states are well administered when friendship is absent, the presence of which, as we were saying, alone secures their good order?

Alcibiades: But I should say that there is friendship among them, for this very reason, that the two parties respectively do their own work.

Socrates: That was not what you were saying before; and what do you mean now by affirming that friendship exists when there is no agreement? How can there be agreement about matters which the one party knows, and of which the other is in ignorance?

Alcibiades: Impossible.

Socrates: And when individuals are doing their own work, are they doing what is just or unjust?

Alcibiades: What is just, certainly.

Socrates: And when individuals do what is just in the state, is there no friendship among them?

Alcibiades: I suppose that there must be, Socrates.

Socrates: Then what do you mean by this friendship or agreement about which we must be wise and discreet in order that we may be good men? I cannot make out where it exists or among whom; according to you, the same persons may sometimes have it, and sometimes not.

Alcibiades: But, indeed, Socrates, I do not know what I am saying; and I have long been, unconsciously to myself, in a most disgraceful state.

Socrates: Nevertheless, cheer up; at fifty, if you had discovered your deficiency, you would have been too old, and the time for taking care of yourself would have passed away, but yours is just the age at which the discovery should be made.

Alcibiades: And what should he do, Socrates, who would make the discovery?

Socrates: Answer questions, Alcibiades; and that is a process which, by the grace of God, if I may put any faith in my oracle, will be very improving to both of us.

Alcibiades: If I can be improved by answering, I will answer.

Socrates: And first of all, that we may not peradventure be deceived by appearances, fancying, perhaps, that we are taking care of ourselves when we are not, what is the meaning of a man taking care of himself? and when does he take care? Does he take care of himself when he takes care of what belongs to him?

Alcibiades: I should think so.

Socrates: When does a man take care of his feet? Does he not take care of them when he takes care of that which belongs to his feet?

Alcibiades: I do not understand.

Socrates: Let me take the hand as an illustration; does not a ring belong to the finger, and to the finger only?

Alcibiades: Yes.

Socrates: And the shoe in like manner to the foot?

Alcibiades: Yes.

Socrates: And when we take care of our shoes, do we not take care of our feet?

Alcibiades: I do not comprehend, Socrates.

Socrates: But you would admit, Alcibiades, that to take proper care of a thing is a correct expression?

Alcibiades: Yes.

Socrates: And taking proper care means improving?

Alcibiades: Yes.

Socrates: And what is the art which improves our shoes?

Alcibiades: Shoemaking.

Socrates: Then by shoemaking we take care of our shoes?

Alcibiades: Yes.

Socrates: And do we by shoemaking take care of our feet, or by some other art which improves the feet?

Alcibiades: By some other art.

Socrates: And the same art improves the feet which improves the rest of the body?

Alcibiades: Very true.

Socrates: Which is gymnastic?

Alcibiades: Certainly.

Socrates: Then by gymnastic we take care of our feet, and by shoemaking of that which belongs to our feet?

Alcibiades: Very true.

Socrates: And by gymnastic we take care of our hands, and by the art of graving rings of that which belongs to our hands?

Alcibiades: Yes.

Socrates: And by gymnastic we take care of the body, and by the art of weaving and the other arts we take care of the things of the body?

Alcibiades: Clearly.

Socrates: Then the art which takes care of each thing is different from that which takes care of the belongings of each thing?

Alcibiades: True.

Socrates: Then in taking care of what belongs to you, you do not take care of yourself?

Alcibiades: Certainly not.

Socrates: For the art which takes care of our belongings appears not to be the same as that which takes care of ourselves?

Alcibiades: Clearly not.

Socrates: And now let me ask you what is the art with which we take care of ourselves?

Alcibiades: I cannot say.

Socrates: At any rate, thus much has been admitted, that the art is not one which makes any of our possessions, but which makes ourselves better?

Alcibiades: True.

Socrates: But should we ever have known what art makes a shoe better, if we did not know a shoe?

Alcibiades: Impossible.

Socrates: Nor should we know what art makes a ring better, if we did not know a ring?

Alcibiades: That is true.

Socrates: And can we ever know what art makes a man better, if we do not know what we are ourselves?

Alcibiades: Impossible.

Socrates: And is self-knowledge such an easy thing, and was he to be lightly esteemed who inscribed the text on the temple at Delphi? Or is self-knowledge a difficult thing, which few are able to attain?

Alcibiades: At times I fancy, Socrates, that anybody can know himself; at other times the task appears to be very difficult.

Socrates: But whether easy or difficult, Alcibiades, still there is no other way; knowing what we are, we shall know how to take care of ourselves, and if we are ignorant we shall not know.

Alcibiades: That is true.

Socrates: Well, then, let us see in what way the self-existent can be discovered by us; that will give us a chance of discovering our own existence, which otherwise we can never know.

Alcibiades: You say truly.

Socrates: Come, now, I beseech you, tell me with whom you are conversing?—with whom but with me?

Alcibiades: Yes.

Socrates: As I am, with you?

Alcibiades: Yes.

Socrates: That is to say, I, Socrates, am talking?

Alcibiades: Yes.

Socrates: And Alcibiades is my hearer?

Alcibiades: Yes.

Socrates: And I in talking use words?

Alcibiades: Certainly.

Socrates: And talking and using words have, I suppose, the same meaning?

Alcibiades: To be sure.

Socrates: And the user is not the same as the thing which he uses?

Alcibiades: What do you mean?

Socrates: I will explain; the shoemaker, for example, uses a square tool, and a circular tool, and other tools for cutting?

Alcibiades: Yes.

Socrates: But the tool is not the same as the cutter and user of the tool?

Alcibiades: Of course not.

Socrates: And in the same way the instrument of the harper is to be distinguished from the harper himself?

Alcibiades: It is.

Socrates: Now the question which I asked was whether you conceive the user to be always different from that which he uses?

Alcibiades: I do.

Socrates: Then what shall we say of the shoemaker? Does he cut with his tools only or with his hands?

Alcibiades: With his hands as well.

Socrates: He uses his hands too?

Alcibiades: Yes.

Socrates: And does he use his eyes in cutting leather?

Alcibiades: He does.

Socrates: And we admit that the user is not the same with the things which he uses?

Alcibiades: Yes.

Socrates: Then the shoemaker and the harper are to be distinguished from the hands and feet which they use?

Alcibiades: Clearly.

Socrates: And does not a man use the whole body?

Alcibiades: Certainly.

Socrates: And that which uses is different from that which is used?

Alcibiades: True.

Socrates: Then a man is not the same as his own body?

Alcibiades: That is the inference.

Socrates: What is he, then?

Alcibiades: I cannot say.

Socrates: Nay, you can say that he is the user of the body.

Alcibiades: Yes.

Socrates: And the user of the body is the soul?

Alcibiades: Yes, the soul.

Socrates: And the soul rules?

Alcibiades: Yes.

Socrates: Let me make an assertion which will, I think, be universally admitted.

Alcibiades: What is it?

Socrates: That man is one of three things.

Alcibiades: What are they?

Socrates: Soul, body, or both together forming a whole.

Alcibiades: Certainly.

Socrates: But did we not say that the actual ruling principle of the body is man?

Alcibiades: Yes, we did.

Socrates: And does the body rule over itself?

Alcibiades: Certainly not.

Socrates: It is subject, as we were saying?

Alcibiades: Yes.

Socrates: Then that is not the principle which we are seeking?

Alcibiades: It would seem not.

Socrates: But may we say that the union of the two rules over the body, and consequently that this is man?

Alcibiades: Very likely.

Socrates: The most unlikely of all things; for if one of the members is subject, the two united cannot possibly rule.

Alcibiades: True.

Socrates: But since neither the body, nor the union of the two, is man, either man has no real existence, or the soul is man?

Alcibiades: Just so.

Socrates: Is anything more required to prove that the soul is man?

Alcibiades: Certainly not; the proof is, I think, quite sufficient.

Socrates: And if the proof, although not perfect, be sufficient, we shall be satisfied;—more precise proof will be supplied when we have discovered that which we were led to omit, from a fear that the enquiry would be too much protracted.

Alcibiades: What was that?

Socrates: What I meant, when I said that absolute existence must be first considered; but now, instead of absolute existence, we have been considering the nature of individual existence, and this may, perhaps, be sufficient; for surely there is nothing which may be called more properly ourselves than the soul?

Alcibiades: There is nothing.

Socrates: Then we may truly conceive that you and I are conversing with one another, soul to soul?

Alcibiades: Very true.

Socrates: And that is just what I was saying before—that I, Socrates, am not arguing or talking with the face of Alcibiades, but with the real Alcibiades; or in other words, with his soul.

Alcibiades: True.

Socrates: Then he who bids a man know himself, would have him know his soul?

Alcibiades: That appears to be true.

Socrates: He whose knowledge only extends to the body, knows the things of a man, and not the man himself?

Alcibiades: That is true.

Socrates: Then neither the physician regarded as a physician, nor the trainer regarded as a trainer, knows himself?

Alcibiades: He does not.

Socrates: The husbandmen and the other craftsmen are very far from knowing themselves, for they would seem not even to know their own belongings? When regarded in relation to the arts which they practise they are even further removed from self-knowledge, for they only know the belongings of the body, which minister to the body.

Alcibiades: That is true.

Socrates: Then if temperance is the knowledge of self, in respect of his art none of them is temperate?

Alcibiades: I agree.

Socrates: And this is the reason why their arts are accounted vulgar, and are not such as a good man would practise?

Alcibiades: Quite true.

Socrates: Again, he who cherishes his body cherishes not himself, but what belongs to him?

Alcibiades: That is true.

Socrates: But he who cherishes his money, cherishes neither himself nor his belongings, but is in a stage yet further removed from himself?

Alcibiades: I agree.

Socrates: Then the money-maker has really ceased to be occupied with his own concerns?

Alcibiades: True.

Socrates: And if any one has fallen in love with the person of Alcibiades, he loves not Alcibiades, but the belongings of Alcibiades?

Alcibiades: True.

Socrates: But he who loves your soul is the true lover?

Alcibiades: That is the necessary inference.

Socrates: The lover of the body goes away when the flower of youth fades?

Alcibiades: True.

Socrates: But he who loves the soul goes not away, as long as the soul follows after virtue?

Alcibiades: Yes.

Socrates: And I am the lover who goes not away, but remains with you, when you are no longer young and the rest are gone?

Alcibiades: Yes, Socrates; and therein you do well, and I hope that you will remain.

Socrates: Then you must try to look your best.

Alcibiades: I will.

Socrates: The fact is, that there is only one lover of Alcibiades the son of Cleinias; there neither is nor ever has been seemingly any other; and he is his darling,—Socrates, the son of Sophroniscus and Phaenarete.

Alcibiades: True.

Socrates: And did you not say, that if I had not spoken first, you were on the point of coming to me, and enquiring why I only remained?

Alcibiades: That is true.

Socrates: The reason was that I loved you for your own sake, whereas other men love what belongs to you; and your beauty, which is not you, is fading away, just as your true self is beginning to bloom. And I will never desert you, if you are not spoiled and deformed by the Athenian people; for the danger which I most fear is that you will become a lover of the people and will be spoiled by them. Many a noble Athenian has been ruined in this way. For the demus of the great-hearted Erechteus is of a fair countenance, but you should see him naked; wherefore observe the caution which I give you.

Alcibiades: What caution?

Socrates: Practise yourself, sweet friend, in learning what you ought to know, before you enter on politics; and then you will have an antidote which will keep you out of harm's way.

Alcibiades: Good advice, Socrates, but I wish that you would explain to me in what way I am to take care of myself.

Socrates: Have we not made an advance? for we are at any rate tolerably well agreed as to what we are, and there is no longer any danger, as we once feared, that we might be taking care not of ourselves, but of something which is not ourselves.

Alcibiades: That is true.

Socrates: And the next step will be to take care of the soul, and look to that?

Alcibiades: Certainly.

Socrates: Leaving the care of our bodies and of our properties to others?

Alcibiades: Very good.

Socrates: But how can we have a perfect knowledge of the things of the soul?—For if we know them, then I suppose we shall know ourselves. Can we really be ignorant of the excellent meaning of the Delphian inscription, of which we were just now speaking?

Alcibiades: What have you in your thoughts, Socrates?

Socrates: I will tell you what I suspect to be the meaning and lesson of that inscription. Let me take an illustration from sight, which I imagine to be the only one suitable to my purpose.

Alcibiades: What do you mean?

Socrates: Consider; if some one were to say to the eye, 'See thyself,' as you might say to a man, 'Know thyself,' what is the nature and meaning of this precept? Would not his meaning be:—That the eye should look at that in which it would see itself?

Alcibiades: Clearly.

Socrates: And what are the objects in looking at which we see ourselves?

Alcibiades: Clearly, Socrates, in looking at mirrors and the like.

Socrates: Very true; and is there not something of the nature of a mirror in our own eyes?

Alcibiades: Certainly.

Socrates: Did you ever observe that the face of the person looking into the eye of another is reflected as in a mirror; and in the visual organ which is over against him, and which is called the pupil, there is a sort of image of the person looking?

Alcibiades: That is quite true.

Socrates: Then the eye, looking at another eye, and at that in the eye which is most perfect, and which is the instrument of vision, will there see itself?

Alcibiades: That is evident.

Socrates: But looking at anything else either in man or in the world, and not to what resembles this, it will not see itself?

Alcibiades: Very true.

Socrates: Then if the eye is to see itself, it must look at the eye, and at that part of the eye where sight which is the virtue of the eye resides?

Alcibiades: True.

Socrates: And if the soul, my dear Alcibiades, is ever to know herself, must she not look at the soul; and especially at that part of the soul in which her virtue resides, and to any other which is like this?

Alcibiades: I agree, Socrates.

Socrates: And do we know of any part of our souls more divine than that which has to do with wisdom and knowledge?

Alcibiades: There is none.

Socrates: Then this is that part of the soul which resembles the divine; and he who looks at this and at the whole class of things divine, will be most likely to know himself?

Alcibiades: Clearly.

Socrates: And self-knowledge we agree to be wisdom?

Alcibiades: True.

Socrates: But if we have no self-knowledge and no wisdom, can we ever know our own good and evil?

Alcibiades: How can we, Socrates?

Socrates: You mean, that if you did not know Alcibiades, there would be no possibility of your knowing that what belonged to Alcibiades was really his?

Alcibiades: It would be quite impossible.

Socrates: Nor should we know that we were the persons to whom anything belonged, if we did not know ourselves?

Alcibiades: How could we?

Socrates: And if we did not know our own belongings, neither should we know the belongings of our belongings?

Alcibiades: Clearly not.

Socrates: Then we were not altogether right in acknowledging just now that a man may know what belongs to him and yet not know himself; nay, rather he cannot even know the belongings of his belongings; for the discernment of the things of self, and of the things which belong to the things of self, appear all to be the business of the same man, and of the same art.

Alcibiades: So much may be supposed.

Socrates: And he who knows not the things which belong to himself, will in like manner be ignorant of the things which belong to others?

Alcibiades: Very true.

Socrates: And if he knows not the affairs of others, he will not know the affairs of states?

Alcibiades: Certainly not.

Socrates: Then such a man can never be a statesman?

Alcibiades: He cannot.

Socrates: Nor an economist?

Alcibiades: He cannot.

Socrates: He will not know what he is doing?

Alcibiades: He will not.

Socrates: And will not he who is ignorant fall into error?

Alcibiades: Assuredly.

Socrates: And if he falls into error will he not fail both in his public and private capacity?

Alcibiades: Yes, indeed.

Socrates: And failing, will he not be miserable?

Alcibiades: Very.

Socrates: And what will become of those for whom he is acting?

Alcibiades: They will be miserable also.

Socrates: Then he who is not wise and good cannot be happy?

Alcibiades: He cannot.

Socrates: The bad, then, are miserable?

Alcibiades: Yes, very.

Socrates: And if so, not he who has riches, but he who has wisdom, is delivered from his misery?

Alcibiades: Clearly.

Socrates: Cities, then, if they are to be happy, do not want walls, or triremes, or docks, or numbers, or size, Alcibiades, without virtue? (Compare Arist. Pol.)

Alcibiades: Indeed they do not.

Socrates: And you must give the citizens virtue, if you mean to administer their affairs rightly or nobly?

Alcibiades: Certainly.

Socrates: But can a man give that which he has not?

Alcibiades: Impossible.

Socrates: Then you or any one who means to govern and superintend, not only himself and the things of himself, but the state and the things of the state, must in the first place acquire virtue.

Alcibiades: That is true.

Socrates: You have not therefore to obtain power or authority, in order to enable you to do what you wish for yourself and the state, but justice and wisdom.

Alcibiades: Clearly.

Socrates: You and the state, if you act wisely and justly, will act according to the will of God?

Alcibiades: Certainly.

Socrates: As I was saying before, you will look only at what is bright and divine, and act with a view to them?

Alcibiades: Yes.

Socrates: In that mirror you will see and know yourselves and your own good?

Alcibiades: Yes.

Socrates: And so you will act rightly and well?

Alcibiades: Yes.

Socrates: In which case, I will be security for your happiness.

Alcibiades: I accept the security.

Socrates: But if you act unrighteously, your eye will turn to the dark and godless, and being in darkness and ignorance of yourselves, you will probably do deeds of darkness.

Alcibiades: Very possibly.

Socrates: For if a man, my dear Alcibiades, has the power to do what he likes, but has no understanding, what is likely to be the result, either to him as an individual or to the state—for example, if he be sick and is able to do what he likes, not having the mind of a physician—having moreover tyrannical power, and no one daring to reprove him, what will happen to him? Will he not be likely to have his constitution ruined?

Alcibiades: That is true.

Socrates: Or again, in a ship, if a man having the power to do what he likes, has no intelligence or skill in navigation, do you see what will happen to him and to his fellow-sailors?

Alcibiades: Yes; I see that they will all perish.

Socrates: And in like manner, in a state, and where there is any power and authority which is wanting in virtue, will not misfortune, in like manner, ensue?

Alcibiades: Certainly.

Socrates: Not tyrannical power, then, my good Alcibiades, should be the aim either of individuals or states, if they would be happy, but virtue.

Alcibiades: That is true.

Socrates: And before they have virtue, to be commanded by a superior is better for men as well as for children? (Compare Arist. Pol.)

Alcibiades: That is evident.

Socrates: And that which is better is also nobler?

Alcibiades: True.

Socrates: And what is nobler is more becoming?

Alcibiades: Certainly.

Socrates: Then to the bad man slavery is more becoming, because better?

Alcibiades: True.

Socrates: Then vice is only suited to a slave?

Alcibiades: Yes.

Socrates: And virtue to a freeman?

Alcibiades: Yes.

Socrates: And, O my friend, is not the condition of a slave to be avoided?

Alcibiades: Certainly, Socrates.

Socrates: And are you now conscious of your own state? And do you know whether you are a freeman or not?

Alcibiades: I think that I am very conscious indeed of my own state.

Socrates: And do you know how to escape out of a state which I do not even like to name to my beauty?

Alcibiades: Yes, I do.

Socrates: How?

Alcibiades: By your help, Socrates.

Socrates: That is not well said, Alcibiades.

Alcibiades: What ought I to have said?

Socrates: By the help of God.

Alcibiades: I agree; and I further say, that our relations are likely to be reversed. From this day forward, I must and will follow you as you have followed me; I will be the disciple, and you shall be my master.

Socrates: O that is rare! My love breeds another love: and so like the stork I shall be cherished by the bird whom I have hatched.

Alcibiades: Strange, but true; and henceforward I shall begin to think about justice.

Socrates: And I hope that you will persist; although I have fears, not because I doubt you; but I see the power of the state, which may be too much for both of us.

Alcibiades II

Persons of the Dialogue: Socrates; Alcibiades.

SOCRATES: ARE YOU GOING, ALCIBIADES, TO OFFER PRAYER TO Zeus?

Alcibiades: Yes, Socrates, I am.

Socrates: you seem to be troubled and to cast your eyes on the ground, as though you were thinking about something.

Alcibiades: Of what do you suppose that I am thinking?

Socrates: Of the greatest of all things, as I believe. Tell me, do you not suppose that the Gods sometimes partly grant and partly reject the requests which we make in public and private, and favour some persons and not others?

Alcibiades: Certainly.

Socrates: Do you not imagine, then, that a man ought to be very careful, lest perchance without knowing it he implore great evils for himself, deeming that he is asking for good, especially if the Gods are in the mood to grant whatever he may request? There is the story of Oedipus, for instance, who prayed that his children might divide their inheritance between them by the sword: he did not, as he might have done, beg that his present evils might be averted, but called down new ones. And was not his prayer accomplished, and did not many and terrible evils thence arise, upon which I need not dilate?

Alcibiades: Yes, Socrates, but you are speaking of a madman: surely you do not think that any one in his senses would venture to make such a prayer?

Socrates: Madness, then, you consider to be the opposite of discretion?

Alcibiades: Of course.

Socrates: And some men seem to you to be discreet, and others the contrary?

Alcibiades: They do.

Socrates: Well, then, let us discuss who these are. We acknowledge that some are discreet, some foolish, and that some are mad?

Alcibiades: Yes.

Socrates: And again, there are some who are in health?

Alcibiades: There are.

Socrates: While others are ailing?

Alcibiades: Yes.

Socrates: And they are not the same?

Alcibiades: Certainly not.

Socrates: Nor are there any who are in neither state?

Alcibiades: No.

Socrates: A man must either be sick or be well?

Alcibiades: That is my opinion.

Socrates: Very good: and do you think the same about discretion and want of discretion?

Alcibiades: How do you mean?

Socrates: Do you believe that a man must be either in or out of his senses; or is there some third or intermediate condition, in which he is neither one nor the other?

Alcibiades: Decidedly not.

Socrates: He must be either sane or insane?

Alcibiades: So I suppose.

Socrates: Did you not acknowledge that madness was the oppo-site of discretion?

Alcibiades: Yes.

Socrates: And that there is no third or middle term between discretion and indiscretion?

Alcibiades: True.

Socrates: And there cannot be two opposites to one thing?

Alcibiades: There cannot.

Socrates: Then madness and want of sense are the same?

Alcibiades: That appears to be the case.

Socrates: We shall be in the right, therefore, Alcibiades, if we say that all who are senseless are mad. For example, if among persons of your own age or older than yourself there are some who are senseless,—as there certainly are,—they are mad. For tell me, by heaven, do you not think that in the city the wise are few, while the foolish, whom you call mad, are many?

Alcibiades: I do.

Socrates: But how could we live in safety with so many crazy people? Should we not long since have paid the penalty at their hands, and have been struck and beaten and endured every other form of ill-usage which madmen are wont to inflict? Consider, my dear friend: may it not be quite otherwise?

Alcibiades: Why, Socrates, how is that possible? I must have been mistaken.

Socrates: So it seems to me. But perhaps we may consider the matter thus:—

Alcibiades: How?

Socrates: I will tell you. We think that some are sick; do we not?

Alcibiades: Yes.

Socrates: And must every sick person either have the gout, or be in a fever, or suffer from ophthalmia? Or do you believe that a man may labour under some other disease, even although he has none of these complaints? Surely, they are not the only maladies which exist?

Alcibiades: Certainly not.

Socrates: And is every kind of ophthalmia a disease?

Alcibiades: Yes.

Socrates: And every disease ophthalmia?

Alcibiades: Surely not. But I scarcely understand what I mean myself.

Socrates: Perhaps, if you give me your best attention, 'two of us' looking together, we may find what we seek.

Alcibiades: I am attending, Socrates, to the best of my power.

Socrates: We are agreed, then, that every form of ophthalmia is a disease, but not every disease ophthalmia?

Alcibiades: We are.

Socrates: And so far we seem to be right. For every one who suffers from a fever is sick; but the sick, I conceive, do not all have fever or gout or ophthalmia, although each of these is a disease, which, according to those whom we call physicians, may require a different treatment. They are not all alike, nor do they produce the same result, but each has its own effect, and yet they are all diseases. May we not take an illustration from the artizans?

Alcibiades: Certainly.

Socrates: There are cobblers and carpenters and sculptors and others of all sorts and kinds, whom we need not stop to enumerate. All have their distinct employments and all are workmen, although they are not all of them cobblers or carpenters or sculptors.

Alcibiades: No, indeed.

Socrates: And in like manner men differ in regard to want of sense. Those who are most out of their wits we call 'madmen,' while we term those who are less far gone 'stupid' or 'idiotic,' or, if we prefer gentler language, describe them as 'romantic' or 'simple-minded,' or, again, as 'innocent' or 'inexperienced' or 'foolish.' You may even find other names, if you seek for them; but by all of them lack of sense is intended. They only differ as one art appeared to us to differ from another or one disease from another. Or what is your opinion?

Alcibiades: I agree with you.

Socrates: Then let us return to the point at which we digressed. We said at first that we should have to consider who were the wise and who the foolish. For we acknowledged that there are these two classes? Did we not?

Alcibiades: To be sure.

Socrates: And you regard those as sensible who know what ought to be done or said?

Alcibiades: Yes.

Socrates: The senseless are those who do not know this?

Alcibiades: True.

Socrates: The latter will say or do what they ought not without their own knowledge?

Alcibiades: Exactly.

Socrates: Oedipus, as I was saying, Alcibiades, was a person of this sort. And even now-a-days you will find many who (have offered inauspicious prayers), although, unlike him, they were not in anger nor thought that they were asking evil. He neither sought, nor supposed that he sought for good, but others have had quite the contrary notion. I believe that if the God whom you are about to consult should appear to you, and, in anticipation of your request, enquired whether you would be contented to become tyrant of Athens, and if this seemed in your eyes a small and mean thing, should add to it the dominion of all Hellas; and seeing that even then you would not be satisfied unless you were ruler of the whole of Europe, should promise, not only that, but, if you so desired, should proclaim to all mankind in one and the same day that Alcibiades, son of Cleinias, was tyrant:—in such a case, I imagine, you would depart full of joy, as one who had obtained the greatest of goods.

Alcibiades: And not only I, Socrates, but any one else who should meet with such luck.

Socrates: Yet you would not accept the dominion and lordship of all the Hellenes and all the barbarians in exchange for your life?

Alcibiades: Certainly not: for then what use could I make of them?

Socrates: And would you accept them if you were likely to use them to a bad and mischievous end?

Alcibiades: I would not.

Socrates: You see that it is not safe for a man either rashly to accept whatever is offered him, or himself to request a thing, if he is likely to suffer thereby or immediately to lose his life. And yet we could tell of many who, having long desired and diligently laboured to obtain a tyranny, thinking that thus they would procure an advantage, have nevertheless fallen victims to designing enemies. You must have heard of what happened only the other day, how Archelaus of Macedonia was slain by his beloved (compare Aristotle, Pol.), whose love for the tyranny was not less than that of Archelaus for him. The tyrannicide expected by his crime to become tyrant and afterwards to have a happy life; but when he had held the tyranny three or four days, he was in his turn conspired against and slain. Or look at certain of our own citizens,—and of their actions we have been not hearers, but eyewitnesses,—who have desired to obtain military command: of those who have gained their object, some are even to this day exiles from the city, while others have lost their lives. And even they who seem to have fared best, have not only gone through many perils and terrors during their office, but after their return home they have been beset by informers worse than they once were by their foes, insomuch that several of them have wished that they had remained in a private station rather than have had the glories of command. If, indeed, such perils and terrors were of profit to the commonwealth, there would be reason in undergoing them; but the very contrary is the case. Again, you will find persons who have prayed for offspring, and when their prayers were heard, have fallen into the greatest pains and sufferings. For some have begotten children who were utterly bad, and have therefore passed all their days in misery, while the parents of good children have undergone the misfortune of losing them, and have been so little happier than the others that they would have preferred never to have had children rather than to have had them and lost them. And yet, although these and the like examples are manifest and known of all, it is rare to find any one who has refused what has been offered him, or, if he were likely to gain aught by prayer, has refrained from making his petition. The mass of mankind would not decline to accept a tyranny, or the command of an army, or any of the numerous things which cause more harm than good: but rather, if they had them not, would have prayed to obtain them. And often in a short space of time they change their tone, and wish their old prayers unsaid. Wherefore also I suspect that men are entirely wrong when they blame the gods as the authors of the ills which befall them (compare Republic): 'their own presumption,' or folly (whichever is the right word)—

'Has brought these unmeasured woes upon them.' (Homer. Odyss.)

He must have been a wise poet, Alcibiades, who, seeing as I believe, his friends foolishly praying for and doing things which would not really profit them, offered up a common prayer in behalf of them all:—

'King Zeus, grant us good whether prayed for or unsought by us; But that which we ask amiss, do thou avert.' (The author of these lines, which are probably of Pythagorean origin, is unknown. They are found also in the Anthology (Anth. Pal.).)

In my opinion, I say, the poet spoke both well and prudently; but if you have anything to say in answer to him, speak out.

Alcibiades: It is difficult, Socrates, to oppose what has been well said. And I perceive how many are the ills of which ignorance is the cause, since, as would appear, through ignorance we not only do, but what is worse, pray for the greatest evils. No man would imagine that he would do so; he would rather suppose that he was quite capable of praying for what was best: to call down evils seems more like a curse than a prayer.

Socrates: But perhaps, my good friend, some one who is wiser than either you or I will say that we have no right to blame ignorance thus rashly, unless we can add what ignorance we mean and of what, and also to whom and how it is respectively a good or an evil?

Alcibiades: How do you mean? Can ignorance possibly be better than knowledge for any person in any conceivable case?

Socrates: So I believe:—you do not think so?

Alcibiades: Certainly not.

Socrates: And yet surely I may not suppose that you would ever wish to act towards your mother as they say that Orestes and Alcmeon and others have done towards their parent.

Alcibiades: Good words, Socrates, prithee.

Socrates: You ought not to bid him use auspicious words, who says that you would not be willing to commit so horrible a deed, but rather him who affirms the contrary, if the act appear to you unfit even to be mentioned. Or do you think that Orestes, had he been in his senses and knew what was best for him to do, would ever have dared to venture on such a crime?

Alcibiades: Certainly not.

Socrates: Nor would any one else, I fancy?

Alcibiades: No.

Socrates: That ignorance is bad then, it would appear, which is of the best and does not know what is best?

Alcibiades: So I think, at least.

Socrates: And both to the person who is ignorant and everybody else?

Alcibiades: Yes.

Socrates: Let us take another case. Suppose that you were suddenly to get into your head that it would be a good thing to kill Pericles, your kinsman and guardian, and were to seize a sword and, going to the doors of his house, were to enquire if he were at home, meaning to slay only him and no one else:—the servants reply, 'Yes': (Mind, I do not mean that you would really do such a thing; but there is nothing, you think, to prevent a man who is ignorant of the best, having occasionally the whim that what is worst is best?

Alcibiades: No.)

Socrates:—If, then, you went indoors, and seeing him, did not know him, but thought that he was some one else, would you venture to slay him?

Alcibiades: Most decidedly not (it seems to me). (These words are omitted in several MSS.)

Socrates: For you designed to kill, not the first who offered, but Pericles himself?

Alcibiades: Certainly.

Socrates: And if you made many attempts, and each time failed to recognize Pericles, you would never attack him?

Alcibiades: Never.

Socrates: Well, but if Orestes in like manner had not known his mother, do you think that he would ever have laid hands upon her?

Alcibiades: No.

Socrates: He did not intend to slay the first woman he came across, nor any one else's mother, but only his own?

Alcibiades: True.

Socrates: Ignorance, then, is better for those who are in such a frame of mind, and have such ideas?

Alcibiades: Obviously.

Socrates: You acknowledge that for some persons in certain cases the ignorance of some things is a good and not an evil, as you formerly supposed?

Alcibiades: I do.

Socrates: And there is still another case which will also perhaps appear strange to you, if you will consider it? (The reading is here uncertain.)

Alcibiades: What is that, Socrates?

Socrates: It may be, in short, that the possession of all the sciences, if unaccompanied by the knowledge of the best, will more often than not injure the possessor. Consider the matter thus:— Must we not, when we intend either to do or say anything, suppose that we know or ought to know that which we propose so confidently to do or say?

Alcibiades: Yes, in my opinion.

Socrates: We may take the orators for an example, who from time to time advise us about war and peace, or the building of walls and the construction of harbours, whether they understand the business in hand, or only think that they do. Whatever the city, in a word, does to another city, or in the management of her own affairs, all happens by the counsel of the orators.

Alcibiades: True.

Socrates: But now see what follows, if I can (make it clear to you). (Some words appear to have dropped out here.) You would distinguish the wise from the foolish?

Alcibiades: Yes.

Socrates: The many are foolish, the few wise?

Alcibiades: Certainly.

Socrates: And you use both the terms, 'wise' and 'foolish,' in reference to something?

Alcibiades: I do.

Socrates: Would you call a person wise who can give advice, but does not know whether or when it is better to carry out the advice?

Alcibiades: Decidedly not.

Socrates: Nor again, I suppose, a person who knows the art of war, but does not know whether it is better to go to war or for how long?

Alcibiades: No.

Socrates: Nor, once more, a person who knows how to kill another or to take away his property or to drive him from his native land, but not when it is better to do so or for whom it is better?

Alcibiades: Certainly not.

Socrates: But he who understands anything of the kind and has at the same time the knowledge of the best course of action:—and the best and the useful are surely the same?—

Alcibiades: Yes.

Socrates:—Such an one, I say, we should call wise and a useful adviser both of himself and of the city. What do you think?

Alcibiades: I agree.

Socrates: And if any one knows how to ride or to shoot with the bow or to box or to wrestle, or to engage in any other sort of contest or to do anything whatever which is in the nature of an art,—what do you call him who knows what is best according to that art? Do you not speak of one who knows what is best in riding as a good rider?

Alcibiades: Yes.

Socrates: And in a similar way you speak of a good boxer or a good flute-player or a good performer in any other art?

Alcibiades: True.

Socrates: But is it necessary that the man who is clever in any of these arts should be wise also in general? Or is there a difference between the clever artist and the wise man?

Alcibiades: All the difference in the world.

Socrates: And what sort of a state do you think that would be which was composed of good archers and flute-players and athletes and masters in other arts, and besides them of those others about whom we spoke, who knew how to go to war and how to kill, as well as of orators puffed up with political pride, but in which not one of them all had this knowledge of the best, and there was no one who could tell when it was better to apply any of these arts or in regard to whom?

Alcibiades: I should call such a state bad, Socrates.

Socrates: You certainly would when you saw each of them rivalling the other and esteeming that of the greatest importance in the state,

'Wherein he himself most excelled.' (Euripides, Antiope.) —I mean that which was best in any art, while he was entirely ignorant of what was best for himself and for the state, because, as I think, he trusts to opinion which is devoid of intelligence. In such a case should we not be right if we said that the state would be full of anarchy and lawlessness?

Alcibiades: Decidedly.

Socrates: But ought we not then, think you, either to fancy that we know or really to know, what we confidently propose to do or say?

Alcibiades: Yes.

Socrates: And if a person does that which he knows or supposes that he knows, and the result is beneficial, he will act advantageously both for himself and for the state?

Alcibiades: True.

Socrates: And if he do the contrary, both he and the state will suffer?

Alcibiades: Yes.

Socrates: Well, and are you of the same mind, as before?

Alcibiades: I am.

Socrates: But were you not saying that you would call the many unwise and the few wise?

Alcibiades: I was.

Socrates: And have we not come back to our old assertion that the many fail to obtain the best because they trust to opinion which is devoid of intelligence?

Alcibiades: That is the case.

Socrates: It is good, then, for the many, if they particularly desire to do that which they know or suppose that they know, neither to know nor to suppose that they know, in cases where if they carry out their ideas in action they will be losers rather than gainers?

Alcibiades: What you say is very true.

Socrates: Do you not see that I was really speaking the truth when I affirmed that the possession of any other kind of knowledge was more likely to injure than to benefit the possessor, unless he had also the knowledge of the best?

Alcibiades: I do now, if I did not before, Socrates.

Socrates: The state or the soul, therefore, which wishes to have a right existence must hold firmly to this knowledge, just as the sick man clings to the physician, or the passenger depends for safety on the pilot. And if the soul does not set sail until she have obtained this she will be all the safer in the voyage through life. But when she rushes in pursuit of wealth or bodily strength or anything else, not having the knowledge of the best, so much the more is she likely to meet with misfortune. And he who has the love of learning (Or, reading polumatheian, 'abundant learning.'), and is skilful in many arts, and does not possess the knowledge of the best, but is under some other guidance, will make, as he deserves, a sorry voyage:—he will, I believe, hurry through the brief space of human life, pilotless in mid-ocean, and the words will apply to him in which the poet blamed his enemy:—

'...Full many a thing he knew; But knew them all badly.' (A fragment from the pseudo-Homeric poem, 'Margites.')

Alcibiades: How in the world, Socrates, do the words of the poet apply to him? They seem to me to have no bearing on the point whatever.

Socrates: Quite the contrary, my sweet friend: only the poet is talking in riddles after the fashion of his tribe. For all poetry has by nature an enigmatical character, and it is by no means everybody who can interpret it. And if, moreover, the spirit of poetry happen to seize on a man who is of a begrudging temper and does not care to manifest his wisdom but keeps it to himself as far as he can, it does indeed require an almost superhuman wisdom to discover what the poet would be at. You surely do not suppose that Homer, the wisest and most divine of poets, was unaware of the impossibility of knowing a thing badly: for it was no less a person than he who said of Margites that 'he knew many things, but knew them all badly.' The solution of the riddle is this, I imagine:—By 'badly' Homer meant 'bad' and 'knew' stands for 'to know.' Put the words together; —the metre will suffer, but the poet's meaning is clear;—'Margites knew all these things, but it was bad for him to know them.' And, obviously, if it was bad for him to know so many things, he must have been a good-for-nothing, unless the argument has played us false.

Alcibiades: But I do not think that it has, Socrates: at least, if the argument is fallacious, it would be difficult for me to find another which I could trust.

Socrates: And you are right in thinking so.

Alcibiades: Well, that is my opinion.

Socrates: But tell me, by Heaven:—you must see now the nature and greatness of the difficulty in which you, like others, have your part. For you change about in all directions, and never come to rest anywhere: what you once most strongly inclined to suppose, you put aside again and quite alter your mind. If the God to whose shrine you are going should appear at this moment, and ask before you made your prayer, 'Whether you would desire to have one of the things which we mentioned at first, or whether he should leave you to make your own request:'—what in either case, think you, would be the best way to take advantage of the opportunity?

Alcibiades: Indeed, Socrates, I could not answer you without consideration. It seems to me to be a wild thing (The Homeric word margos is said to be here employed in allusion to the quotation from the 'Margites' which Socrates has just made; but it is not used in the sense which it has in Homer.) to make such a request; a man must be very careful lest he pray for evil under the idea that he is asking for good, when shortly after he may have to recall his prayer, and, as you were saying, demand the opposite of what he at first requested.

Socrates: And was not the poet whose words I originally quoted wiser than we are, when he bade us (pray God) to defend us from evil even though we asked for it?

Alcibiades: I believe that you are right.

Socrates: The Lacedaemonians, too, whether from admiration of the poet or because they have discovered the idea for themselves, are wont to offer the prayer alike in public and private, that the Gods will give unto them the beautiful as well as the good:—no one is likely to hear them make any further petition. And yet up to the present time they have not been less fortunate than other men; or if they have sometimes met with misfortune, the fault has not been due to their prayer. For surely, as I conceive, the Gods have power either to grant our requests, or to send us the contrary of what we ask.

And now I will relate to you a story which I have heard from certain of our elders. It chanced that when the Athenians and Lacedaemonians were at war, our city lost every battle by land and sea and never gained a victory. The Athenians being annoyed and perplexed how to find a remedy for their troubles, decided to send and enquire at the shrine of Ammon. Their envoys were also to ask, 'Why the Gods always granted the victory to the Lacedaemonians?' 'We,' (they were to say,) 'offer them more and finer sacrifices than any other Hellenic state, and adorn their temples with gifts, as nobody else does; moreover, we make the most solemn and costly processions to them every year, and spend more money in their service than all the rest of the Hellenes put together. But the Lacedaemonians take no thought of such matters, and pay so little respect to the Gods that they have a habit of sacrificing blemished animals to them, and in various ways are less zealous than we are, although their wealth is quite equal to ours.' When they had thus spoken, and had made their request to know what remedy they could find against the evils which troubled them, the prophet made no direct answer,— clearly because he was not allowed by the God to do so;—but he summoned them to him and said: 'Thus saith Ammon to the Athenians: "The silent worship of the Lacedaemonians pleaseth me better than all the offerings of the other Hellenes."' Such were the words of the God, and nothing more. He seems to have meant by 'silent worship' the prayer of the Lacedaemonians, which is indeed widely different from the usual requests of the Hellenes. For they either bring to the altar bulls with gilded horns or make offerings to the Gods, and beg at random for what they need, good or bad. When, therefore, the Gods hear them using words of ill omen they reject these costly processions and sacrifices of theirs. And we ought, I think, to be very careful and consider well what we should say and what leave unsaid. Homer, too, will furnish us with similar stories. For he tells us how the Trojans in making their encampment,

'Offered up whole hecatombs to the immortals,'

and how the 'sweet savour' was borne 'to the heavens by the winds;

'But the blessed Gods were averse and received it not.

For exceedingly did they hate the holy Ilium,

Both Priam and the people of the spear-skilled king.'

So that it was in vain for them to sacrifice and offer gifts, seeing that they were hateful to the Gods, who are not, like vile usurers, to be gained over by bribes. And it is foolish for us to boast that we are superior to the Lacedaemonians by reason of our much worship. The idea is inconceivable that the Gods have regard, not to the justice and purity of our souls, but to costly processions and sacrifices, which men may celebrate year after year, although they have committed innumerable crimes against the Gods or against their fellow-men or the state. For the Gods, as Ammon and his prophet declare, are no receivers of gifts, and they scorn such unworthy service. Wherefore also it would seem that wisdom and justice are especially honoured both by the Gods and by men of sense; and they are the wisest and most just who know how to speak and act towards Gods and men. But I should like to hear what your opinion is about these matters.

Alcibiades: I agree, Socrates, with you and with the God, whom, indeed, it would be unbecoming for me to oppose.

Socrates: Do you not remember saying that you were in great perplexity, lest perchance you should ask for evil, supposing that you were asking for good?

Alcibiades: I do.

Socrates: You see, then, that there is a risk in your approaching the God in prayer, lest haply he should refuse your sacrifice when he hears the blasphemy which you utter, and make you partake of other evils as well. The wisest plan, therefore, seems to me that you should keep silence; for your 'highmindedness'—to use the mildest term which men apply to folly—will most likely prevent you from using the prayer of the Lacedaemonians. You had better wait until we find out how we should behave towards the Gods and towards men.

Alcibiades: And how long must I wait, Socrates, and who will be my teacher? I should be very glad to see the man.

Socrates: It is he who takes an especial interest in you. But first of all, I think, the darkness must be taken away in which your soul is now enveloped, just as Athene in Homer removes the mist from the eyes of Diomede that

'He may distinguish between God and mortal man.'

Afterwards the means may be given to you whereby you may distinguish between good and evil. At present, I fear, this is beyond your power.

Alcibiades: Only let my instructor take away the impediment, whether it pleases him to call it mist or anything else! I care not who he is; but I am resolved to disobey none of his commands, if I am likely to be the better for them.

Socrates: And surely he has a wondrous care for you.

Alcibiades: It seems to be altogether advisable to put off the sacrifice until he is found.

Socrates: You are right: that will be safer than running such a tremendous risk.

Alcibiades: But how shall we manage, Socrates?—At any rate I will set this crown of mine upon your head, as you have given me such excellent advice, and to the Gods we will offer crowns and perform the other customary rites when I see that day approaching: nor will it be long hence, if they so will.

Socrates: I accept your gift, and shall be ready and willing to receive whatever else you may proffer. Euripides makes Creon say in the play, when he beholds Teiresias with his crown and hears that he has gained it by his skill as the first-fruits of the spoil:—

'An auspicious omen I deem thy victor's wreath: For well thou knowest that wave and storm oppress us.'

And so I count your gift to be a token of good-fortune; for I am in no less stress than Creon, and would fain carry off the victory over your lovers.

Lesser Hippias

Persons of the Dialogue: Eudicus; Socrates; Hippias.

EUDICUS: WHY ARE YOU SILENT, SOCRATES, AFTER THE MAGNIFICENT display which Hippias has been making? Why do you not either refute his words, if he seems to you to have been wrong in any point, or join with us in commending him? There is the more reason why you should speak, because we are now alone, and the audience is confined to those who may fairly claim to take part in a philosophical discussion.

Socrates: I should greatly like, Eudicus, to ask Hippias the meaning of what he was saying just now about Homer. I have heard your father, Apemantus, declare that the Iliad of Homer is a finer poem than the Odyssey in the same degree that Achilles was a better man than Odysseus; Odysseus, he would say, is the central figure of the one poem and Achilles of the other. Now, I should like to know, if Hippias has no objection to tell me, what he thinks about these two heroes, and which of them he maintains to be the better;

he has already told us in the course of his exhibition many things of various kinds about Homer and divers other poets.

Eudicus: I am sure that Hippias will be delighted to answer anything which you would like to ask; tell me, Hippias, if Socrates asks you a question, will you answer him?

Hippias: Indeed, Eudicus, I should be strangely inconsistent if I refused to answer Socrates, when at each Olympic festival, as I went up from my house at Elis to the temple of Olympia, where all the Hellenes were assembled, I continually professed my willingness to perform any of the exhibitions which I had prepared, and to answer any questions which any one had to ask.

Socrates: Truly, Hippias, you are to be congratulated, if at every Olympic festival you have such an encouraging opinion of your own wisdom when you go up to the temple. I doubt whether any muscular hero would be so fearless and confident in offering his body to the combat at Olympia, as you are in offering your mind.

Hippias: And with good reason, Socrates; for since the day when I first entered the lists at Olympia I have never found any man who was my superior in anything. (Compare Gorgias.)

Socrates: What an ornament, Hippias, will the reputation of your wisdom be to the city of Elis and to your parents! But to return: what say you of Odysseus and Achilles? Which is the better of the two? and in what particular does either surpass the other? For when you were exhibiting and there was company in the room, though I could not follow you, I did not like to ask what you meant, because a crowd of people were present, and I was afraid that the question might interrupt your exhibition. But now that there are not so many of us, and my friend Eudicus bids me ask, I wish you would tell me what you were saying about these two heroes, so that I may clearly understand; how did you distinguish them?

Hippias: I shall have much pleasure, Socrates, in explaining to you more clearly than I could in public my views about these and also about other heroes. I say that Homer intended Achilles to be the bravest of the men who went to Troy, Nestor the wisest, and Odysseus the wiliest.

Socrates: O rare Hippias, will you be so good as not to laugh, if I find a difficulty in following you, and repeat my questions several times over? Please to answer me kindly and gently.

Hippias: I should be greatly ashamed of myself, Socrates, if I, who teach others and take money of them, could not, when I was asked by you, answer in a civil and agreeable manner.

Socrates: Thank you: the fact is, that I seemed to understand what you meant when you said that the poet intended Achilles to be the bravest of men, and also that he intended Nestor to be the wisest; but when you said that he meant Odysseus to be the wiliest, I must confess that I could not understand what you were saying. Will you tell me, and then I shall perhaps understand you better; has not Homer made Achilles wily?

Hippias: Certainly not, Socrates; he is the most straight-forward of mankind, and when Homer introduces them talking with one another in the passage called the Prayers, Achilles is supposed by the poet to say to Odysseus:—

'Son of Laertes, sprung from heaven, crafty Odysseus, I will speak out plainly the word which I intend to carry out in act, and which will, I believe, be accomplished. For I hate him like the gates of death who thinks one thing and says another. But I will speak that which shall be accomplished.'

Now, in these verses he clearly indicates the character of the two men; he shows Achilles to be true and simple, and Odysseus to be wily and false; for he supposes Achilles to be addressing Odysseus in these lines.

Socrates: Now, Hippias, I think that I understand your meaning; when you say that Odysseus is wily, you clearly mean that he is false?

Hippias: Exactly so, Socrates; it is the character of Odysseus, as he is represented by Homer in many passages both of the Iliad and Odyssey.

Socrates: And Homer must be presumed to have meant that the true man is not the same as the false?

Hippias: Of course, Socrates.

Socrates: And is that your own opinion, Hippias?

Hippias: Certainly; how can I have any other?

Socrates: Well, then, as there is no possibility of asking Homer what he meant in these verses of his, let us leave him; but as you show a willingness to take up his cause, and your opinion agrees with what you declare to be his, will you answer on behalf of yourself and him?

Hippias: I will; ask shortly anything which you like.

Socrates: Do you say that the false, like the sick, have no power to do things, or that they have the power to do things?

Hippias: I should say that they have power to do many things, and in particular to deceive mankind.

Socrates: Then, according to you, they are both powerful and wily, are they not?

Hippias: Yes.

Socrates: And are they wily, and do they deceive by reason of their simplicity and folly, or by reason of their cunning and a certain sort of prudence?

Hippias: By reason of their cunning and prudence, most certainly.

Socrates: Then they are prudent, I suppose?

Hippias: So they are—very.

Socrates: And if they are prudent, do they know or do they not know what they do?

Hippias: Of course, they know very well; and that is why they do mischief to others.

Socrates: And having this knowledge, are they ignorant, or are they wise?

Hippias: Wise, certainly; at least, in so far as they can deceive.

Socrates: Stop, and let us recall to mind what you are saying; are you not saying that the false are powerful and prudent and knowing and wise in those things about which they are false?

Hippias: To be sure.

Socrates: And the true differ from the false—the true and the false are the very opposite of each other?

Hippias: That is my view.

Socrates: Then, according to your view, it would seem that the false are to be ranked in the class of the powerful and wise?

Hippias: Assuredly.

Socrates: And when you say that the false are powerful and wise in so far as they are false, do you mean that they have or have not the power of uttering their falsehoods if they like?

Hippias: I mean to say that they have the power.

Socrates: In a word, then, the false are they who are wise and have the power to speak falsely?

Hippias: Yes.

Socrates: Then a man who has not the power of speaking falsely and is ignorant cannot be false?

Hippias: You are right.

Socrates: And every man has power who does that which he wishes at the time when he wishes. I am not speaking of any special case in which he is prevented by disease or something of that sort, but I am speaking generally, as I might say of you, that you are able to write my name when you like. Would you not call a man able who could do that?

Hippias: Yes.

Socrates: And tell me, Hippias, are you not a skilful calculator and arithmetician?

Hippias: Yes, Socrates, assuredly I am.

Socrates: And if some one were to ask you what is the sum of 3 multiplied by 700, you would tell him the true answer in a moment, if you pleased?

Hippias: certainly I should.

Socrates: Is not that because you are the wisest and ablest of men in these matters?

Hippias: Yes.

Socrates: And being as you are the wisest and ablest of men in these matters of calculation, are you not also the best?

Hippias: To be sure, Socrates, I am the best.

Socrates: And therefore you would be the most able to tell the truth about these matters, would you not?

Hippias: Yes, I should.

Socrates: And could you speak falsehoods about them equally well? I must beg, Hippias, that you will answer me with the same frankness and magnanimity which has hitherto characterized you. If a person were to ask you what is the sum of 3 multiplied by 700, would not you be the best and most consistent teller of a falsehood, having always the power of speaking falsely as you have of speaking truly, about these same matters, if you wanted to tell a falsehood, and not to answer truly? Would the ignorant man be better able to tell a falsehood in matters of calculation than you would be, if you chose? Might he not sometimes stumble upon the truth, when he wanted to tell a lie, because he did not know, whereas you who are the wise man, if you wanted to tell a lie would always and consistently lie?

Hippias: Yes, there you are quite right.

Socrates: Does the false man tell lies about other things, but not about number, or when he is making a calculation?

Hippias: To be sure; he would tell as many lies about number as about other things.

Socrates: Then may we further assume, Hippias, that there are men who are false about calculation and number?

Hippias: Yes.

Socrates: Who can they be? For you have already admitted that he who is false must have the ability to be false: you said, as you will remember, that he who is unable to be false will not be false?

Hippias: Yes, I remember; it was so said.

Socrates: And were you not yourself just now shown to be best able to speak falsely about calculation?

Hippias: Yes; that was another thing which was said.

Socrates: And are you not likewise said to speak truly about calculation?

Hippias: Certainly.

Socrates: Then the same person is able to speak both falsely and truly about calculation? And that person is he who is good at calculation—the arithmetician?

Hippias: Yes.

Socrates: Who, then, Hippias, is discovered to be false at calculation? Is he not the good man? For the good man is the able man, and he is the true man.

Hippias: That is evident.

Socrates: Do you not see, then, that the same man is false and also true about the same matters? And the true man is not a whit better than the false; for indeed he is the same with him and not the very opposite, as you were just now imagining.

Hippias: Not in that instance, clearly.

Socrates: Shall we examine other instances?

Hippias: Certainly, if you are disposed.

Socrates: Are you not also skilled in geometry?

Hippias: I am.

Socrates: Well, and does not the same hold in that science also? Is not the same person best able to speak falsely or to speak truly about diagrams; and he is—the geometrician?

Hippias: Yes.

Socrates: He and no one else is good at it?

Hippias: Yes, he and no one else.

Socrates: Then the good and wise geometer has this double power in the highest degree; and if there be a man who is false about diagrams the good man will be he, for he is able to be false; whereas the bad is unable, and for this reason is not false, as has been admitted.

Hippias: True.

Socrates: Once more—let us examine a third case; that of the astronomer, in whose art, again, you, Hippias, profess to be a still greater proficient than in the preceding—do you not?

Hippias: Yes, I am.

Socrates: And does not the same hold of astronomy?

Hippias: True, Socrates.

Socrates: And in astronomy, too, if any man be able to speak falsely he will be the good astronomer, but he who is not able will not speak falsely, for he has no knowledge.

Hippias: Clearly not.

Socrates: Then in astronomy also, the same man will be true and false?

Hippias: It would seem so.

Socrates: And now, Hippias, consider the question at large about all the sciences, and see whether the same principle does not always hold. I know that in most arts you are the wisest of men, as I have heard you boasting in the agora at the tables of the money-changers, when you were setting forth the great and enviable stores of your wisdom; and you said that upon one occasion, when you went to the Olympic games, all that you had on your person was made by yourself. You began with your ring, which was of your own workmanship, and you said that you could engrave rings; and you had another seal which was also of your own workmanship, and a strigil and an oil flask, which you had made yourself; you said also that you had made the shoes which you had on your feet, and the cloak and the short tunic; but what appeared to us all most extraordinary and a proof of singular art, was the girdle of your tunic, which, you said, was as fine as the most costly Persian fabric, and of your own weaving; moreover, you told us that you had brought with you poems, epic, tragic, and dithyrambic, as well as prose writings of the most various kinds; and you said that your skill was also pre-eminent in the arts which I was just now mentioning, and in the true principles of rhythm and harmony and of orthography; and if I remember rightly, there were a great many other accomplishments in which you excelled. I have forgotten to mention your art of memory, which you regard as your special glory, and I dare say that I have forgotten many other things; but, as I was saying, only look to your own arts—and there are plenty of them—and to those of others; and tell me, having regard to the admissions which you and I have made, whether you discover any department of art or any description of wisdom or cunning, whichever name you use, in which the true and false are different and not the same: tell me, if you can, of any. But you cannot.

Hippias: Not without consideration, Socrates.

Socrates: Nor will consideration help you, Hippias, as I believe; but then if I am right, remember what the consequence will be.

Hippias: I do not know what you mean, Socrates.

Socrates: I suppose that you are not using your art of memory, doubtless because you think that such an accomplishment is not needed on the present occasion. I will therefore remind you of what you were saying: were you not saying that Achilles was a true man, and Odysseus false and wily?

Hippias: I was.

Socrates: And now do you perceive that the same person has turned out to be false as well as true? If Odysseus is false he is also true, and if Achilles is true he is also false, and so the two men are not opposed to one another, but they are alike.

Hippias: O Socrates, you are always weaving the meshes of an argument, selecting the most difficult point, and fastening upon details instead of grappling with the matter in hand as a whole. Come now, and I will demonstrate to you, if you will allow me, by many satisfactory proofs, that Homer has made Achilles a better man than Odysseus, and a truthful man too; and that he has made the other crafty, and a teller of many untruths, and inferior to Achilles. And then, if you please, you shall make a speech on the other side, in order to prove that Odysseus is the better man; and this may be compared to mine, and then the company will know which of us is the better speaker.

Socrates: O Hippias, I do not doubt that you are wiser than I am. But I have a way, when anybody else says anything, of giving close attention to him, especially if the speaker appears to me to be a wise man. Having a desire to understand, I question him, and I examine and analyse and put together what he says, in order that I may understand; but if the speaker appears to me to be a poor hand, I do not interrogate him, or trouble myself about him, and you may know by this who they are whom I deem to be wise men, for you will see that when I am talking with a wise man, I am very attentive to what he says; and I ask questions of him, in order that I may learn, and be improved by him. And I could not help remarking while you were speaking, that when you recited the verses in which Achilles, as you argued, attacks Odysseus as a deceiver, that you must be strangely mistaken, because Odysseus, the man of wiles, is never found to tell a lie; but Achilles is found to be wily on your own showing. At any rate he speaks falsely; for first he utters these words, which you just now repeated,—

'He is hateful to me even as the gates of death who thinks one thing and says another:'—

And then he says, a little while afterwards, he will not be persuaded by Odysseus and Agamemnon, neither will he remain at Troy; but, says he,—

'To-morrow, when I have offered sacrifices to Zeus and all the Gods, having loaded my ships well, I will drag them down into the deep; and then you shall see, if you have a mind, and if such things are a care to you, early in the morning my ships sailing over the fishy Hellespont, and my men eagerly plying the oar; and, if the illustrious shaker of the earth gives me a good voyage, on the third day I shall reach the fertile Phthia.'

And before that, when he was reviling Agamemnon, he said,—

'And now to Phthia I will go, since to return home in the beaked ships is far better, nor am I inclined to stay here in dishonour and amass wealth and riches for you.'

But although on that occasion, in the presence of the whole army, he spoke after this fashion, and on the other occasion to his companions, he appears never to have made any preparation or attempt to draw down the ships, as if he had the least intention of sailing home; so nobly regardless was he of the truth. Now I, Hippias, originally asked you the question, because I was in doubt as to which of the two heroes was intended by the poet to be the best, and because I thought that both of them were the best, and that it would be difficult to decide which was the better of them, not only in respect of truth and falsehood, but of virtue generally, for even in this matter of speaking the truth they are much upon a par.

Hippias: There you are wrong, Socrates; for in so far as Achilles speaks falsely, the falsehood is obviously unintentional. He is compelled against his will to remain and rescue the army in their misfortune. But when Odysseus speaks falsely he is voluntarily and intentionally false.

Socrates: You, sweet Hippias, like Odysseus, are a deceiver yourself.

Hippias: Certainly not, Socrates; what makes you say so?

Socrates: Because you say that Achilles does not speak falsely from design, when he is not only a deceiver, but besides being a braggart, in Homer's description of him is so cunning, and so far superior to Odysseus in lying and pretending, that he dares to contradict himself, and Odysseus does not find him out; at any rate he does not appear to say anything to him which would imply that he perceived his falsehood.

Hippias: What do you mean, Socrates?

Socrates: Did you not observe that afterwards, when he is speaking to Odysseus, he says that he will sail away with the early dawn; but to Ajax he tells quite a different story?

Hippias: Where is that?

Socrates: Where he says,—

'I will not think about bloody war until the son of warlike Priam, illustrious Hector, comes to the tents and ships of the Myrmidons, slaughtering the Argives, and burning the ships with fire; and about my tent and dark ship, I suspect that Hector, although eager for the battle, will nevertheless stay his hand.'

Now, do you really think, Hippias, that the son of Thetis, who had been the pupil of the sage Cheiron, had such a bad memory, or would have carried the art of lying to such an extent (when he had been assailing liars in the most violent terms only the instant before) as to say to Odysseus that he would sail away, and to Ajax that he would remain, and that he was not rather practising upon the simplicity of Odysseus, whom he regarded as an ancient, and thinking that he would get the better of him by his own cunning and falsehood?

Hippias: No, I do not agree with you, Socrates; but I believe that Achilles is induced to say one thing to Ajax, and another to Odysseus in the innocence of his heart, whereas Odysseus, whether he speaks falsely or truly, speaks always with a purpose.

Socrates: Then Odysseus would appear after all to be better than Achilles?

Hippias: Certainly not, Socrates.

Socrates: Why, were not the voluntary liars only just now shown to be better than the involuntary?

Hippias: And how, Socrates, can those who intentionally err, and voluntarily and designedly commit iniquities, be better than those who err and do wrong involuntarily? Surely there is a great excuse to be made for a man telling a falsehood, or doing an injury or any sort of harm to another in ignorance. And the laws are obviously far more severe on those who lie or do evil, voluntarily, than on those who do evil involuntarily.

Socrates: You see, Hippias, as I have already told you, how pertinacious I am in asking questions of wise men. And I think that this is the only good point about me, for I am full of defects, and always getting wrong in some way or other. My deficiency is proved to me by the fact that when I meet one of you who are famous for wisdom, and to whose wisdom all the Hellenes are witnesses, I am found out to know nothing. For speaking generally, I hardly ever have the same opinion about anything which you have, and what proof of ignorance can be greater than to differ from wise men? But I have one singular good quality, which is my salvation; I am not ashamed to learn, and I ask and enquire, and am very grateful to those who answer me, and never fail to give them my grateful thanks; and when I learn a thing I never deny my teacher, or pretend that the lesson is a discovery of my own; but I praise his wisdom, and proclaim what I have learned from him. And now I cannot agree in what you are saying, but I strongly disagree. Well, I know that this is my own fault, and is a defect in my character, but I will not pretend to be more than I am; and my opinion, Hippias, is the very contrary of what you are saying. For I maintain that those who hurt or injure mankind, and speak falsely and deceive, and err voluntarily, are better far than those who do wrong involuntarily. Sometimes, however, I am of the opposite opinion; for I am all abroad in my ideas about this matter, a condition obviously occasioned by ignorance. And just now I happen to be in a crisis of my disorder at which those who err voluntarily appear to me better than those who err involuntarily. My present state of mind is due to our previous argument, which inclines me to believe that in general those who do wrong involuntarily are worse than those who do wrong voluntarily, and therefore I hope that you will be good to me, and not refuse to heal me; for you will do me a much greater benefit if you cure my soul of ignorance, than you would if you were to cure my body of disease. I must, however, tell you beforehand, that if you make a long oration to me you will not cure me, for I shall not be able to follow you; but if you will answer me, as you did just now, you will do me a great deal of good, and I do not think that you will be any the worse yourself. And I have some claim upon you also, O son of Apemantus, for you incited me to converse with Hippias; and now, if Hippias will not answer me, you must entreat him on my behalf.

Eudicus: But I do not think, Socrates, that Hippias will require any entreaty of mine; for he has already said that he will refuse to answer no man.—Did you not say so, Hippias?

Hippias: Yes, I did; but then, Eudicus, Socrates is always troublesome in an argument, and appears to be dishonest. (Compare Gorgias; Republic.)

Socrates: Excellent Hippias, I do not do so intentionally (if I did, it would show me to be a wise man and a master of wiles, as you would argue), but unintentionally, and therefore you must pardon me; for, as you say, he who is unintentionally dishonest should be pardoned.

Eudicus: Yes, Hippias, do as he says; and for our sake, and also that you may not belie your profession, answer whatever Socrates asks you.

Hippias: I will answer, as you request me; and do you ask whatever you like.

Socrates: I am very desirous, Hippias, of examining this question, as to which are the better—those who err voluntarily or involuntarily? And if you will answer me, I think that I can put you in the way of approaching the subject: You would admit, would you not, that there are good runners?

Hippias: Yes.

Socrates: And there are bad runners?

Hippias: Yes.

Socrates: And he who runs well is a good runner, and he who runs ill is a bad runner?

Hippias: Very true.

Socrates: And he who runs slowly runs ill, and he who runs quickly runs well?

Hippias: Yes.

Socrates: Then in a race, and in running, swiftness is a good, and slowness is an evil quality?

Hippias: To be sure.

Socrates: Which of the two then is a better runner? He who runs slowly voluntarily, or he who runs slowly involuntarily?

Hippias: He who runs slowly voluntarily.

Socrates: And is not running a species of doing?

Hippias: Certainly.

Socrates: And if a species of doing, a species of action?

Hippias: Yes.

Socrates: Then he who runs badly does a bad and dishonourable action in a race?

Hippias: Yes; a bad action, certainly.

Socrates: And he who runs slowly runs badly?

Hippias: Yes.

Socrates: Then the good runner does this bad and disgraceful action voluntarily, and the bad involuntarily?

Hippias: That is to be inferred.

Socrates: Then he who involuntarily does evil actions, is worse in a race than he who does them voluntarily?

Hippias: Yes, in a race.

Socrates: Well, but at a wrestling match—which is the better wrestler, he who falls voluntarily or involuntarily?

Hippias: He who falls voluntarily, doubtless.

Socrates: And is it worse or more dishonourable at a wrestling match, to fall, or to throw another?

Hippias: To fall.

Socrates: Then, at a wrestling match, he who voluntarily does base and dishonourable actions is a better wrestler than he who does them involuntarily?

Hippias: That appears to be the truth.

Socrates: And what would you say of any other bodily exercise —is not he who is better made able to do both that which is strong and that which is weak—that which is fair and that which is foul?— so that when he does bad actions with the body, he who is better made does them voluntarily, and he who is worse made does them involuntarily.

Hippias: Yes, that appears to be true about strength.

Socrates: And what do you say about grace, Hippias? Is not he who is better made able to assume evil and disgraceful figures and postures voluntarily, as he who is worse made assumes them involuntarily?

Hippias: True.

Socrates: Then voluntary ungracefulness comes from excellence of the bodily frame, and involuntary from the defect of the bodily frame?

Hippias: True.

Socrates: And what would you say of an unmusical voice; would you prefer the voice which is voluntarily or involuntarily out of tune?

Hippias: That which is voluntarily out of tune.

Socrates: The involuntary is the worse of the two?

Hippias: Yes.

Socrates: And would you choose to possess goods or evils?

Hippias: Goods.

Socrates: And would you rather have feet which are voluntarily or involuntarily lame?

Hippias: Feet which are voluntarily lame.

Socrates: But is not lameness a defect or deformity?

Hippias: Yes.

Socrates: And is not blinking a defect in the eyes?

Hippias: Yes.

Socrates: And would you rather always have eyes with which you might voluntarily blink and not see, or with which you might involuntarily blink?

Hippias: I would rather have eyes which voluntarily blink.

Socrates: Then in your own case you deem that which voluntarily acts ill, better than that which involuntarily acts ill?

Hippias: Yes, certainly, in cases such as you mention.

Socrates: And does not the same hold of ears, nostrils, mouth, and of all the senses—those which involuntarily act ill are not to be desired, as being defective; and those which voluntarily act ill are to be desired as being good?

Hippias: I agree.

Socrates: And what would you say of instruments;—which are the better sort of instruments to have to do with?—those with which a man acts ill voluntarily or involuntarily? For example, had a man better have a rudder with which he will steer ill, voluntarily or involuntarily?

Hippias: He had better have a rudder with which he will steer ill voluntarily.

Socrates: And does not the same hold of the bow and the lyre, the flute and all other things?

Hippias: Very true.

Socrates: And would you rather have a horse of such a temper that you may ride him ill voluntarily or involuntarily?

Hippias: I would rather have a horse which I could ride ill voluntarily.

Socrates: That would be the better horse?

Hippias: Yes.

Socrates: Then with a horse of better temper, vicious actions would be produced voluntarily; and with a horse of bad temper involuntarily?

Hippias: Certainly.

Socrates: And that would be true of a dog, or of any other animal?

Hippias: Yes.

Socrates: And is it better to possess the mind of an archer who voluntarily or involuntarily misses the mark?

Hippias: Of him who voluntarily misses.

Socrates: This would be the better mind for the purposes of archery?

Hippias: Yes.

Socrates: Then the mind which involuntarily errs is worse than the mind which errs voluntarily?

Hippias: Yes, certainly, in the use of the bow.

Socrates: And what would you say of the art of medicine;—has not the mind which voluntarily works harm to the body, more of the healing art?

Hippias: Yes.

Socrates: Then in the art of medicine the voluntary is better than the involuntary?

Hippias: Yes.

Socrates: Well, and in lute-playing and in flute-playing, and in all arts and sciences, is not that mind the better which voluntarily does what is evil and dishonourable, and goes wrong, and is not the worse that which does so involuntarily?

Hippias: That is evident.

Socrates: And what would you say of the characters of slaves? Should we not prefer to have those who voluntarily do wrong and make mistakes, and are they not better in their mistakes than those who commit them involuntarily?

Hippias: Yes.

Socrates: And should we not desire to have our own minds in the best state possible?

Hippias: Yes.

Socrates: And will our minds be better if they do wrong and make mistakes voluntarily or involuntarily?

Hippias: O, Socrates, it would be a monstrous thing to say that those who do wrong voluntarily are better than those who do wrong involuntarily!

Socrates: And yet that appears to be the only inference.

Hippias: I do not think so.

Socrates: But I imagined, Hippias, that you did. Please to answer once more: Is not justice a power, or knowledge, or both? Must not justice, at all events, be one of these?

Hippias: Yes.

Socrates: But if justice is a power of the soul, then the soul which has the greater power is also the more just; for that which has the greater power, my good friend, has been proved by us to be the better.

Hippias: Yes, that has been proved.

Socrates: And if justice is knowledge, then the wiser will be the juster soul, and the more ignorant the more unjust?

Hippias: Yes.

Socrates: But if justice be power as well as knowledge—then will not the soul which has both knowledge and power be the more just, and that which is the more ignorant be the more unjust? Must it not be so?

Hippias: Clearly.

Socrates: And is not the soul which has the greater power and wisdom also better, and better able to do both good and evil in every action?

Hippias: Certainly.

Socrates: The soul, then, which acts ill, acts voluntarily by power and art—and these either one or both of them are elements of justice?

Hippias: That seems to be true.

Socrates: And to do injustice is to do ill, and not to do injustice is to do well?

Hippias: Yes.

Socrates: And will not the better and abler soul when it does wrong, do wrong voluntarily, and the bad soul involuntarily?

Hippias: Clearly.

Socrates: And the good man is he who has the good soul, and the bad man is he who has the bad?

Hippias: Yes.

Socrates: Then the good man will voluntarily do wrong, and the bad man involuntarily, if the good man is he who has the good soul?

Hippias: Which he certainly has.

Socrates: Then, Hippias, he who voluntarily does wrong and disgraceful things, if there be such a man, will be the good man?

Hippias: There I cannot agree with you.

Socrates: Nor can I agree with myself, Hippias; and yet that seems to be the conclusion which, as far as we can see at present, must follow from our argument. As I was saying before, I am all abroad, and being in perplexity am always changing my opinion. Now, that I or any ordinary man should wander in perplexity is not surprising; but if you wise men also wander, and we cannot come to you and rest from our wandering, the matter begins to be serious both to us and to you.

Greater Hippias

Persons of the Dialogue: Socrates; Hippias.

SOCRATES: HIPPIAS, BEAUTIFUL AND WISE, WHAT A LONG TIME IT IS since you have put in at the port of Athens!

Hippias: I am too busy, Socrates. For whenever Elis needs to have any business transacted with any of the states, she always comes to me first of her citizens and chooses me as envoy, thinking that I am the ablest judge and messenger of the words that are spoken by the several states. So I have often gone as envoy to other states, but most often and concerning the most numerous and important matters to Lacedaemon. For that reason, then, since you ask me, I do not often come to this neighborhood.

Socrates: That's what it is, Hippias, to be a truly wise and perfect man! For you are both in your private capacity able to earn much money from the young and to confer upon them still greater benefits than you receive, and in public affairs you are able to benefit your own state, as a man must who is to be not despised but held in high repute among the many. And yet, Hippias, what in the world is the reason why those men of old whose names are called great in respect to wisdom — Pittacus, and Bias, and the Milesian Thales with his followers and also the later ones, down to Anaxagoras, are all, or most of them, found to refrain from affairs of state?

Hippias: What else do you suppose, Socrates, than that they were not able to compass by their wisdom both public and private matters?

Socrates: Then for Heaven's sake, just as the other arts have progressed, and the ancients are of no account in comparison with the artisans of today, shall we say that your art also has progressed and those of the ancients who were concerned with wisdom are of no account in comparison with you?

Hippias: Yes, you are quite right.

Socrates: Then, Hippias, if Bias were to come to life again now, he would be a laughing-stock in comparison with you, just as the sculptors say that Daedalus, if he were to be born now and were to create such works as those from which he got his reputation, would be ridiculous.

Hippias: That, Socrates, is exactly as you say. I, however, am in the habit of praising the ancients and our predecessors rather than the men of the present day, and more greatly, as a precaution against the envy of the living and through fear of the wrath of those who are dead.

Socrates: Yours, Hippias, is a most excellent way, at any rate, of speaking about them and of thinking, it seems to me and I can bear you witness that you speak the truth, and that your art really has progressed in the direction of ability to carry on public together with private affairs. For this man Gorgias, the sophist from Leontini, came here from home in the public capacity of envoy, as being best able of all the citizens of Leontini to attend to the interests of the community, and it was the general opinion that he spoke excellently in the public assembly, and in his private capacity, by giving exhibitions and associating with the young, he earned and received a great deal of money from this city; or, if you like, our friend here, Prodicus, often went to other places in a public capacity, and the last time, just lately, when he came here in a public capacity from Ceos, he gained great reputation by his speaking before the Council, and in his private capacity, by giving exhibitions and associating with the young, he received a marvellous sum of money; but none of those ancients ever thought fit to exact the money as payment for his wisdom or to give exhibitions among people of various places; so simple-minded were they, and so unconscious of the fact that money is of the greatest value. But either of these two has earned more money from his wisdom than any artisan from his art. And even before these Protagoras did so.

Hippias: Why, Socrates, you know nothing of the beauties of this. For if you were to know how much money I have made, you would be amazed. I won't mention the rest, but once, when I went to Sicily, although Protagoras was staying there and had a great reputation and was the older, I, who was much younger, made in a very short time more than one hundred and fifty minas, and in one very small place, Inycus, more than twenty minas; and when I came home, I took this and gave it to my father, so that he and the other citizens were overwhelmed with amazement. And I pretty well think I have made more money than any other two sophists together.

Socrates: That's a fine thing you say, Hippias, and strong testimony to your wisdom and that of the men of today and to their great superiority to the ancients. For the earlier sophists of the school of Anaxagoras must have been very ignorant to judge from what is said, according to your view; for they say that what happened to Anaxagoras was the opposite of what happens to you; for though much money was left him, he neglected it and lost it all so senseless was his wisdom. And they tell similar tales about others among the ancients. So this seems to me fine testimony that you adduce for the wisdom of the men of today as compared with the earlier men, and many people agree with me that the wise man must be wise for himself especially; and the test of this is, who makes the most money. Well, so much for that. But tell me this: at which of the cities that you go to did you make the most money? Or are we to take it that it was at Lacedaemon, where your visits have been most frequent?

Hippias: No, by Zeus, it was not, Socrates.

Socrates: What's that you say? But did you make least there?

Hippias: Why, I never made anything at all.

Socrates: That is a prodigious marvel that you tell, Hippias; and say now: is not your wisdom such as to make those who are in contact with it and learn it, better men in respect to virtue?

Hippias: Yes, much better, Socrates.

Socrates: But you were able to make the sons of the Inycenes better, and had no power to improve the sons of the Spartans?

Hippias: That is far from true.

Socrates: Well, then, the Siceliotes desire to become better, and the Lacedaemonians do not?

Hippias: No certainly, Socrates, the Lacedaemonians also desire it.

Socrates: Then it was for lack of money that they avoided intercourse with you?

Hippias: Not at all, since they have plenty of money.

Socrates: What, then, could be the reason, that when they desired it and had money, and you had power to confer upon them the greatest benefits, they did not send you away loaded with money? But I see; perhaps the Lacedaemonians might educate their own children better than you? Shall we state it so, and do you agree?

Hippias: Not in the least.

Socrates: Then were you not able to persuade the young men at Lacedaemon that they would make more progress towards virtue by associating with you than with their own people, or were you powerless to persuade their fathers that they ought rather to hand them over to you than to care for them themselves, if they are at all concerned for their sons? For surely they did not begrudge it to their children to become as good as possible.

Hippias: I do not think they begrudged it.

Socrates: But certainly Lacedaemon is well governed.

Hippias: Of course it is.

Socrates: And in well-governed states virtue is most highly honored.

Hippias: Certainly.

Socrates: And you know best of all men how to transmit that to another.

Hippias: Much best, Socrates.

Socrates: Well, he who knows best how to transmit horsemanship would be most honored in Thessaly of all parts of Greece and would receive most money — and anywhere else where horsemanship is a serious interest, would he not?

Hippias: Very likely.

Socrates: Then will not he who is able to transmit the doctrines that are of most value for the acquisition of virtue be most highly honored in Lacedaemon and make most money, if he so wishes, and in any other of the Greek states that is well governed? But do you, my friend, think he will fare better in Sicily and at Inycus? Are we to believe that, Hippias? For if you tell us to do so, we must believe it.

Hippias: Yes, for it is not the inherited usage of the Lacedaemonians to change their laws or to educate their children differently from what is customary.

Socrates: What? For the Lacedaemonians is it the hereditary usage not to act rightly, but to commit errors?

Hippias: I wouldn't say so, Socrates.

Socrates: Would they, then, not act rightly in educating the young men better, but not in educating them worse?

Hippias: Yes, they would; but it is not lawful for them to give them a foreign education; for you may be sure that if anybody had ever received money there in payment for education, I should have received by far the most; they certainly enjoy hearing me and they applaud me; but, as I say, it is not the law.

Socrates: But, Hippias, do you say that law is an injury to the state, or a benefit?

Hippias: It is made, I think, with benefit in view, but sometimes, if the law is badly made, it is injurious.

Socrates: Well, then, is it not true that those who make the law make it as the greatest good to the state, and that without this it is impossible to enjoy good government?

Hippias: What you say is true.

Socrates: Then, when those who make the laws miss the good, they have missed the lawful and the law; or what do you say?

Hippias: Speaking accurately, Socrates, that is true; however, men are not accustomed to think so.

Socrates: The men who know, Hippias, or those who do not know?

Hippias: The many.

Socrates: Are these, the many, those who know the truth?

Hippias: Certainly not.

Socrates: But surely those who know, think that in truth for all men that which is more beneficial is more lawful than that which is less beneficial; or do you not agree?

Hippias: Yes, I agree that they think it is so in truth.

Socrates: Well, it actually is as those who know think it is, is it not?

Hippias: Certainly.

Socrates: But or the Lacedaemonians, as you say, it is more beneficial to be educated in your education, which is foreign, than in the local education.

Hippias: Yes, and what I say is true.

Socrates: And do you say this also, Hippias, that beneficial things are more lawful?

Hippias: Yes, I said so.

Socrates: Then, according to what you say, it is more lawful for the sons of the Lacedaemonians to be educated by Hippias and less lawful for them to be educated by their fathers, if in reality they will be more benefited by you.

Hippias: But certainly they will be benefited, Socrates.

Socrates: Then the Lacedaemonians in not giving you money and entrusting their sons to you, act contrary to law.

Hippias: I agree to that; for you seem to be making your argument in my favour, and there is no need of my opposing it.

Socrates: Then my friends, we find that the Lacedaemonians are law-breakers, and that too in the most important affairs — they who are regarded as the most law-abiding of men. But then, for Heaven's sake, Hippias, what sort of discourses are those for which they applaud you and which they enjoy hearing? Or are they evidently those which you understand most admirably, those about the stars and the phenomena of the heavens?

Hippias: Not in the least; they won't even endure those.

Socrates: But they enjoy hearing about geometry?

Hippias: Not at all, since one might say that many of them do not even know how to count.

Socrates: Then they are far from enduring a lecture by you on the processes of thought.

Hippias: Far from it indeed, by Zeus.

Socrates: Well, then, those matters which you of all men know best how to discuss, concerning the value of letters and syllables and rhythms and harmonies?

Hippias: Harmonies indeed, my good fellow, and letters!

Socrates: But then what are the things about which they like to listen to you and which they applaud? Tell me yourself, for I cannot discover them.

Hippias: They are very fond of hearing about the genealogies of heroes and men, Socrates, and the foundations of cities in ancient times and, in short, about antiquity in general, so that for their sake I have been obliged to learn all that sort of thing by heart and practise it thoroughly.

Socrates: By Zeus, Hippias, it is lucky for you that the Lacedaemonians do not enjoy hearing one recite the list of our archons from Solon's time; if they did, you would have trouble in learning it by heart.

Hippias: How so, Socrates? After hearing them once, I can remember fifty names.

Socrates: True, but I did not understand that you possess the science of memory; and so I understand that the Lacedaemonians naturally enjoy you as one who knows many things, and they make use of you as children make use of old women, to tell stories agreeably.

Hippias: And by Zeus, Socrates, I have just lately gained reputation there by telling about noble or beautiful pursuits, recounting what those of a young man should be. For I have a very beautiful discourse composed about them, well arranged in its words and also in other respects. And the plan of the discourse, and its beginning, is something like this: After the fall of Troy, the story goes that Neoptolemus asked Nestor what the noble and beautiful pursuits were, by following which a young man would become most famous; so after that we have Nestor speaking and suggesting to him very many lawful and most beautiful pursuits. That discourse, then, I delivered there and intend to deliver here the day after tomorrow in Pheidostratus's schoolroom, with many other things worth hearing; for Eudicus, the son of Apemantus, asked me to do so. Now be sure to be there yourself and to bring others who are able to judge of discourses that they hear.

Socrates: Well, that shall be done, God willing, Hippias. Now, however, give me a brief answer to a question about your discourse, for you reminded me of the beautiful just at the right moment. For recently, my most excellent friend, as I was finding fault with some things in certain speeches as ugly and praising other things as beautiful, a man threw me into confusion by questioning me very insolently somewhat after this fashion: "How, if you please, do you know, Socrates," said he, "what sort of things are beautiful and ugly? For, come now, could you tell me what the beautiful is?" And I, being of no account, was at a loss and could not answer him properly; and so, as I was going away from the company, I was angry with myself and reproached myself, and threatened that the first time I met one of you wise men, I would hear and learn and practise and then go back to the man who questioned me to renew the wordy strife. So now, as I say, you have come at the right moment; just teach me satisfactorily what the absolute beautiful is, and try in replying to speak as accurately as possible, that I may not be confuted a second time and be made ridiculous again. For you doubtless know clearly, and this would doubtless be but a small example of your wide learning.

Hippias: Yes, surely, by Zeus, a small one, Socrates, and, I may say, of no value.

Socrates: Then I shall learn it easily, and nobody will confute me any more.

Hippias: Nobody, surely; for in that case my profession would be worthless and ordinary.

Socrates: That is good, by Hera, Hippias, if we are to worst the fellow. But may I without hindering you imitate him, and when you answer, take exception to what you say, in order that you may give me as much practice as possible? For I am more or less experienced in taking exceptions. So, if it is all the same to you, I wish to take exceptions, that I may learn more vigorously.

Hippias: Oh yes, take exceptions. For, as I said just now, the question is no great matter, but I could teach you to answer much harder ones than this, so that nobody in the world could confute you.

Socrates: Oh how good that is! But come, since you tell me to do so, now let me try to play that man's part, so far as possible, and ask you questions. For if you were to deliver for him this discourse that you mention, the one about beautiful pursuits, when he had heard it, after you had stopped speaking, the very first thing he would ask about would be the beautiful; for he has that sort of habit, and he would say, "Stranger from Elis, is it not by justice that the just are just?" So answer, Hippias, as though he were asking the question.

Hippias: I shall answer that it is by justice.

Socrates: "Then this — I mean justice — is something?"

Hippias: Certainly.

Socrates: "Then, too, by wisdom the wise are wise and by the good all things are good, are they not?"

Hippias: Of course.

Socrates: "And justice, wisdom, and so forth are something; for the just, wise, and so forth would not be such by them, if they were not something."

Hippias: To be sure, they are something.

Socrates: "Then are not all beautiful things beautiful by the beautiful?"

Hippias: Yes, by the beautiful.

Socrates: "By the beautiful, which is something?"

Hippias: Yes, for what alternative is there?

Socrates: "Tell me, then, stranger," he will say, "what is this, the beautiful?"

Hippias: Well, Socrates, does he who asks this question want to find out anything else than what is beautiful?

Socrates: I do not think that is what he wants to find out, but what the beautiful is.

Hippias: And what difference is there between the two?

Socrates: Do you think there is none?

Hippias: Yes, for there is no difference.

Socrates: Well, surely it is plain that you know best; but still, my good friend, consider; for he asked you, not what is beautiful, but what the beautiful is.

Hippias: I understand, my good friend, and I will answer and tell him what the beautiful is, and I shall never be confuted. For be assured, Socrates, if I must speak the truth, a beautiful maiden is beautiful.

Socrates: Beautifully answered, Hippias, by the dog, and notably! Then if I give this answer, I shall have answered the question that was asked, and shall have answered it correctly, and shall never be confuted?

Hippias: Yes, for how could you, Socrates, be confuted, when you say what everybody thinks, and when all who hear it will bear witness that what you say is correct?

Socrates: Very well; certainly. Come, then, Hippias, let me rehearse to myself what you say. The man will question me in some such fashion as this: "Come Socrates, answer me. All these things which you say are beautiful, if the absolute beautiful is anything, would be beautiful?" And I shall say that if a beautiful maiden is beautiful, there is something by reason of which these things would be beautiful.

Hippias: Do you think, then, that he will still attempt to refute you and to show that what you say is not beautiful, or, if he does attempt it, that he will not be ridiculous?

Socrates: That he will attempt it, my admirable friend, I am sure but whether the attempt will make him ridiculous, the event will show. However, I should like to tell you what he will ask.

Hippias: Do so.

Socrates: "How charming you are, Socrates!" he will say. "But is not a beautiful mare beautiful, which even the god praised in his oracle?" What shall we say, Hippias? Shall we not say that the mare is beautiful, I mean the beautiful mare? For how could we dare to deny that the beautiful thing is beautiful?

Hippias: Quite true, Socrates for what the god said is quite correct, too; for very beautiful mares are bred in our country.

Socrates: "Very well," he will say, "and how about a beautiful lyre? Is it not beautiful?" Shall we agree, Hippias?

Hippias: Yes.

Socrates: After this, then, the man will ask, I am sure, judging by his character: "You most excellent man, how about a beautiful pot? Is it, then, not beautiful?"

Hippias: Socrates, who is the fellow? What an uncultivated person, who has the face to mention such worthless things in a dignified discussion!

Socrates: That's the kind of person he is, Hippias, not elegant, but vulgar, thinking of nothing but the truth. But nevertheless the man must be answered, and I will declare my opinion beforehand: if the pot were made by a good potter, were smooth and round and well fired, as are some of the two-handled pots, those that hold six choes, very beautiful ones — if that were the kind of pot he asked about, we must agree that it is beautiful; for how could we say that being beautiful it is not beautiful?

Hippias: We could not at all, Socrates.

Socrates: "Then," he will say, "a beautiful pot also is beautiful, is it not?" Answer.

Hippias: Well, Socrates, it is like this, I think. This utensil, when well wrought, is beautiful, but absolutely considered it does not deserve to be regarded as beautiful in comparison with a mare and a maiden and all the beautiful things.

Socrates: Very well I understand, Hippias, that the proper reply to him who asks these questions is this: "Sir, you are not aware that the saying of Heracleitus is good, that 'the most beautiful of monkeys is ugly compared with the race of man,' and the most beautiful of pots is ugly compared with the race of maidens, as Hippias the wise man says." Is it not so, Hippias?

Hippias: Certainly, Socrates; you replied rightly.

Socrates: Listen then. For I am sure that after this he will say: "Yes, but, Socrates, if we compare maidens with gods, will not the same thing happen to them that happened to pots when compared with maidens? Will not the most beautiful maiden appear ugly? Or does not Heracleitus, whom you cite, mean just this, that the wisest of men, if compared with a god, will appear a monkey, both in wisdom and in beauty and in everything else?" Shall we agree, Hippias, that the most beautiful maiden is ugly if compared with the gods?

Hippias: Yes, for who would deny that, Socrates?

Socrates: If, then, we agree to that, he will laugh and say: "Socrates, do you remember the question you were asked?" "I do," I shall say, "the question was what the absolute beautiful is." "Then," he will say, "when you were asked for the beautiful, do you give as your reply what is, as you yourself say, no more beautiful than ugly?" "So it seems," I shall say; or what do you, my friend, advise me to say?

Hippias: That is what I advise; for, of course, in saying that the human race is not beautiful in comparison with gods, you will be speaking the truth.

Socrates: "But if I had asked you," he will say, "in the beginning what is beautiful and ugly, if you had replied as you now do, would you not have replied correctly? But do you still think that the absolute beautiful, by the addition of which all other things are adorned and made to appear beautiful, when its form is added to any of them — do you think that is a maiden or a mare or a lyre?"

Hippias: Well, certainly, Socrates, if that is what he is looking for, nothing is easier than to answer and tell him what the beautiful is, by which all other things are adorned and by the addition of which they are made to appear beautiful. So the fellow is very simple-minded and knows nothing about beautiful possessions. For if you reply to him: "This that you ask about, the beautiful, is nothing else but gold," he will be thrown into confusion and will not attempt to confute you. For we all know, I fancy, that wherever this is added, even what before appears ugly will appear beautiful when adorned with gold.

Socrates: You don't know the man, Hippias, what a wretch he is, and how certain not to accept anything easily.

Hippias: What of that, then, Socrates? For he must perforce accept what is correct, or if he does not accept it, be ridiculous.

Socrates: This reply, my most excellent friend, he not only will certainly not accept, but he will even jeer at me grossly and will say: "You lunatic, do you think Pheidias is a bad craftsman?" And I shall say, "Not in the least."

Hippias: And you will be right, Socrates.

Socrates: Yes, to be sure. Consequently when I agree that Pheidias is a good craftsman, "Well, then," he will say, "do you imagine that Pheidias did not know this beautiful that you speak of?" "Why do you ask that?" I shall say. "Because," he will say, "he did not make the eyes of his Athena of gold, nor the rest of her face, nor her hands and feet, if, that is, they were sure to appear most beautiful provided only they were made of gold, but he made them of ivory; evidently he made this mistake through ignorance, not knowing that it is gold which makes everything beautiful to which it is added." When he says that, what reply shall we make to him, Hippias?

Hippias: That is easy; for we shall say that Pheidias did right; for ivory, I think, is beautiful.

Socrates: "Why, then," he will say, "did he not make the middle parts of the eyes also of ivory, but of stone, procuring stone as similar as possible to the ivory? Or is beautiful stone also beautiful?" Shall we say that it is, Hippias?

Hippias: Surely we shall say so, that is, where it is appropriate.

Socrates: "But ugly when not appropriate?" Shall I agree, or not?

Hippias: Agree, that is, when it is not appropriate.

Socrates: "What then? Do not gold and ivory," he will say, "when they are appropriate, make things beautiful, and when they are not appropriate, ugly?" Shall we deny that, or agree that what he says is correct?

Hippias: We shall agree to this, at any rate, that whatever is appropriate to any particular thing makes that thing beautiful.

Socrates: "Well, then," he will say, "when some one has boiled the pot of which we were speaking just now, the beautiful one, full of beautiful soup, is a golden ladle appropriate to it, or one made of fig wood?"

Hippias: Heracles! What a fellow this is that you speak of! Won't you tell me who he is?

Socrates: You would not know him if I should tell you his name.

Hippias: But even now I know that he is an ignoramus.

Socrates: He is a great nuisance, Hippias, but yet, what shall we say? Which of the two ladles shall we say is appropriate to the soup and the pot? Is it not evidently the one of fig wood? For it is likely to make the soup smell better, and besides, my friend, it would not break the pot, thereby spilling the soup, putting out the fire, and making those who are to be entertained go without their splendid soup; whereas the golden ladle would do all those things, so that it seems to me that we must say that the wooden ladle is more appropriate than the golden one, unless you disagree.

Hippias: No, for it is more appropriate, Socrates; however, I, for my part, would not talk with the fellow when he asks such questions.

Socrates: Quite right, my friend; for it would not be appropriate for you to be filled up with such words, you who are so beautifully clad, so beautifully shod, and so famous for your wisdom among all the Greeks; but for me it doesn't matter if I do associate with the fellow; so instruct me and for my sake answer him. "For if the wooden one is more appropriate than the golden one," the fellow will say, "would it not be more beautiful, since you agreed, Socrates, that the appropriate is more beautiful than that which is not appropriate?" Shall we not agree, Hippias, that the wooden one is more beautiful than the golden?

Hippias: Do you wish me to tell you, Socrates, what definition of the beautiful will enable you to free yourself from long discussion?

Socrates: Certainly; but not until after you have told me which of the two ladles I just spoke of I shall reply is appropriate and more beautiful.

Hippias: Well, if you like, reply to him that it is the one made of fig wood.

Socrates: Now, then, say what you were just now going to say. For by this reply, if I say that the beautiful is gold, it seems to me that gold will be shown to be no more beautiful than fig wood; but what do you now, once more, say that the beautiful is?

Hippias: I will tell you; for you seem to me to be seeking to reply that the beautiful is something of such sort that it will never appear ugly anywhere to anybody.

Socrates: Certainly, Hippias; now you understand beautifully.

Hippias: Listen, then; for, mind you, if anyone has anything to say against this, you may say I know nothing at all.

Socrates: Then for Heaven's sake, speak as quickly as you can.

Hippias: I say, then, that for every man and everywhere it is most beautiful to be rich and healthy, and honored by the Greeks, to reach old age, and, after providing a beautiful funeral for his deceased parents, to be beautifully and splendidly buried by his own offspring.

Socrates: Bravo, bravo, Hippias! You have spoken in a way that is wonderful and great and worthy of you; and now, by Hera, I thank you, because you are kindly coming to my assistance to the best of your ability. But our shots are not hitting the man; no, he will laugh at us now more than ever, be sure of that.

Hippias: A wretched laugh, Socrates; for when he has nothing to say to this, but laughs, he will be laughing at himself and will himself be laughed at by those present.

Socrates: Perhaps that is so perhaps, however, after this reply, he will, I foresee, be likely to do more than laugh at me.

Hippias: Why do you say that, pray?

Socrates: Because, if he happens to have a stick, unless I get away in a hurry, he will try to fetch me a good one.

Hippias: What? Is the fellow some sort of master of yours, and if he does that, will he not be arrested and have to pay for it? Or does your city disregard justice and allow the citizens to beat one another unjustly?

Socrates: Oh no that is not allowed at all.

Hippias: Then he will have to pay a penalty for beating you unjustly.

Socrates: I do not think so, Hippias. No, if I were to make that reply, the beating would be just, I think.

Hippias: Then I think so, too, Socrates, since that is your own belief.

Socrates: Shall I, then, not tell you why it is my own belief that the beating would be just, if I made that reply? Or will you also beat me without trial? Or will you listen to what I have to say?

Hippias: It would be shocking if I would not listen; but what have you to say?

Socrates: I will tell you, imitating him in the same way as a while ago, that I may not use to you such harsh and uncouth words as he uses to me. For you may be sure, "Tell me, Socrates," he will say, "do you think it would be unjust if you got a beating for singing such a long dithyramb so unmusically and so far from the question?" "How so?" I shall say. "How so?" he will say; "are you not able to remember that I asked for the absolute beautiful, by which everything to which it is added has the property of being beautiful, both stone and stick and man and god and every act and every acquisition of knowledge? For what I am asking is this, man: what is absolute beauty? and I cannot make you hear what I say any more than if you were a stone sitting beside me, and a millstone at that, having neither ears nor brain." Would you, then, not be angry, Hippias, if I should be frightened and should reply in this way? "Well, but Hippias said that this was the beautiful; and yet I asked him, just as you asked me, what is beautiful to all and always." What do you say? Will you not be angry if I say that?

Hippias: I know very well, Socrates, that this which I said was beautiful is beautiful to all and will seem so.

Socrates: And will it be so, too he will say for the beautiful is always beautiful, is it not?

Hippias: Certainly.

Socrates: "Then was it so, too?" he will say.

Hippias: It was so, too.

Socrates: "And," he will say, "did the stranger from Elis say also that for Achilles it was beautiful to be buried later than his parents, and for his grandfather Aeacus, and all the others who were born of gods, and for the gods themselves?"

Hippias: What's that? Confound it! These questions of the fellow's are not even respectful to religion.

Socrates: Well, then, when another asks the question, perhaps it is not quite disrespectful to religion to say that these things are so?

Hippias: Perhaps.

Socrates: "Perhaps, then, you are the man," he will say, "who says that it is beautiful for every one and always to be buried by one's offspring, and to bury one's parents; or was not Heracles included in 'every one,' he and all those whom we just now mentioned?"

Hippias: But I did not say it was so for the gods.

Socrates: "Nor for the heroes either, apparently."

Hippias: Not those who were children of gods.

Socrates: "But those who were not?"

Hippias: Certainly.

Socrates: "Then again, according to your statement, among the heroes it is terrible and impious and disgraceful for Tantalus and Dardanus and Zethus, but beautiful for Pelops and the others who were born as he was?"

Hippias: I think so.

Socrates: "You think, then, what you did not say just now, that to bury one's parents and be buried by one's offspring is sometimes and for some persons disgraceful; and it is still more impossible, as it seems, for this to become and to be beautiful for all, so that the same thing has happened to this as to the things we mentioned before, the maiden and the pot, in a still more ridiculous way than to them; it is beautiful for some and not beautiful for others. And you are not able yet, even today, Socrates," he will say, "to answer what is asked about the beautiful, namely what it is." With these words and the like he will rebuke me, if I reply to him in this way. For the most

part, Hippias, he talks with me in some such way as that but sometimes, as if in pity for my inexperience and lack of training, he
himself volunteers a question, and asks whether I think the beautiful
is so and so or whatever else it is which happens to be the subject of
our questions and our discussion.

Hippias: What do you mean by that, Socrates?

Socrates: I will tell you. "Oh, my dear Socrates," he says, "stop
making replies of this sort and in this way — for they are too silly
and easy to refute; but see if something like this does not seem to
you to be beautiful, which we got hold of just now in our reply,
when we said that gold was beautiful for those things for which it
was appropriate, but not for those for which it was not, and that all
the other things were beautiful to which this quality pertains; so
examine this very thing, the appropriate, and see if it is perchance
the beautiful." Now I am accustomed to agree to such things every
time for I don't know what to say; but now does it seem to you that
the appropriate is the beautiful?

Hippias: Yes, certainly, Socrates.

Socrates: Let us consider, lest we make a mistake somehow.

Hippias: Yes, we must consider.

Socrates: See, then; do we say that the appropriate is that which,
when it is added, makes each of those things to which it is added
appear beautiful, or which makes them be beautiful, or neither of
these?

Hippias: I think so.

Socrates: Which?

Hippias: That which makes them appear beautiful; as when a
man takes clothes or shoes that fit, even if he be ridiculous, he
appears more beautiful.

Socrates: Then if the appropriate makes him appear more beautiful than he is, the appropriate would be a sort of deceit in respect
to the beautiful, and would not be that which we are looking for,
would it, Hippias? For we were rather looking for that by which all
beautiful things are beautiful — like that by which all great things
are great, that is, excess; for it is by this that all great things are
great; for even if they do not appear great, but exceed, they are of

necessity great; so, then, we say, what would the beautiful be, by which all things are beautiful, whether they appear so or not? For it could not be the appropriate, since that, by your statement, makes things appear more beautiful than they are, but does not let them appear such as they are. But we must try to say what that is which makes things be beautiful, as I said just now, whether they appear so or not; for that is what we are looking for, since we are looking for the beautiful.

Hippias: But the appropriate, Socrates, makes things both be and appear beautiful by its presence.

Socrates: Is it impossible, then, for things which are really beautiful not to appear to be beautiful, at any rate when that is present which makes them appear so?

Hippias: It is impossible.

Socrates: Shall we, then, agree to this, Hippias, that all things which are really beautiful, both uses and pursuits, are always believed to be beautiful by all, and appear so to them, or, quite the contrary, that people are ignorant about them, and that there is more strife and contention about them than about anything else, both in private between individuals and in public between states?

Hippias: The latter rather, Socrates; that people are ignorant about them.

Socrates: They would not be so, if the appearance of beauty were added to them; and it would be added, if the appropriate were beautiful and made things not only to be beautiful, but also to appear so. So that the appropriate, if it is that which makes things be beautiful, would be the beautiful which we are looking for, but would not be that which makes things appear beautiful; but if, on the other hand, the appropriate is that which makes things appear beautiful, it would not be the beautiful for which we are looking. For that makes things be beautiful, but the same element could not make things both appear and be beautiful, nor could it make them both appear and be anything else whatsoever. Let us choose, then, whether we think that the appropriate is that which makes things appear or be beautiful.

Hippias: That which makes them appear so, in my opinion, Socrates.

Socrates: Whew! Our perception of what the beautiful is has fled away and gone, Hippias, since the appropriate has been found to be something other than the beautiful.

Hippias: Yes, by Zeus, Socrates, and to me that is very queer.

Socrates: However, my friend, let us not yet give it up, for I still have hopes that what the beautiful is will be made clear.

Hippias: Certainly, to be sure, Socrates, for it is not hard to find. Now I know that if I should go away into solitude and meditate alone by myself, I could tell it to you with the most perfect accuracy.

Socrates: Ah, don't boast, Hippias. You see how much trouble it has caused us already; I'm afraid it may get angry and run away more than ever. And yet that is nonsense; for you, I think, will easily find it when you go away by yourself. But for Heaven's sake, find it in my presence, or, if you please, join me, as you are now doing, in looking for it. And if we find it, that will be splendid, but if we do not, I shall, I suppose, accept my lot, and you will go away and find it easily. And if we find it now, I shall certainly not be a nuisance to you by asking what that was which you found by yourself; but now once more see if this is in your opinion the beautiful : I say, then, that it is — but consider, paying close attention to me, that I may not talk nonsense — for I say, then, whatever is useful shall be for us beautiful. But I said it with this reason for my thought; beautiful eyes, we say, are not such as seem to be so, which are unable to see, but those which are able and useful for seeing. Is that right?

Hippias: Yes.

Socrates: Then, too, in the same way we say that the whole body is beautiful, part of it for running, part for wrestling; and again all the animals, a beautiful horse or cock or quail and all utensils and land vehicles, and on the sea freight-ships and ships of war; and all instruments in music and in the other arts, and, if you like, customs and laws also — pretty well all these we call beautiful in the same way looking at each of them — how it is formed by nature, how it is wrought, how it has been enacted — the useful we call beautiful, and beautiful in the way in which it is useful, and for the purpose for which it is useful, and at the time when it is useful; and that which is in all these aspects useless we say is ugly. Now is not this your opinion also, Hippias?

Hippias: It is.

Socrates: Then are we right in saying that the useful rather than everything else is beautiful?

Hippias: We are right, surely, Socrates.

Socrates: Now that which has power to accomplish anything is useful for that for which it has power, but that which is powerless is useless, is it not?

Hippias: Certainly.

Socrates: Power, then, is beautiful, and want of power is disgraceful or ugly.

Hippias: Decidedly. Now other things, Socrates, testify for us that this is so, but especially political affairs; for in political affairs and in one's own state to be powerful is the most beautiful of all things, but to be powerless is the most disgraceful of all.

Socrates: Good! Then, for Heaven's sake, Hippias, is wisdom also for this reason the most beautiful of all things and ignorance the most disgraceful of all things?

Hippias: Well, what do you suppose, Socrates?

Socrates: Just keep quiet, my dear friend; I am so afraid and wondering what in the world we are saying again.

Hippias: What are you afraid of again, Socrates, since now your discussion has gone ahead most beautifully?

Socrates: I wish that might be the case; but consider this point with me: could a person do what he did not know how and was utterly powerless to do?

Hippias: By no means; for how could he do what he was powerless to do?

Socrates: Then those who commit errors and accomplish and do bad things involuntarily, if they were powerless to do those things, would not do them?

Hippias: Evidently not.

Socrates: But yet it is by power that those are powerful who are powerful for surely it is not by powerlessness.

Hippias: Certainly not.

Socrates: And all who do, have power to do what they do?

Hippias: Yes.

Socrates: Men do many more bad things than good, from childhood up, and commit many errors involuntarily.

Hippias: That is true.

Socrates: Well, then, this power and these useful things, which are useful for accomplishing something bad — shall we say that they are beautiful, or far from it?

Hippias: Far from it, in my opinion, Socrates.

Socrates: Then, Hippias, the powerful and the useful are not, as it seems, our beautiful.

Hippias: They are, Socrates, if they are powerful and useful for good.

Socrates: Then that assertion, that the powerful and useful are beautiful without qualification, is gone; but was this, Hippias, what our soul wished to say, that the useful and the powerful for doing something good is the beautiful?

Hippias: Yes, in my opinion.

Socrates: But surely this is beneficial; or is it not?

Hippias: Certainly.

Socrates: So by this argument the beautiful persons and beautiful customs and all that we mentioned just now are beautiful because they are beneficial.

Hippias: Evidently.

Socrates: Then the beneficial seems to us to be the beautiful, Hippias.

Hippias: Yes, certainly, Socrates.

Socrates: But the beneficial is that which creates good.

Hippias: Yes, it is.

Socrates: But that which creates is nothing else than the cause; am I right?

Hippias: It is so.

Socrates: Then the beautiful is the cause of the good.

Hippias: Yes, it is.

Socrates: But surely, Hippias, the cause and that of which the cause is the cause are different; for the cause could not well be the cause of the cause. But look at it in this way was not the cause seen to be creating?

Hippias: Yes, certainly.

Socrates: By that which creates, then, only that is created which comes into being, but not that which creates. Is not that true?

Hippias: That is true.

Socrates: The cause, then, is not the cause of the cause, but of that which comes into being through it.

Hippias: Certainly.

Socrates: If, then, the beautiful is the cause of good, the good would come into being through the beautiful; and this is why we are eager for wisdom and all the other beautiful things, because their offspring, the good, is worthy of eagerness, and, from what we are finding, it looks as if the beautiful were a sort of father of the good.

Hippias: Certainly for what you say is well said, Socrates.

Socrates: Then is this well said, too, that the father is not the son, and the son not father?

Hippias: To be sure it is well said.

Socrates: And neither is the cause that which comes into being, nor is that which comes into being the cause.

Hippias: True.

Socrates: By Zeus, my good friend, then neither is the beautiful good, nor the good beautiful; or does it seem to you possible, after what has been said?

Hippias: No, by Zeus, it does not appear so to me.

Socrates: Does it please us, and should we be willing to say that the beautiful is not good, and the good not beautiful?

Hippias: No, by Zeus, it does not please me at all.

Socrates: Right, by Zeus, Hippias! And it pleases me least of all the things we have said.

Hippias: Yes, that is likely.

Socrates: Then there is a good chance that the statement that the beneficial and the useful and the powerful to create something good are beautiful, is not, as it appeared to be, the most beautiful of of statements, but, if that be possible, is even more ridiculous than those first ones in which we thought the maiden was the beautiful, and each of the various other things we spoke of before.

Hippias: That is likely.

Socrates: And Hippias, I no longer know where to turn; I am at a loss; but have you anything to say?

Hippias: Not at the moment, but, as I said just now, I am sure I shall find it after meditation.

Socrates: But it seems to me that I am so eager to know that I cannot wait for you while you delay; for I believe I have just now found a way out. Just see; how would it help us towards our goal if we were to say that that is beautiful which makes us feel joy; I do not mean all pleasures, but that which makes us feel joy through hearing and sight? For surely beautiful human beings, Hippias, and all decorations and paintings and works of sculpture which are beautiful, delight us when we see them; and beautiful sounds and music in general and speeches and stories do the same thing, so that if we were to reply to that impudent fellow, "My excellent man, the beautiful is that which is pleasing through hearing and sight," don't you think that we should put a stop to his impudence?

Hippias: To me, at any rate, Socrates, it seems that the nature of the beautiful is now well stated.

Socrates: But what then? Shall we say, Hippias, that beautiful customs and laws are beautiful because they are pleasing through hearing and sight, or that they have some other form of beauty?

Hippias: Perhaps, Socrates, these things might slip past the man unnoticed.

Socrates: No, by dog, Hippias — not past the man before whom I should be most ashamed of talking nonsense and pretending that I was talking sense when I was not.

Hippias: What man is that?

Socrates: Socrates, the son of Sophroniscus, who would no more permit me to say these things carelessly without investigation than to say that I know what I do not know.

Hippias: But certainly I also, now that you have mentioned it, think that this about the laws is something different.

Socrates: Not too fast, Hippias; for very likely we have fallen into the same perplexity about the beautiful in which we were a while ago, although we think we have found another way out.

Hippias: What do you mean by that, Socrates?

Socrates: I will tell you what presents itself to me, if perhaps there may be some sense in it. For perhaps these matters of laws and customs might be shown to be not outside of the perception which we have through hearing and sight; but let us stick to the statement that that which is pleasing through the senses is beautiful, without interjecting the matter of the laws. But if this man of whom I speak, or anyone else whosoever, should ask us: "Hippias and Socrates, did you make the distinction that in the category of the pleasing that which is pleasing in the way you mention is beautiful, whereas you say that that which is pleasing according to the other senses — those concerned with food and drink and sexual love and all such things — is not beautiful? Or do you say that such things are not even pleasing and that there is no pleasure at all in them, nor in anything else except sight and hearing?" What shall we say, Hippias?

Hippias: Certainly, by all means, Socrates, we shall say that there are very great pleasures in the other things also.

Socrates: "Why, then," he will say, "if they are pleasures no less than the others, do you take from them this designation and deprive them of being beautiful?" "Because," we shall say, "everybody would laugh at us if we should say that eating is not pleasant but is beautiful, and that a pleasant odor is not pleasant but is beautiful; and as to the act of sexual love, we should all, no doubt, contend that it is most pleasant, but that one must, if he perform it, do it so that no one else shall see, because it is most repulsive to see." If we say this, Hippias, "I too understand," he will perhaps say, "that you have all along been ashamed to say that these pleasures are beautiful, because they do not seem so to people; but that is not what I asked, what seems to most people to be beautiful, but what is so." We shall, then, I fancy, say, as we suggested, "We say that that part of the pleasant which comes by sight and hearing is beautiful." Do you think the statement is of any use, Hippias, or shall we say something else?

Hippias: Inevitably, in view of what has been said, Socrates, we must say just that.

Socrates: "Excellent!" he will say. "Then if that which is pleasant through sight and hearing is beautiful, that among pleasant things which does not happen to be of that sort would evidently not be beautiful?" Shall we agree?

Hippias: Yes.

Socrates: "Is, then, that which is pleasant through sight," he will say, "pleasant through sight and hearing, or is that which is pleasant through hearing pleasant through hearing and sight?" "No," we shall say, "that which is pleasant through each of these would not in the least be pleasant through both — for that is what you appear to us to mean — but we said that either of these pleasant things would be beautiful alone by itself, and both together." Is not that the reply we shall make?

Hippias: Certainly.

Socrates: "Does, then," he will say, "any pleasant thing whatsoever differ from any pleasant thing whatsoever by this, by being pleasant? I ask not whether any pleasure is greater or smaller or more or less, but whether it differs by just this very thing, by the fact that one of the pleasures is a pleasure and the other is not a pleasure." "We do not think so." Do we?

Hippias: No, we do not.

Socrates: "Is it not," then, he will say, "for some other reason than because they are pleasures that you chose these pleasures out from the other pleasures — it was because you saw some quality in both, since they have something different from the others, in view of which you say that they are beautiful? For the reason why that which is pleasant through sight is beautiful, is not, I imagine, because it is through sight; for if that were the cause of its being beautiful, the other pleasure, that through hearing, would not be beautiful; it certainly is not pleasure through sight." Shall we say "What you say is true"?

Hippias: Yes, we shall.

Socrates: "Nor, again, is the pleasure through hearing beautiful for the reason that it is through hearing; for in that case, again, the pleasure through sight would not be beautiful; it certainly is not pleasure through hearing." Shall we say, Hippias, that the man who says that speaks the truth?

Hippias: Yes, he speaks the truth.

Socrates: "But yet both are beautiful, as you say." We do say that, do we not?

Hippias: We do.

Socrates: "They have, then, something identical which makes them to be beautiful, this common quality which pertains to both of them in common and to each individually; for otherwise they would not both collectively and each individually be beautiful." Answer me, as if you were answering him.

Hippias: I answer, and I think it is as you say.

Socrates: If, then, these pleasures are both affected in any way collectively, but each individually is not so affected, it is not by this affection that they would be beautiful.

Hippias: And how could that be, Socrates, when neither of them individually is affected by some affection or other, that then both are affected by that affection by which neither is affected?

Socrates: You think it cannot be?

Hippias: I should have to be very inexperienced both in the nature of these things and in the language of our present discussion.

Socrates: Very pretty, Hippias. But there is a chance that I think I see a case of that kind which you say is impossible, but do not really see it.

Hippias: There's no chance about it, Socrates, but you quite purposely see wrongly.

Socrates: And certainly many such cases appear before my mind, but I mistrust them because they do not appear to you, a man who has made more money by wisdom than anyone now living, but to me who never made any money at all; and the thought disturbs me that you are playing with me and purposely deceiving me, they appear to me in such numbers and with such force.

Hippias: Nobody, Socrates, will know better than you whether I am playing with you or not, if you proceed to tell these things that appear to you; for it will be apparent to you that you are talking nonsense. For you will never find that you and I are both affected by an affection by which neither of us is affected.

Socrates: What are you saying, Hippias? Perhaps you are talking sense, and I fail to understand; but let me tell more clearly what I wish to say. For it appears to me that it is possible for us both to be so affected as to be something which I am not so affected as to be, and which I am not and you are not either; and again for neither of us to be so affected as to be other things which we both are.

Hippias: Your reply, Socrates, seems to involve miracles again even greater than those of your previous reply. For consider: if we are both just, would not each of us be just also, and if each is unjust, would not both again also be unjust, or if both are healthy, each of us also? Or if each of us were to be tired or wounded or struck or affected in any other way whatsoever, should we not both of us be affected in the same way? Then, too, if we were to be golden or of silver or of ivory, or, if you please, noble or wise or honored or old or young or whatever else you like of all that flesh is heir to, is it not quite inevitable that each of us be that also?

Socrates: Absolutely.

Hippias: But you see, Socrates, you do not consider the entirety of things, nor do they with whom you are in the habit of conversing, but you all test the beautiful and each individual entity by taking them separately and cutting them to pieces. For this reason you fail to observe that embodiments of reality are by nature so great and undivided. And now you have failed to observe to such a degree that you think there is some affection or reality which pertains to both of these together, but not to each individually, or again to each, but not to both; so unreasoning and undiscerning and foolish and unreflecting is your state of mind.

Socrates: Human affairs, Hippias, are not what a man wishes, but what he can, as the proverb goes which people are constantly citing; but you are always aiding us with admonitions. For now too, until we were admonished by you of our foolish state of mind — shall I continue to speak and make you a still further exhibition of our thoughts on the subject, or shall I not speak?

Hippias: You will speak to one who knows, Socrates, for I know the state of mind of all who are concerned with discussions; but nevertheless, if you prefer, speak.

Socrates: Well, I do prefer. For we, my friend, were so stupid, before you spoke, as to have an opinion concerning you and me, that each of us was one, but that we were not both that which each of us was — for we are not one, but two — so foolish were we. But now we have been taught by you that if we are both two, then each of us is inevitably two, and if each is one, then both are inevitably one; for it is impossible, by the continuous doctrine of reality according to Hippias, that it be otherwise, but what we both are, that each is, and what each is, both are. So now I have been convinced by you, and I hold this position. But first, Hippias, refresh my memory: Are you and I one, or are you two and I two?

Hippias: What do you mean, Socrates?

Socrates: Just what I say; for I am afraid to speak plainly to you, because you are vexed with me, when you think you are talking sensibly; however, tell me further: is not each of us one and affected in such a way as to be one?

Hippias: Certainly.

Socrates: Then each of us, if one, would be an odd number; or do you not consider one an odd number?

Hippias: I do.

Socrates: Then are we both an odd number, being two?

Hippias: That could not be, Socrates.

Socrates: But we are both an even number, are we not?

Hippias: Certainly.

Socrates: Then because we are both even, is each of us on that account even?

Hippias: No, surely not.

Socrates: Then it is not absolutely inevitable, as you said just now, that what both are, each is, and what each is, both are.

Hippias: Not things of this sort, but such as I mentioned before.

Socrates: That suffices, Hippias; for even this is welcome, since it appears that some things are so and some are not so. For I said, if you remember the beginning of this discussion, that pleasure through sight and through hearing were beautiful, not by that by which each of them was so affected as to be beautiful, but not both, nor both but not each, but by that by which both and each were so affected, because you conceded that both and each were beautiful. For this reason I thought that if both are beautiful they must be beautiful by that essence which belongs to both, but not by that which is lacking in each; and I still think so. But tell me, as in the beginning: If pleasure through sight and pleasure through hearing are both and each beautiful, does not that which makes them beautiful belong to both and to each?

Hippias: Certainly.

Socrates: Is it, then, for this reason, because each is a pleasure and both are pleasures, that they would be beautiful? Or would all other pleasures be for this reason no less beautiful than they? For we saw, if you remember, that they were no less pleasures.

Hippias: Yes, I remember.

Socrates: But for this reason, because these pleasures were through sight and hearing, it was said that they are beautiful.

Hippias: Yes, that is what was said.

Socrates: See if what I say is true. For it was said, if my memory serves me, that this "pleasant" was beautiful, not all "pleasant," but that which is through sight and hearing.

Hippias: True.

Socrates: Now this quality belongs to both, but not to each, does it not? For surely each of them, as was said before, is not through both senses, but both are through both, and each is not. Is that true?

Hippias: It is.

Socrates: Then it is not by that which does not belong to each that each of them is beautiful; for "both" does not belong to each; so that it is possible, according to our hypothesis, to say that they both are beautiful, but not to say that each is so; or what shall we say? Is that not inevitable?

Hippias: It appears so.

Socrates: Shall we say, then, that both are beautiful, but that each is not?

Hippias: What is to prevent?

Socrates: This seems to me, my friend, to prevent, that there were some attributes thus belonging to individual things, which belonged, we thought, to each, if they belonged to both, and to both, if they belonged to each — I mean all those attributes which you specified. Am I right?

Hippias: Yes.

Socrates: But those again which I specified did not; and among those were precisely "each" and "both". Is that so?

Hippias: It is.

Socrates: To which group, then, Hippias, does the beautiful seem to you to belong? To the group of those that you mentioned? If I am strong and you also, are we both collectively strong, and if I am just and you also, are we both collectively just, and if both collectively, then each individually so, too, if I am beautiful and you also, are we both collectively beautiful, and if both collectively, then each individually? Or is there nothing to prevent this, as in the case that when given things are both collectively even, they may perhaps individually be odd, or perhaps even, and again, when things are individually irrational quantities they may perhaps both collectively be rational, or perhaps irrational, and countless other cases which, you know, I said appeared before my mind? To which group do you assign the beautiful? Or have you the same view about it as I? For to me it seems great foolishness that we collectively are beautiful, but each of us is not so, or that each of us is so, but both are not, or anything else of that sort. Do you choose in this way, as I do, or in some other way?

Hippias: In this way, Socrates.

Socrates: You choose well, Hippias, that we may be free from the need of further search; for if the beautiful is in this group, that which is pleasing through sight and hearing would no longer be the beautiful. For the expression through sight and hearing makes both collectively beautiful, but not each individually; and this was impossible, as you and I agree.

Hippias: Yes, we agree.

Socrates: It is, then, impossible that the pleasant through sight and hearing be the beautiful, since in becoming beautiful it offers an impossibility.

Hippias: That is true.

Socrates: "Then tell us again," he will say, "from the beginning, since you failed this time; what do you say that this 'beautiful', belonging to both the pleasures, is, on account of which you honored them before the rest and called them beautiful?" It seems to me, Hippias, inevitable that we say that these are the most harmless and the best of pleasures, both of them collectively and each of them individually; or have you anything else to suggest, by which they excel the rest?

Hippias: Not at all; for really they are the best.

Socrates: "This, then," he will say, "you say is the beautiful, beneficial pleasure?" "It seems that we do," I shall say; and you?

Hippias: I also.

Socrates: "Well, then," he will say, "beneficial is that which creates the good, but that which creates and that which is created were just now seen to be different, and our argument has come round to the earlier argument, has it not? For neither could the good be beautiful nor the beautiful good, if each of them is different from the other." "Absolutely true," we shall say, if we are reasonable; for it is inadmissible to disagree with him who says what is right.

Hippias: But now, Socrates, what do you think all this amounts to? It is mere scrapings and shavings of discourse, as I said a while ago, divided into bits; but that other ability is beautiful and of great worth, the ability to produce a discourse well and beautifully in a court of law or a council-house or before any other public body before which the discourse may be delivered, to convince the audience and to carry off, not the smallest, but the greatest of prizes, the salvation of oneself, one's property, and one's friends. For these things, therefore, one must strive, renouncing these petty arguments, that one may not, by busying oneself, as at present, with mere talk and nonsense, appear to be a fool.

Socrates: My dear Hippias, you are blessed because you know the things a man ought to practise, and have, as you say, practised them satisfactorily. But I, as it seems, am possessed by some accursed fortune, so that I am always wandering and perplexed, and, exhibiting my perplexity to you wise men, am in turn reviled by you in speech whenever I exhibit it. For you say of me, what you are now saying, that I busy myself with silly little matters of no account; but when in turn I am convinced by you and say what you say, that it is by far the best thing to be able to produce a discourse well and beautifully and gain one's end in a court of law or in any other assemblage, I am called everything that is bad by some other men here and especially by that man who is continually refuting me; for he is a very near relative of mine and lives in the same house. So whenever I go home to my own house, and he hears me saying these things, he asks me if I am not ashamed that I have the face to talk about beautiful practices, when it is so plainly shown, to my confusion, that I do not even know what the beautiful itself is. "And yet how are you to know," he will say, "either who produced a discourse, or anything else whatsoever, beautifully, or not, when you are ignorant of the beautiful? And when you are in such a condition, do you think it is better for you to be alive than dead?" So it has come about, as I say, that I am abused and reviled by you and by him. But perhaps it is necessary to endure all this, for it is quite reasonable that I might be benefited by it. So I think, Hippias, that I have been benefited by conversation with both of you; for I think I know the meaning of the proverb "beautiful things are difficult".

Eryxias

Persons of the Dialogue: Socrates, Eryxias, Erasistratus, Critias.

Scene: The portico of a temple of Zeus.

IT HAPPENED BY CHANCE THAT ERYXIAS THE STEIRIAN WAS WALKING with me in the Portico of Zeus the Deliverer, when there came up to us Critias and Erasistratus, the latter the son of Phaeax, who was the nephew of Erasistratus. Now Erasistratus had just arrived from Sicily and that part of the world. As they approached, he said, Hail, Socrates!

Socrates: The same to you, I said; have you any good news from Sicily to tell us?

Erasistratus: Most excellent. But, if you please, let us first sit down; for I am tired with my yesterday's journey from Megara.

Socrates: Gladly, if that is your desire.

Erasistratus: What would you wish to hear first? he said. What the Sicilians are doing, or how they are disposed towards our city? To my mind, they are very like wasps: so long as you only cause them a little annoyance they are quite unmanageable; you must destroy their nests if you wish to get the better of them. And in a similar way, the Syracusans, unless we set to work in earnest, and go against them with a great expedition, will never submit to our rule. The petty injuries which we at present inflict merely irritate them enough to make them utterly intractable. And now they have sent ambassadors to Athens, and intend, I suspect, to play us some trick. —While we were talking, the Syracusan envoys chanced to go by, and Erasistratus, pointing to one of them, said to me, That, Socrates, is the richest man in all Italy and Sicily. For who has larger estates or more land at his disposal to cultivate if he please? And they are of a quality, too, finer than any other land in Hellas. Moreover, he has all the things which go to make up wealth, slaves and horses innumerable, gold and silver without end.

I saw that he was inclined to expatiate on the riches of the man; so I asked him, Well, Erasistratus, and what sort of character does he bear in Sicily?

Erasistratus: He is esteemed to be, and really is, the wickedest of all the Sicilians and Italians, and even more wicked than he is rich; indeed, if you were to ask any Sicilian whom he thought to be the worst and the richest of mankind, you would never hear any one else named.

I reflected that we were speaking, not of trivial matters, but about wealth and virtue, which are deemed to be of the greatest moment, and I asked Erasistratus whom he considered the wealthier,—he who was the possessor of a talent of silver or he who had a field worth two talents?

Erasistratus: The owner of the field.

Socrates: And on the same principle he who had robes and bedding and such things which are of greater value to him than to a stranger would be richer than the stranger?

Erasistratus: True.

Socrates: And if any one gave you a choice, which of these would you prefer?

Erasistratus: That which was most valuable.

Socrates: In which way do you think you would be the richer?

Erasistratus: By choosing as I said.

Socrates: And he appears to you to be the richest who has goods of the greatest value?

Erasistratus: He does.

Socrates: And are not the healthy richer than the sick, since health is a possession more valuable than riches to the sick? Surely there is no one who would not prefer to be poor and well, rather than to have all the King of Persia's wealth and to be ill. And this proves that men set health above wealth, else they would never choose the one in preference to the other.

Erasistratus: True.

Socrates: And if anything appeared to be more valuable than health, he would be the richest who possessed it?

Erasistratus: He would.

Socrates: Suppose that some one came to us at this moment and were to ask, Well, Socrates and Eryxias and Erasistratus, can you tell me what is of the greatest value to men? Is it not that of which the possession will best enable a man to advise how his own and his friend's affairs should be administered?—What will be our reply?

Erasistratus: I should say, Socrates, that happiness was the most precious of human possessions.

Socrates: Not a bad answer. But do we not deem those men who are most prosperous to be the happiest?

Erasistratus: That is my opinion.

Socrates: And are they not most prosperous who commit the fewest errors in respect either of themselves or of other men?

Erasistratus: Certainly.

Socrates: And they who know what is evil and what is good; what should be done and what should be left undone;—these behave the most wisely and make the fewest mistakes?

Erasistratus agreed to this.

Socrates: Then the wisest and those who do best and the most fortunate and the richest would appear to be all one and the same, if wisdom is really the most valuable of our possessions?

Yes, said Eryxias, interposing, but what use would it be if a man had the wisdom of Nestor and wanted the necessaries of life, food

and drink and clothes and the like? Where would be the advantage
of wisdom then? Or how could he be the richest of men who might
even have to go begging, because he had not wherewithal to live?

I thought that what Eryxias was saying had some weight, and I
replied, Would the wise man really suffer in this way, if he were so
ill-provided; whereas if he had the house of Polytion, and the house
were full of gold and silver, he would lack nothing?

Eryxias: Yes; for then he might dispose of his property and
obtain in exchange what he needed, or he might sell it for money
with which he could supply his wants and in a moment procure
abundance of everything.

Socrates: True, if he could find some one who preferred such a
house to the wisdom of Nestor. But if there are persons who set
great store by wisdom like Nestor's and the advantages accruing
from it, to sell these, if he were so disposed, would be easier still. Or
is a house a most useful and necessary possession, and does it make
a great difference in the comfort of life to have a mansion like Polytion's instead of living in a shabby little cottage, whereas wisdom is
of small use and it is of no importance whether a man is wise or
ignorant about the highest matters? Or is wisdom despised of men
and can find no buyers, although cypress wood and marble of
Pentelicus are eagerly bought by numerous purchasers? Surely the
prudent pilot or the skilful physician, or the artist of any kind who is
proficient in his art, is more worth than the things which are especially reckoned among riches; and he who can advise well and
prudently for himself and others is able also to sell the product of
his art, if he so desire.

Eryxias looked askance, as if he had received some unfair treatment, and said, I believe, Socrates, that if you were forced to speak
the truth, you would declare that you were richer than Callias the
son of Hipponicus. And yet, although you claimed to be wiser about
things of real importance, you would not any the more be richer
than he.

I dare say, Eryxias, I said, that you may regard these arguments
of ours as a kind of game; you think that they have no relation to
facts, but are like the pieces in the game of draughts which the

player can move in such a way that his opponents are unable to make any countermove. (Compare Republic.) And perhaps, too, as regards riches you are of opinion that while facts remain the same, there are arguments, no matter whether true or false, which enable the user of them to prove that the wisest and the richest are one and the same, although he is in the wrong and his opponents are in the right. There would be nothing strange in this; it would be as if two persons were to dispute about letters, one declaring that the word Socrates began with an S, the other that it began with an A, and the latter could gain the victory over the former.

Eryxias glanced at the audience, laughing and blushing at once, as if he had had nothing to do with what had just been said, and replied,—No, indeed, Socrates, I never supposed that our arguments should be of a kind which would never convince any one of those here present or be of advantage to them. For what man of sense could ever be persuaded that the wisest and the richest are the same? The truth is that we are discussing the subject of riches, and my notion is that we should argue respecting the honest and dishonest means of acquiring them, and, generally, whether they are a good thing or a bad.

Very good, I said, and I am obliged to you for the hint: in future we will be more careful. But why do not you yourself, as you introduced the argument, and do not think that the former discussion touched the point at issue, tell us whether you consider riches to be a good or an evil?

I am of opinion, he said, that they are a good. He was about to add something more, when Critias interrupted him:—Do you really suppose so, Eryxias?

Certainly, replied Eryxias; I should be mad if I did not: and I do not fancy that you would find any one else of a contrary opinion.

And I, retorted Critias, should say that there is no one whom I could not compel to admit that riches are bad for some men. But surely, if they were a good, they could not appear bad for any one?

Here I interposed and said to them: If you two were having an argument about equitation and what was the best way of riding, supposing that I knew the art myself, I should try to bring you to an agreement. For I should be ashamed if I were present and did not do what I could to prevent your difference. And I should do the same if you were quarrelling about any other art and were likely, unless you agreed on the point in dispute, to part as enemies instead of as friends. But now, when we are contending about a thing of which the usefulness continues during the whole of life, and it makes an enormous difference whether we are to regard it as beneficial or not,—a thing, too, which is esteemed of the highest importance by the Hellenes:—(for parents, as soon as their children are, as they think, come to years of discretion, urge them to consider how wealth may be acquired, since by riches the value of a man is judged):—When, I say, we are thus in earnest, and you, who agree in other respects, fall to disputing about a matter of such moment, that is, about wealth, and not merely whether it is black or white, light or heavy, but whether it is a good or an evil, whereby, although you are now the dearest of friends and kinsmen, the most bitter hatred may arise betwixt you, I must hinder your dissension to the best of my power. If I could, I would tell you the truth, and so put an end to the dispute; but as I cannot do this, and each of you supposes that you can bring the other to an agreement, I am prepared, as far as my capacity admits, to help you in solving the question. Please, therefore, Critias, try to make us accept the doctrines which you yourself entertain.

Critias: I should like to follow up the argument, and will ask Eryxias whether he thinks that there are just and unjust men?

Eryxias: Most decidedly.

Critias: And does injustice seem to you an evil or a good?

Eryxias: An evil.

Critias: Do you consider that he who bribes his neighbour's wife and commits adultery with her, acts justly or unjustly, and this although both the state and the laws forbid?

Eryxias: Unjustly.

Critias: And if the wicked man has wealth and is willing to spend it, he will carry out his evil purposes? whereas he who is short of means cannot do what he fain would, and therefore does not sin? In such a case, surely, it is better that a person should not be wealthy, if his poverty prevents the accomplishment of his desires, and his desires are evil? Or, again, should you call sickness a good or an evil?

Eryxias: An evil.

Critias: Well, and do you think that some men are intemperate?

Eryxias: Yes.

Critias: Then, if it is better for his health that the intemperate man should refrain from meat and drink and other pleasant things, but he cannot owing to his intemperance, will it not also be better that he should be too poor to gratify his lust rather than that he should have a superabundance of means? For thus he will not be able to sin, although he desire never so much.

Critias appeared to be arguing so admirably that Eryxias, if he had not been ashamed of the bystanders, would probably have got up and struck him. For he thought that he had been robbed of a great possession when it became obvious to him that he had been wrong in his former opinion about wealth. I observed his vexation, and feared that they would proceed to abuse and quarrelling: so I said,—I heard that very argument used in the Lyceum yesterday by a wise man, Prodicus of Ceos; but the audience thought that he was talking mere nonsense, and no one could be persuaded that he was speaking the truth. And when at last a certain talkative young gentleman came in, and, taking his seat, began to laugh and jeer at Prodicus, tormenting him and demanding an explanation of his argument, he gained the ear of the audience far more than Prodicus.

Can you repeat the discourse to us? Said Erasistratus.

Socrates: If I can only remember it, I will. The youth began by asking Prodicus, In what way did he think that riches were a good and in what an evil? Prodicus answered, as you did just now, that they were a good to good men and to those who knew in what way they should be employed, while to the bad and the ignorant they were an evil. The same is true, he went on to say, of all other things; men make them to be what they are themselves. The saying of Archilochus is true:—

'Men's thoughts correspond to the things which they meet with.'

Well, then, replied the youth, if any one makes me wise in that wisdom whereby good men become wise, he must also make everything else good to me. Not that he concerns himself at all with these other things, but he has converted my ignorance into wisdom. If, for example, a person teach me grammar or music, he will at the same time teach me all that relates to grammar or music, and so when he makes me good, he makes things good to me.

Prodicus did not altogether agree: still he consented to what was said.

And do you think, said the youth, that doing good things is like building a house,—the work of human agency; or do things remain what they were at first, good or bad, for all time?

Prodicus began to suspect, I fancy, the direction which the argument was likely to take, and did not wish to be put down by a mere stripling before all those present:—(if they two had been alone, he would not have minded):—so he answered, cleverly enough: I think that doing good things is a work of human agency.

And is virtue in your opinion, Prodicus, innate or acquired by instruction?

The latter, said Prodicus.

Then you would consider him a simpleton who supposed that he could obtain by praying to the Gods the knowledge of grammar or music or any other art, which he must either learn from another or find out for himself?

Prodicus agreed to this also.

And when you pray to the Gods that you may do well and receive good, you mean by your prayer nothing else than that you desire to become good and wise:—if, at least, things are good to the good and wise and evil to the evil. But in that case, if virtue is acquired by instruction, it would appear that you only pray to be taught what you do not know.

Hereupon I said to Prodicus that it was no misfortune to him if he had been proved to be in error in supposing that the Gods immediately granted to us whatever we asked:—if, I added, whenever you go up to the Acropolis you earnestly entreat the Gods to grant you good things, although you know not whether they can yield your request, it is as though you went to the doors of the grammarian and begged him, although you had never made a study of the art, to give you a knowledge of grammar which would enable you forthwith to do the business of a grammarian.

While I was speaking, Prodicus was preparing to retaliate upon his youthful assailant, intending to employ the argument of which you have just made use; for he was annoyed to have it supposed that he offered a vain prayer to the Gods. But the master of the gymnasium came to him and begged him to leave because he was teaching the youths doctrines which were unsuited to them, and therefore bad for them.

I have told you this because I want you to understand how men are circumstanced in regard to philosophy. Had Prodicus been present and said what you have said, the audience would have thought him raving, and he would have been ejected from the gymnasium. But you have argued so excellently well that you have not only persuaded your hearers, but have brought your opponent to an agreement. For just as in the law courts, if two witnesses testify to the same fact, one of whom seems to be an honest fellow and the other a rogue, the testimony of the rogue often has the contrary effect on the judges' minds to what he intended, while the same evidence if given by the honest man at once strikes them as perfectly true. And probably the audience have something of the same feeling about yourself and Prodicus; they think him a Sophist and a braggart, and regard you as a gentleman of courtesy and worth. For they do not pay attention to the argument so much as to the character of the speaker.

But truly, Socrates, said Erasistratus, though you may be joking, Critias does seem to me to be saying something which is of weight.

Socrates: I am in profound earnest, I assure you. But why, as you have begun your argument so prettily, do you not go on with the rest? There is still something lacking, now you have agreed that (wealth) is a good to some and an evil to others. It remains to enquire what constitutes wealth; for unless you know this, you cannot possibly come to an understanding as to whether it is a good or an evil. I am ready to assist you in the enquiry to the utmost of my power: but first let him who affirms that riches are a good, tell us what, in his opinion, is wealth.

Erasistratus: Indeed, Socrates, I have no notion about wealth beyond that which men commonly have. I suppose that wealth is a quantity of money (compare Arist. Pol.); and this, I imagine, would also be Critias' definition.

Socrates: Then now we have to consider, What is money? Or else later on we shall be found to differ about the question. For instance, the Carthaginians use money of this sort. Something which is about the size of a stater is tied up in a small piece of leather: what it is, no one knows but the makers. A seal is next set upon the leather, which then passes into circulation, and he who has the largest number of such pieces is esteemed the richest and best off. And yet if any one among us had a mass of such coins he would be no wealthier than if he had so many pebbles from the mountain. At Lacedaemon, again, they use iron by weight which has been rendered useless: and he who has the greatest mass of such iron is thought to be the richest, although elsewhere it has no value. In Ethiopia engraved stones are employed, of which a Lacedaemonian could make no use. Once more, among the Nomad Scythians a man who owned the house of Polytion would not be thought richer than one who possessed Mount Lycabettus among ourselves. And clearly those things cannot all be regarded as possessions; for in some cases the possessors would appear none the richer thereby: but, as I was saying, some one of them is thought in one place to be money, and the possessors of it are the wealthy, whereas in some other place it is not money, and the ownership of it does not confer wealth; just as the standard of morals varies, and what is honourable to some men is dishonourable to others. And if we wish to enquire why a house is valuable to us but not to the Scythians, or why the Carthaginians value leather which is worthless to us, or the Lacedaemonians find wealth in iron and we do not, can we not get an answer in some such way as this: Would an Athenian, who had a thousand talents weight of the stones which lie about in the Agora and which we do not employ for any purpose, be thought to be any the richer?

Erasistratus: He certainly would not appear so to me.

Socrates: But if he possessed a thousand talents weight of some precious stone, we should say that he was very rich?

Erasistratus: Of course.

Socrates: The reason is that the one is useless and the other useful?

Erasistratus: Yes.

Socrates: And in the same way among the Scythians a house has no value because they have no use for a house, nor would a Scythian set so much store on the finest house in the world as on a leather coat, because he could use the one and not the other. Or again, the Carthaginian coinage is not wealth in our eyes, for we could not employ it, as we can silver, to procure what we need, and therefore it is of no use to us.

Erasistratus: True.

Socrates: What is useful to us, then, is wealth, and what is useless to us is not wealth?

But how do you mean, Socrates? said Eryxias, interrupting. Do we not employ in our intercourse with one another speech and violence (?) and various other things? These are useful and yet they are not wealth.

Socrates: Clearly we have not yet answered the question, What is wealth? That wealth must be useful, to be wealth at all,—thus much is acknowledged by every one. But what particular thing is wealth, if not all things? Let us pursue the argument in another way; and then we may perhaps find what we are seeking. What is the use of wealth, and for what purpose has the possession of riches been invented,—in the sense, I mean, in which drugs have been discovered for the cure of disease? Perhaps in this way we may throw some light on the question. It appears to be clear that whatever constitutes wealth must be useful, and that wealth is one class of useful things; and now we have to enquire, What is the use of those useful things which constitute wealth? For all things probably may be said to be useful which we use in production, just as all things which have life are animals, but there is a special kind of animal which we call 'man.' Now if any one were to ask us, What is that of which, if we were rid, we should not want medicine and the

instruments of medicine, we might reply that this would be the case
if disease were absent from our bodies and either never came to
them at all or went away again as soon as it appeared; and we may
therefore conclude that medicine is the science which is useful for
getting rid of disease. But if we are further asked, What is that from
which, if we were free, we should have no need of wealth? can we
give an answer? If we have none, suppose that we restate the question thus:—If a man could live without food or drink, and yet suffer
neither hunger nor thirst, would he want either money or anything
else in order to supply his needs?

Eryxias: He would not.

Socrates: And does not this apply in other cases? If we did not
want for the service of the body the things of which we now stand
in need, and heat and cold and the other bodily sensations were
unperceived by us, there would be no use in this so-called wealth, if
no one, that is, had any necessity for those things which now make
us wish for wealth in order that we may satisfy the desires and needs
of the body in respect of our various wants. And therefore if the
possession of wealth is useful in ministering to our bodily wants, and
bodily wants were unknown to us, we should not need wealth, and
possibly there would be no such thing as wealth.

Eryxias: Clearly not.

Socrates: Then our conclusion is, as would appear, that wealth is
what is useful to this end?

Eryxias once more gave his assent, but the small argument
considerably troubled him.

Socrates: And what is your opinion about another question:—
Would you say that the same thing can be at one time useful and at
another useless for the production of the same result?

Eryxias: I cannot say more than that if we require the same
thing to produce the same result, then it seems to me to be useful; if
not, not.

Socrates: Then if without the aid of fire we could make a
brazen statue, we should not want fire for that purpose; and if we
did not want it, it would be useless to us? And the argument applies
equally in other cases.

Eryxias: Clearly.

Socrates: And therefore conditions which are not required for the existence of a thing are not useful for the production of it?

Eryxias: Of course not.

Socrates: And if without gold or silver or anything else which we do not use directly for the body in the way that we do food and drink and bedding and houses,—if without these we could satisfy the wants of the body, they would be of no use to us for that purpose?

Eryxias: They would not.

Socrates: They would no longer be regarded as wealth, because they are useless, whereas that would be wealth which enabled us to obtain what was useful to us?

Eryxias: O Socrates, you will never be able to persuade me that gold and silver and similar things are not wealth. But I am very strongly of opinion that things which are useless to us are not wealth, and that the money which is useful for this purpose is of the greatest use; not that these things are not useful towards life, if by them we can procure wealth.

Socrates: And how would you answer another question? There are persons, are there not, who teach music and grammar and other arts for pay, and thus procure those things of which they stand in need?

Eryxias: There are.

Socrates: And these men by the arts which they profess, and in exchange for them, obtain the necessities of life just as we do by means of gold and silver?

Eryxias: True.

Socrates: Then if they procure by this means what they want for the purposes of life, that art will be useful towards life? For do we not say that silver is useful because it enables us to supply our bodily needs?

Eryxias: We do.

Socrates: Then if these arts are reckoned among things useful, the arts are wealth for the same reason as gold and silver are, for, clearly, the possession of them gives wealth. Yet a little while ago we found it difficult to accept the argument which proved that the wisest are the wealthiest. But now there seems no escape from this conclusion. Suppose that we are asked, 'Is a horse useful to everybody?' will not our reply be, 'No, but only to those who know how to use a horse?'

Eryxias: Certainly.

Socrates: And so, too, physic is not useful to every one, but only to him who knows how to use it?

Eryxias: True.

Socrates: And the same is the case with everything else?

Eryxias: Yes.

Socrates: Then gold and silver and all the other elements which are supposed to make up wealth are only useful to the person who knows how to use them?

Eryxias: Exactly.

Socrates: And were we not saying before that it was the business of a good man and a gentleman to know where and how anything should be used?

Eryxias: Yes.

Socrates: The good and gentle, therefore will alone have profit from these things, supposing at least that they know how to use them. But if so, to them only will they seem to be wealth. It appears, however, that where a person is ignorant of riding, and has horses which are useless to him, if some one teaches him that art, he makes him also richer, for what was before useless has now become useful to him, and in giving him knowledge he has also conferred riches upon him.

Eryxias: That is the case.

Socrates: Yet I dare be sworn that Critias will not be moved a whit by the argument.

Critias: No, by heaven, I should be a madman if I were. But why do you not finish the argument which proves that gold and silver and other things which seem to be wealth are not real wealth? For I have been exceedingly delighted to hear the discourses which you have just been holding.

Socrates: My argument, Critias (I said), appears to have given you the same kind of pleasure which you might have derived from some rhapsode's recitation of Homer; for you do not believe a word of what has been said. But come now, give me an answer to this question. Are not certain things useful to the builder when he is building a house?

Critias: They are.

Socrates: And would you say that those things are useful which are employed in house building,—stones and bricks and beams and the like, and also the instruments with which the builder built the house, the beams and stones which they provided, and again the instruments by which these were obtained?

Critias: It seems to me that they are all useful for building.

Socrates: And is it not true of every art, that not only the materials but the instruments by which we procure them and without which the work could not go on, are useful for that art?

Critias: Certainly.

Socrates: And further, the instruments by which the instruments are procured, and so on, going back from stage to stage ad infinitum,—are not all these, in your opinion, necessary in order to carry out the work?

Critias: We may fairly suppose such to be the case.

Socrates: And if a man has food and drink and clothes and the other things which are useful to the body, would he need gold or silver or any other means by which he could procure that which he now has?

Critias: I do not think so.

Socrates: Then you consider that a man never wants any of these things for the use of the body?

Critias: Certainly not.

Socrates: And if they appear useless to this end, ought they not always to appear useless? For we have already laid down the principle that things cannot be at one time useful and at another time not, in the same process.

Critias: But in that respect your argument and mine are the same. For you maintain if they are useful to a certain end, they can never become useless; whereas I say that in order to accomplish some results bad things are needed, and good for others.

Socrates: But can a bad thing be used to carry out a good purpose?

Critias: I should say not.

Socrates: And we call those actions good which a man does for the sake of virtue?

Critias: Yes.

Socrates: But can a man learn any kind of knowledge which is imparted by word of mouth if he is wholly deprived of the sense of hearing?

Critias: Certainly not, I think.

Socrates: And will not hearing be useful for virtue, if virtue is taught by hearing and we use the sense of hearing in giving instruction?

Critias: Yes.

Socrates: And since medicine frees the sick man from his disease, that art too may sometimes appear useful in the acquisition of virtue, e.g. when hearing is procured by the aid of medicine.

Critias: Very likely.

Socrates: But if, again, we obtain by wealth the aid of medicine, shall we not regard wealth as useful for virtue?

Critias: True.

Socrates: And also the instruments by which wealth is procured?

Critias: Certainly.

Socrates: Then you think that a man may gain wealth by bad and disgraceful means, and, having obtained the aid of medicine which enables him to acquire the power of hearing, may use that very faculty for the acquisition of virtue?

Critias: Yes, I do.

Socrates: But can that which is evil be useful for virtue?

Critias: No.

Socrates: It is not therefore necessary that the means by which we obtain what is useful for a certain object should always be useful for the same object: for it seems that bad actions may sometimes serve good purposes? The matter will be still plainer if we look at it in this way:—If things are useful towards the several ends for which they exist, which ends would not come into existence without them, how would you regard them? Can ignorance, for instance, be useful for knowledge, or disease for health, or vice for virtue?

Critias: Never.

Socrates: And yet we have already agreed—have we not?—that there can be no knowledge where there has not previously been ignorance, nor health where there has not been disease, nor virtue where there has not been vice?

Critias: I think that we have.

Socrates: But then it would seem that the antecedents without which a thing cannot exist are not necessarily useful to it. Otherwise ignorance would appear useful for knowledge, disease for health, and vice for virtue.

Critias still showed great reluctance to accept any argument which went to prove that all these things were useless. I saw that it was as difficult to persuade him as (according to the proverb) it is to boil a stone, so I said: Let us bid 'good-bye' to the discussion, since we cannot agree whether these things are useful and a part of wealth or not. But what shall we say to another question: Which is the happier and better man,—he who requires the greatest quantity of necessaries for body and diet, or he who requires only the fewest and least? The answer will perhaps become more obvious if we suppose some one, comparing the man himself at different times, to consider whether his condition is better when he is sick or when he is well?

Critias: That is not a question which needs much consideration.

Socrates: Probably, I said, every one can understand that health is a better condition than disease. But when have we the greatest and the most various needs, when we are sick or when we are well?

Critias: When we are sick.

Socrates: And when we are in the worst state we have the greatest and most especial need and desire of bodily pleasures?

Critias: True.

Socrates: And seeing that a man is best off when he is least in need of such things, does not the same reasoning apply to the case of any two persons, of whom one has many and great wants and desires, and the other few and moderate? For instance, some men are gamblers, some drunkards, and some gluttons: and gambling and the love of drink and greediness are all desires?

Critias: Certainly.

Socrates: But desires are only the lack of something: and those who have the greatest desires are in a worse condition than those who have none or very slight ones?

Critias: Certainly I consider that those who have such wants are bad, and that the greater their wants the worse they are.

Socrates: And do we think it possible that a thing should be useful for a purpose unless we have need of it for that purpose?

Critias: No.

Socrates: Then if these things are useful for supplying the needs of the body, we must want them for that purpose?

Critias: That is my opinion.

Socrates: And he to whom the greatest number of things are useful for his purpose, will also want the greatest number of means of accomplishing it, supposing that we necessarily feel the want of all useful things?

Critias: It seems so.

Socrates: The argument proves then that he who has great riches has likewise need of many things for the supply of the wants of the body; for wealth appears useful towards that end. And the richest must be in the worst condition, since they seem to be most in want of such things.

Menexenus

Persons of the Dialogue: Socrates and Menexenus.

SOCRATES: WHENCE COME YOU, MENEXENUS? ARE YOU FROM THE
Agora?

Menexenus: Yes, Socrates; I have been at the Council.

Socrates: And what might you be doing at the Council? And yet
I need hardly ask, for I see that you, believing yourself to have
arrived at the end of education and of philosophy, and to have had
enough of them, are mounting upwards to things higher still, and,
though rather young for the post, are intending to govern us elder
men, like the rest of your family, which has always provided some
one who kindly took care of us.

Menexenus: Yes, Socrates, I shall be ready to hold office, if you
allow and advise that I should, but not if you think otherwise. I went
to the council chamber because I heard that the Council was about
to choose some one who was to speak over the dead. For you know
that there is to be a public funeral?

Socrates: Yes, I know. And whom did they choose?

Menexenus: No one; they delayed the election until tomorrow, but I believe that either Archinus or Dion will be chosen.

Socrates: O Menexenus! Death in battle is certainly in many respects a noble thing. The dead man gets a fine and costly funeral, although he may have been poor, and an elaborate speech is made over him by a wise man who has long ago prepared what he has to say, although he who is praised may not have been good for much. The speakers praise him for what he has done and for what he has not done—that is the beauty of them—and they steal away our souls with their embellished words; in every conceivable form they praise the city; and they praise those who died in war, and all our ancestors who went before us; and they praise ourselves also who are still alive, until I feel quite elevated by their laudations, and I stand listening to their words, Menexenus, and become enchanted by them, and all in a moment I imagine myself to have become a greater and nobler and finer man than I was before. And if, as often happens, there are any foreigners who accompany me to the speech, I become suddenly conscious of having a sort of triumph over them, and they seem to experience a corresponding feeling of admiration at me, and at the greatness of the city, which appears to them, when they are under the influence of the speaker, more wonderful than ever. This consciousness of dignity lasts me more than three days, and not until the fourth or fifth day do I come to my senses and know where I am; in the meantime I have been living in the Islands of the Blest. Such is the art of our rhetoricians, and in such manner does the sound of their words keep ringing in my ears.

Menexenus: You are always making fun of the rhetoricians, Socrates; this time, however, I am inclined to think that the speaker who is chosen will not have much to say, for he has been called upon to speak at a moment's notice, and he will be compelled almost to improvise.

Socrates: But why, my friend, should he not have plenty to say? Every rhetorician has speeches ready made; nor is there any difficulty in improvising that sort of stuff. Had the orator to praise Athenians among Peloponnesians, or Peloponnesians among Athenians, he must be a good rhetorician who could succeed and gain credit.

But there is no difficulty in a man's winning applause when he is contending for fame among the persons whom he is praising.

Menexenus: Do you think not, Socrates?

Socrates: Certainly 'not.'

Menexenus: Do you think that you could speak yourself if there should be a necessity, and if the Council were to choose you?

Socrates: That I should be able to speak is no great wonder, Menexenus, considering that I have an excellent mistress in the art of rhetoric,—she who has made so many good speakers, and one who was the best among all the Hellenes—Pericles, the son of Xanthippus.

Menexenus: And who is she? I suppose that you mean Aspasia.

Socrates: Yes, I do; and besides her I had Connus, the son of Metrobius, as a master, and he was my master in music, as she was in rhetoric. No wonder that a man who has received such an education should be a finished speaker; even the pupil of very inferior masters, say, for example, one who had learned music of Lamprus, and rhetoric of Antiphon the Rhamnusian, might make a figure if he were to praise the Athenians among the Athenians.

Menexenus: And what would you be able to say if you had to speak?

Socrates: Of my own wit, most likely nothing; but yesterday I heard Aspasia composing a funeral oration about these very dead. For she had been told, as you were saying, that the Athenians were going to choose a speaker, and she repeated to me the sort of speech which he should deliver, partly improvising and partly from previous thought, putting together fragments of the funeral oration which Pericles spoke, but which, as I believe, she composed.

Menexenus: And can you remember what Aspasia said?

Socrates: I ought to be able, for she taught me, and she was ready to strike me because I was always forgetting.

Menexenus: Then why will you not rehearse what she said?

Socrates: Because I am afraid that my mistress may be angry with me if I publish her speech.

Menexenus: Nay, Socrates, let us have the speech, whether Aspasia's or any one else's, no matter. I hope that you will oblige me.

Socrates: But I am afraid that you will laugh at me if I continue the games of youth in old age.

Menexenus: Far otherwise, Socrates; let us by all means have the speech.

Socrates: Truly I have such a disposition to oblige you, that if you bid me dance naked I should not like to refuse, since we are alone. Listen then: If I remember rightly, she began as follows, with the mention of the dead:—(Thucyd.)

There is a tribute of deeds and of words. The departed have already had the first, when going forth on their destined journey they were attended on their way by the state and by their friends; the tribute of words remains to be given to them, as is meet and by law ordained. For noble words are a memorial and a crown of noble actions, which are given to the doers of them by the hearers. A word is needed which will duly praise the dead and gently admonish the living, exhorting the brethren and descendants of the departed to imitate their virtue, and consoling their fathers and mothers and the survivors, if any, who may chance to be alive of the previous generation. What sort of a word will this be, and how shall we rightly begin the praises of these brave men? In their life they rejoiced their own friends with their valour, and their death they gave in exchange for the salvation of the living. And I think that we should praise them in the order in which nature made them good, for they were good because they were sprung from good fathers. Wherefore let us first of all praise the goodness of their birth; secondly, their nurture and education; and then let us set forth how noble their actions were, and how worthy of the education which they had received.

And first as to their birth. Their ancestors were not strangers, nor are these their descendants sojourners only, whose fathers have come from another country; but they are the children of the soil, dwelling and living in their own land. And the country which brought them up is not like other countries, a stepmother to her children, but their own true mother; she bore them and nourished them and received them, and in her bosom they now repose. It is meet and right, therefore, that we should begin by praising the land which is their mother, and that will be a way of praising their noble birth.

The country is worthy to be praised, not only by us, but by all mankind; first, and above all, as being dear to the Gods. This is proved by the strife and contention of the Gods respecting her. And ought not the country which the Gods praise to be praised by all mankind? The second praise which may be fairly claimed by her, is that at the time when the whole earth was sending forth and creating diverse animals, tame and wild, she our mother was free and pure from savage monsters, and out of all animals selected and brought forth man, who is superior to the rest in understanding, and alone has justice and religion. And a great proof that she brought forth the common ancestors of us and of the departed, is that she provided the means of support for her offspring. For as a woman proves her motherhood by giving milk to her young ones (and she who has no fountain of milk is not a mother), so did this our land prove that she was the mother of men, for in those days she alone and first of all brought forth wheat and barley for human food, which is the best and noblest sustenance for man, whom she regarded as her true offspring. And these are truer proofs of motherhood in a country than in a woman, for the woman in her conception and generation is but the imitation of the earth, and not the earth of the woman. And of the fruit of the earth she gave a plenteous supply, not only to her own, but to others also; and afterwards she made the olive to spring up to be a boon to her children, and to help them in their toils. And when she had herself nursed them and brought them up to manhood, she gave them Gods to be their rulers and teachers, whose names are well known, and need not now be repeated. They are the Gods who first ordered our lives, and instructed us in the arts for the supply of our daily needs, and taught us the acquisition and use of arms for the defence of the country.

Thus born into the world and thus educated, the ancestors of the departed lived and made themselves a government, which I ought briefly to commemorate. For government is the nurture of man, and the government of good men is good, and of bad men bad. And I must show that our ancestors were trained under a good

government, and for this reason they were good, and our contempo-
raries are also good, among whom our departed friends are to be
reckoned. Then as now, and indeed always, from that time to this,
speaking generally, our government was an aristocracy—a form of
government which receives various names, according to the fancies
of men, and is sometimes called democracy, but is really an aristocracy or government of the best which has the approval of the many.
For kings we have always had, first hereditary and then elected, and
authority is mostly in the hands of the people, who dispense offices
and power to those who appear to be most deserving of them.
Neither is a man rejected from weakness or poverty or obscurity of
origin, nor honoured by reason of the opposite, as in other states,
but there is one principle—he who appears to be wise and good is a
governor and ruler. The basis of this our government is equality of
birth; for other states are made up of all sorts and unequal conditions of men, and therefore their governments are unequal; there
are tyrannies and there are oligarchies, in which the one party are
slaves and the others masters. But we and our citizens are brethren,
the children all of one mother, and we do not think it right to be
one another's masters or servants; but the natural equality of birth
compels us to seek for legal equality, and to recognize no superiority
except in the reputation of virtue and wisdom.

And so their and our fathers, and these, too, our brethren, being
nobly born and having been brought up in all freedom, did both in
their public and private capacity many noble deeds famous over the
whole world. They were the deeds of men who thought that they
ought to fight both against Hellenes for the sake of Hellenes on
behalf of freedom, and against barbarians in the common interest
of Hellas. Time would fail me to tell of their defence of their
country against the invasion of Eumolpus and the Amazons, or of
their defence of the Argives against the Cadmeians, or of the Hera-
cleids against the Argives; besides, the poets have already declared in
song to all mankind their glory, and therefore any commemoration
of their deeds in prose which we might attempt would hold a second
place. They already have their reward, and I say no more of them;
but there are other worthy deeds of which no poet has worthily

sung, and which are still wooing the poet's muse. Of these I am bound to make honourable mention, and shall invoke others to sing of them also in lyric and other strains, in a manner becoming the actors. And first I will tell how the Persians, lords of Asia, were enslaving Europe, and how the children of this land, who were our fathers, held them back. Of these I will speak first, and praise their valour, as is meet and fitting. He who would rightly estimate them should place himself in thought at that time, when the whole of Asia was subject to the third king of Persia. The first king, Cyrus, by his valour freed the Persians, who were his countrymen, and subjected the Medes, who were their lords, and he ruled over the rest of Asia, as far as Egypt; and after him came his son, who ruled all the accessible part of Egypt and Libya; the third king was Darius, who extended the land boundaries of the empire to Scythia, and with his fleet held the sea and the islands. None presumed to be his equal; the minds of all men were enthralled by him—so many and mighty and warlike nations had the power of Persia subdued. Now Darius had a quarrel against us and the Eretrians, because, as he said, we had conspired against Sardis, and he sent 500,000 men in transports and vessels of war, and 300 ships, and Datis as commander, telling him to bring the Eretrians and Athenians to the king, if he wished to keep his head on his shoulders. He sailed against the Eretrians, who were reputed to be amongst the noblest and most warlike of the Hellenes of that day, and they were numerous, but he conquered them all in three days; and when he had conquered them, in order that no one might escape, he searched the whole country after this manner: his soldiers, coming to the borders of Eretria and spreading from sea to sea, joined hands and passed through the whole country, in order that they might be able to tell the king that no one had escaped them. And from Eretria they went to Marathon with a like intention, expecting to bind the Athenians in the same yoke of necessity in which they had bound the Eretrians. Having effected one-half of their purpose, they were in the act of attempting the other, and none of the Hellenes dared to assist either the Eretrians or the Athenians, except the Lacedaemonians, and they arrived a day too late for the battle; but the rest were panic-stricken and kept quiet, too happy in having escaped for a time. He who has present to his mind that conflict will know what manner of men they were who received the onset of the barbarians at Marathon, and chastened the pride of the whole of Asia, and by the victory which they gained over the barbarians first taught other men that the power of the Persians was not invincible, but that hosts of men and the multitude of riches alike yield to valour. And I assert that those men are the fathers not only of ourselves, but of our liberties and of the liberties of all who are on the continent, for that was the action to which the Hellenes looked back when they ventured to fight for their own safety in the battles which ensued: they became disciples of the men of Marathon. To them, therefore, I assign in my speech the first place, and the second to those who fought and conquered in the sea fights at Salamis and Artemisium; for of them, too, one might have many things to say—of the assaults which they endured by sea and land, and how they repelled them. I will mention only that act of theirs which appears to me to be the noblest, and which followed that of Marathon and came nearest to it; for the men of Marathon only showed the Hellenes that it was possible to ward off the barbarians by land, the many by the few; but there was no proof that they could be defeated by ships, and at sea the Persians retained the reputation of being invincible in numbers and wealth and skill and strength. This is the glory of the men who fought at sea, that they dispelled the second terror which had hitherto possessed the Hellenes, and so made the fear of numbers, whether of ships or men, to cease among them. And so the soldiers of Marathon and the sailors of Salamis became the schoolmasters of Hellas; the one teaching and habituating the Hellenes not to fear the barbarians at sea, and the others not to fear them by land. Third in order, for the number and valour of the combatants, and third in the salvation of Hellas, I place the battle of Plataea. And now the Lacedaemonians as well as the Athenians took part in the struggle; they were all united in this greatest and most terrible conflict of all; wherefore their virtues will be cele-brated in times to come, as they are now celebrated by us. But at a later period many Hellenic tribes were still on the side of the barbarians, and there was a report that the great king was going to make a new attempt upon the Hellenes, and therefore justice requires that we should also make mention of those who crowned the previous work of our salvation, and drove and purged away all barbarians from the sea. These were the men who fought by sea at the river Eurymedon, and who went on the expedition to Cyprus, and who sailed to Egypt and divers other places; and they should be gratefully remembered by us, because they compelled the king in fear for himself to look to his own safety instead of plotting the destruction of Hellas.

And so the war against the barbarians was fought out to the end by the whole city on their own behalf, and on behalf of their countrymen. There was peace, and our city was held in honour; and then, as prosperity makes men jealous, there succeeded a jealousy of her, and jealousy begat envy, and so she became engaged against her will in a war with the Hellenes. On the breaking out of war, our citizens met the Lacedaemonians at Tanagra, and fought for the freedom of the Boeotians; the issue was doubtful, and was decided by the engagement which followed. For when the Lacedaemonians had gone on their way, leaving the Boeotians, whom they were aiding, on the third day after the battle of Tanagra, our countrymen conquered at Oenophyta, and righteously restored those who had been unrighteously exiled. And they were the first after the Persian war who fought on behalf of liberty in aid of Hellenes against Hellenes; they were brave men, and freed those whom they aided, and were the first too who were honourably interred in this sepulchre by the state. Afterwards there was a mighty war, in which all the Hellenes joined, and devastated our country, which was very ungrateful of them; and our countrymen, after defeating them in a naval engagement and taking their leaders, the Spartans, at Sphagia, when they might have destroyed them, spared their lives, and gave them back, and made peace, considering that they should war with the fellow-countrymen only until they gained a victory over them, and not because of the private anger of the state destroy the common interest of Hellas; but that with barbarians they should war to the death. Worthy of praise are they also who waged this

war, and are here interred; for they proved, if any one doubted the
superior prowess of the Athenians in the former war with the
barbarians, that their doubts had no foundation—showing by their
victory in the civil war with Hellas, in which they subdued the other
chief state of the Hellenes, that they could conquer single-handed
those with whom they had been allied in the war against the barbarians. After the peace there followed a third war, which was of a
terrible and desperate nature, and in this many brave men who are
here interred lost their lives—many of them had won victories in
Sicily, whither they had gone over the seas to fight for the liberties of
the Leontines, to whom they were bound by oaths; but, owing to the
distance, the city was unable to help them, and they lost heart and
came to misfortune, their very enemies and opponents winning
more renown for valour and temperance than the friends of others.
Many also fell in naval engagements at the Hellespont, after having
in one day taken all the ships of the enemy, and defeated them in
other naval engagements. And what I call the terrible and desperate
nature of the war, is that the other Hellenes, in their extreme
animosity towards the city, should have entered into negotiations
with their bitterest enemy, the king of Persia, whom they, together
with us, had expelled;—him, without us, they again brought back,
barbarian against Hellenes, and all the hosts, both of Hellenes and
barbarians, were united against Athens. And then shone forth the
power and valour of our city. Her enemies had supposed that she
was exhausted by the war, and our ships were blockaded at Mity-
lene. But the citizens themselves embarked, and came to the rescue
with sixty other ships, and their valour was confessed of all men, for
they conquered their enemies and delivered their friends. And yet by
some evil fortune they were left to perish at sea, and therefore are
not interred here. Ever to be remembered and honoured are they,
for by their valour not only that sea-fight was won for us, but the
entire war was decided by them, and through them the city gained
the reputation of being invincible, even though attacked by all
mankind. And that reputation was a true one, for the defeat which
came upon us was our own doing. We were never conquered by
others, and to this day we are still unconquered by them; but we

were our own conquerors, and received defeat at our own hands. Afterwards there was quiet and peace abroad, but there sprang up war at home; and, if men are destined to have civil war, no one could have desired that his city should take the disorder in a milder form. How joyful and natural was the reconciliation of those who came from the Piraeus and those who came from the city; with what moderation did they order the war against the tyrants in Eleusis, and in a manner how unlike what the other Hellenes expected! And the reason of this gentleness was the veritable tie of blood, which created among them a friendship as of kinsmen, faithful not in word only, but in deed. And we ought also to remember those who then fell by one another's hands, and on such occasions as these to reconcile them with sacrifices and prayers, praying to those who have power over them, that they may be reconciled even as we are reconciled. For they did not attack one another out of malice or enmity, but they were unfortunate. And that such was the fact we ourselves are witnesses, who are of the same race with them, and have mutually received and granted forgiveness of what we have done and suffered. After this there was perfect peace, and the city had rest; and her feeling was that she forgave the barbarians, who had severely suffered at her hands and severely retaliated, but that she was indignant at the ingratitude of the Hellenes, when she remembered how they had received good from her and returned evil, having made common cause with the barbarians, depriving her of the ships which had once been their salvation, and dismantling our walls, which had preserved their own from falling. She thought that she would no longer defend the Hellenes, when enslaved either by one another or by the barbarians, and did accordingly. This was our feeling, while the Lacedaemonians were thinking that we who were the champions of liberty had fallen, and that their business was to subject the remaining Hellenes. And why should I say more? for the events of which I am speaking happened not long ago and we can all of us remember how the chief peoples of Hellas, Argives and Boeotians and Corinthians, came to feel the need of us, and, what is the greatest miracle of all, the Persian king himself was driven to such extremity as to come round to the opinion, that from this city,

of which he was the destroyer, and from no other, his salvation
would proceed.

And if a person desired to bring a deserved accusation against
our city, he would find only one charge which he could justly urge—
that she was too compassionate and too favourable to the weaker
side. And in this instance she was not able to hold out or keep her
resolution of refusing aid to her injurers when they were being
enslaved, but she was softened, and did in fact send out aid, and
delivered the Hellenes from slavery, and they were free until they
afterwards enslaved themselves. Whereas, to the great king she
refused to give the assistance of the state, for she could not forget
the trophies of Marathon and Salamis and Plataea; but she allowed
exiles and volunteers to assist him, and they were his salvation. And
she herself, when she was compelled, entered into the war, and built
walls and ships, and fought with the Lacedaemonians on behalf of
the Parians. Now the king fearing this city and wanting to stand
aloof, when he saw the Lacedaemonians growing weary of the war
at sea, asked of us, as the price of his alliance with us and the other
allies, to give up the Hellenes in Asia, whom the Lacedaemonians
had previously handed over to him, he thinking that we should
refuse, and that then he might have a pretence for withdrawing from
us. About the other allies he was mistaken, for the Corinthians and
Argives and Boeotians, and the other states, were quite willing to let
them go, and swore and covenanted, that, if he would pay them
money, they would make over to him the Hellenes of the continent,
and we alone refused to give them up and swear. Such was the
natural nobility of this city, so sound and healthy was the spirit of
freedom among us, and the instinctive dislike of the barbarian,
because we are pure Hellenes, having no admixture of barbarism in
us. For we are not like many others, descendants of Pelops or
Cadmus or Egyptus or Danaus, who are by nature barbarians, and
yet pass for Hellenes, and dwell in the midst of us; but we are pure
Hellenes, uncontaminated by any foreign element, and therefore the
hatred of the foreigner has passed unadulterated into the life-blood
of the city. And so, notwithstanding our noble sentiments, we were
again isolated, because we were unwilling to be guilty of the base

and unholy act of giving up Hellenes to barbarians. And we were in the same case as when we were subdued before; but, by the favour of Heaven, we managed better, for we ended the war without the loss of our ships or walls or colonies; the enemy was only too glad to be quit of us. Yet in this war we lost many brave men, such as were those who fell owing to the ruggedness of the ground at the battle of Corinth, or by treason at Lechaeum. Brave men, too, were those who delivered the Persian king, and drove the Lacedaemonians from the sea. I remind you of them, and you must celebrate them together with me, and do honour to their memories.

Such were the actions of the men who are here interred, and of others who have died on behalf of their country; many and glorious things I have spoken of them, and there are yet many more and more glorious things remaining to be told—many days and nights would not suffice to tell of them. Let them not be forgotten, and let every man remind their descendants that they also are soldiers who must not desert the ranks of their ancestors, or from cowardice fall behind. Even as I exhort you this day, and in all future time, when-ever I meet with any of you, shall continue to remind and exhort you, O ye sons of heroes, that you strive to be the bravest of men. And I think that I ought now to repeat what your fathers desired to have said to you who are their survivors, when they went out to battle, in case anything happened to them. I will tell you what I heard them say, and what, if they had only speech, they would fain be saying, judging from what they then said. And you must imagine that you hear them saying what I now repeat to you:—

'Sons, the event proves that your fathers were brave men; for we might have lived dishonourably, but have preferred to die honourably rather than bring you and your children into disgrace, and rather than dishonour our own fathers and forefathers; consid-ering that life is not life to one who is a dishonour to his race, and that to such a one neither men nor Gods are friendly, either while he is on the earth or after death in the world below. Remember our words, then, and whatever is your aim let virtue be the condition of the attainment of your aim, and know that without this all posses-sions and pursuits are dishonourable and evil. For neither does

wealth bring honour to the owner, if he be a coward; of such a one
the wealth belongs to another, and not to himself. Nor does beauty
and strength of body, when dwelling in a base and cowardly man,
appear comely, but the reverse of comely, making the possessor
more conspicuous, and manifesting forth his cowardice. And all
knowledge, when separated from justice and virtue, is seen to be
cunning and not wisdom; wherefore make this your first and last
and constant and all-absorbing aim, to exceed, if possible, not only
us but all your ancestors in virtue; and know that to excel you in
virtue only brings us shame, but that to be excelled by you is a
source of happiness to us. And we shall most likely be defeated, and
you will most likely be victors in the contest, if you learn so to order
your lives as not to abuse or waste the reputation of your ancestors,
knowing that to a man who has any self-respect, nothing is more
dishonourable than to be honoured, not for his own sake, but on
account of the reputation of his ancestors. The honour of parents is
a fair and noble treasure to their posterity, but to have the use of a
treasure of wealth and honour, and to leave none to your successors,
because you have neither money nor reputation of your own, is
alike base and dishonourable. And if you follow our precepts you
will be received by us as friends, when the hour of destiny brings
you hither; but if you neglect our words and are disgraced in your
lives, no one will welcome or receive you. This is the message which
is to be delivered to our children.

'Some of us have fathers and mothers still living, and we would
urge them, if, as is likely, we shall die, to bear the calamity as lightly
as possible, and not to condole with one another; for they have
sorrows enough, and will not need any one to stir them up. While
we gently heal their wounds, let us remind them that the Gods have
heard the chief part of their prayers; for they prayed, not that their
children might live for ever, but that they might be brave and
renowned. And this, which is the greatest good, they have attained.
A mortal man cannot expect to have everything in his own life
turning out according to his will; and they, if they bear their misfortunes bravely, will be truly deemed brave fathers of the brave. But if
they give way to their sorrows, either they will be suspected of not

being our parents, or we of not being such as our panegyrists declare. Let not either of the two alternatives happen, but rather let them be our chief and true panegyrists, who show in their lives that they are true men, and had men for their sons. Of old the saying, "Nothing too much," appeared to be, and really was, well said. For he whose happiness rests with himself, if possible, wholly, and if not, as far as is possible,—who is not hanging in suspense on other men, or changing with the vicissitude of their fortune,—has his life ordered for the best. He is the temperate and valiant and wise; and when his riches come and go, when his children are given and taken away, he will remember the proverb—"Neither rejoicing overmuch nor grieving overmuch," for he relies upon himself. And such we would have our parents to be—that is our word and wish, and as such we now offer ourselves, neither lamenting overmuch, nor fearing overmuch, if we are to die at this time. And we entreat our fathers and mothers to retain these feelings throughout their future life, and to be assured that they will not please us by sorrowing and lamenting over us. But, if the dead have any knowledge of the living, they will displease us most by making themselves miserable and by taking their misfortunes too much to heart, and they will please us best if they bear their loss lightly and temperately. For our life will have the noblest end which is vouchsafed to man, and should be glorified rather than lamented. And if they will direct their minds to the care and nurture of our wives and children, they will soonest forget their misfortunes, and live in a better and nobler way, and be dearer to us.

'This is all that we have to say to our families: and to the state we would say—Take care of our parents and of our sons: let her worthily cherish the old age of our parents, and bring up our sons in the right way. But we know that she will of her own accord take care of them, and does not need any exhortation of ours.'

This, O ye children and parents of the dead, is the message which they bid us deliver to you, and which I do deliver with the utmost seriousness. And in their name I beseech you, the children, to imitate your fathers, and you, parents, to be of good cheer about yourselves; for we will nourish your age, and take care of you both publicly and privately in any place in which one of us may meet one of you who are the parents of the dead. And the care of you which the city shows, you know yourselves; for she has made provision by law concerning the parents and children of those who die in war; the highest authority is specially entrusted with the duty of watching over them above all other citizens, and they will see that your fathers and mothers have no wrong done to them. The city herself shares in the education of the children, desiring as far as it is possible that their orphanhood may not be felt by them; while they are children she is a parent to them, and when they have arrived at man's estate she sends them to their several duties, in full armour clad; and bringing freshly to their minds the ways of their fathers, she places in their hands the instruments of their fathers' virtues; for the sake of the omen, she would have them from the first begin to rule over their own houses arrayed in the strength and arms of their fathers. And as for the dead, she never ceases honouring them, celebrating in common for all rites which become the property of each; and in addition to this, holding gymnastic and equestrian contests, and musical festivals of every sort. She is to the dead in the place of a son and heir, and to their sons in the place of a father, and to their parents and elder kindred in the place of a guardian—ever and always caring for them. Considering this, you ought to bear your calamity the more gently; for thus you will be most endeared to the dead and to the living, and your sorrows will heal and be healed. And now do you and all, having lamented the dead in common according to the law, go your ways.

You have heard, Menexenus, the oration of Aspasia the Milesian.

Menexenus: Truly, Socrates, I marvel that Aspasia, who is only a woman, should be able to compose such a speech; she must be a rare one.

Socrates: Well, if you are incredulous, you may come with me and hear her.

Menexenus: I have often met Aspasia, Socrates, and know what she is like.

Socrates: Well, and do you not admire her, and are you not grateful for her speech?

Menexenus: Yes, Socrates, I am very grateful to her or to him who told you, and still more to you who have told me.

Socrates: Very good. But you must take care not to tell of me, and then at some future time I will repeat to you many other excellent political speeches of hers.

Menexenus: Fear not, only let me hear them, and I will keep the secret.

Socrates: Then I will keep my promise.

Book IX

_____

Translated by
GEORGE BURGES

The Epinomis, or the Philosopher

Persons of the Dialogue: An Athenian Guest, Clinias a Cretan, and Megillus a Lacedæmonian.

CLINIAS: ACCORDING TO OUR AGREEMENT, WE HAVE ALL OF US, guest, come correctly, being three, I, and you, and Megillus here, to consider the question of intellect, in what manner it is meet to go through in a discourse that, which we say belongs to the constitution of man, (and which,) when it has been thought upon, causes it to be in the best state with regard to itself, as far as it is possible for man to possess it. For, as we assert, we have gone through all the other matters, that existed, relating to the laying down of laws. But that, which is of the greatest moment to discover and to speak of, namely, by learning what will a mortal man become wise, this we have neither spoken of nor discovered. Now then let us endeavour not to leave this behind. For we should nearly do that imperfectly, for the sake of which we have all rushed onwards, with the view of making clear (every thing) from the beginning to the end.

Athenian: You speak well, friend Clinias. But I think you will now hear a strange discourse, and on the other hand in a certain respect not strange. For many, who meet us in life, tell the same story, that the human race will be neither blessed nor happy. Follow me, then, and see whether to you I likewise appear together with them to speak correctly on a point like this. I assert then that it is not possible for men, except a few, to be blessed and happy; I limit this to as long as we live; but there is a fair hope that a person will after death obtain every thing, for the sake of which he would desire, when alive, to live in the best manner he could, and dying to meet with such an end. And I assert nothing (very) wise, but what all of us, both Greeks and Barbarians, after a certain manner know, that to be produced is at the beginning difficult for every animal. In the first place, it is difficult to partake of the state of conception, next to be born, and, further still, to be brought up and educated; (for) all these things take place, as we all say, through ten thousand troubles. The time too would be short, not only with respect to the calculation of annoyances, but what every one would imagine to be moderate; and this seems to make almost a kind of breathing-time in the middle of the life of man. Old age however, quickly overtaking a person, would make him not at all willing to live his life over again, after he has considered the life he has lived, unless he happens to be full of the thoughts of a child. Now of this what is to me the proof? It is, because what is sought for in our discourse exists naturally in this way. Now we are seeking by what manner we shall be come wise, as if there were to each of us some such power as this. But it flies quickly away then, when any one proceeds to an investigation of the so-called arts or notions, or any other things of that kind, which we imagine to be sciences; whereas not one of them is worthy to be called by the name of that wisdom, which is conversant with the affairs of man; while on the other hand, the soul is very confident, and divines, as if this wisdom were existing in her by some gift of nature; but what it is, and when, and how it exists, it is wholly unable to discover. Does not then in this manner our difficulty about, and search after, wisdom, seem somehow greatly to be full of the hope, which exists to each of those amongst us, who are able to examine both themselves prudently, and others harmoniously, through reasonings of all kinds and spoken in every manner? Shall we agree that these things are not thus, or thus?

Clinias: We will agree in this, O guest, in the hope perhaps, which will arise in the course of time, of having hereafter with you opinions the most true on these points.

Athenian: We must then first go through the other sciences, as they are called, but which do not render him wise, who receives and possesses them, in order that, by putting them out of the way, we may endeavour to place by our side those, of which we are in want, and, after placing them by our side, learn them. Let us, then, first look into the sciences, of which the race of man is first in want; since these are nearly the most necessary, and truly the first. Now he, who becomes skilled in these, even though he seemed at first to be wise, yet now he is not considered to be wise, but obtains rather a disgrace by a science of this kind. We will therefore mention what they are, and (show) that nearly every one, to whom is proposed the contest of seeming to become the best man, avoids them through the possession of intellect and study. Let the first art then be that, which, withdrawing us from eating human flesh, that, as the story goes, took place formerly amongst mankind after the manner of savage animals, has recalled us to a more lawful food. And may those before be propitious to us, and they are. For whosoever we are, who have spoken, let them be bidden the first farewell. The manufacture of wheaten flour and barley meal and moreover the food is in deed beautiful and good; but it will never be able to work out the man completely wise. For this very thing, under the appellation of a manufacture, would produce a difficult handling of the things manufactured. Nor would the cultivation of nearly the whole country (do so); for we all appear to take in hand the earth, not by art, but by nature, according to a god. Nor yet would the weaving together of dwellings nor the whole of house-building, and the manufacture of all kinds of utensils, and copper-work, and the preparing of instruments for carpenters and moulders, and weavers, and trades in general, although possessing what is useful for the common people, be suited for virtue. Nor yet does the whole of hunting, although various and full of art, contribute what is greatly becoming together with what is wise. Nor yet does the diviner's and interpreter's art at all; for such merely knows what is said, but has not learnt whether it is true. Since then we see that the possession of necessaries is worked out indeed by art, but that not one of these arts makes any person wise, there would be left after this a certain sport, imitative for the most part, but by no means a serious pursuit. For persons do with many instruments, and with many imitations, effected by their own bodies, not altogether graceful, make an imitation of things, expressed in prose and verse, and of those, of which painting is the mother, while colours many and various are worked out, by many substances moist and dry; by operating upon none of which with the greatest care does the imitative art render a person wise. And when all has been done, there would be something remaining in the assistance without number given to persons without number; the greatest of which and for the most numerous occasions is the art of war, called by the name of generalship, of the highest repute in the case of need, but requiring the greatest good fortune, and that which is assigned naturally rather to bravery than wisdom. And what persons call the medical art is surely itself an assistance nearly of such (ills) as the seasons cause by cold and unseasonable heat, and make by all such matters, the nature of animals their spoil. But not one of these (arts) is in good repute for the truest wisdom; for being made the subject of conjecture, they are carried along without measure by opinions. And assistants we will call pilots and sailors likewise. But not one of these let any person, by cheating us with words, proclaim a wise man on every ground. For not one of them would know the rage of the winds or their kindness, which is the most acceptable thing in the whole of the pilot's art. Nor yet such as say they are assistants in lawsuits by their power in speaking, and, by their memory and practice, give their minds to unusual opinions, but stumble outside the truth in cases of real justice. There still remains a certain strange power with respect to the opinion of wisdom, which the many would then call by the name of nature rather than wisdom, when any one perceives that he is easily learning, what even a child could learn, and is remembering many things and firmly so, and can call to mind what is suited to each thing, and quickly do it, when it would be becoming, if it took place. Now all this some will place under nature, others under wisdom, and others under a cleverness of nature. But no prudent person would ever be willing to call any one of these a truly wise man. It is however necessary for a certain science to be come apparent, by which he, who possesses it, would be wise in reality, and not be so in opinion merely. Let us, then, consider. For we are endeavouring by a reasoning, difficult in every way, to find some other science beyond those already mentioned, which may be truly and with propriety called wisdom; while he, who receives it, will be a person neither vulgar nor silly, but wise and good through it; and, whether he governs or is governed by the state, injustice become an elegant person. Let us, therefore, consider that science first, which singly proceeds from human nature, and which, amongst all that are present, would, by not being present, render the race of man of (all) animals the most senseless and thoughtless. Now this it is not very difficult for any one to consider. For that, which has given number to the whole race of man, would, so to say, being compared one against one, effect this. I conceive however that a certain god himself, rather than a certain accident, gave it to us to preserve us; but whom I conceive to have been the god, it is necessary to state, strange although it be, and, on the other hand, somehow not strange. For how must we not conceive that he, who is the cause to us of every good thing, should not have been the cause likewise of intellect, the greatest good by far? Now what god am I speaking of, Megillus and Clinias, and making an object of worship? It is almost Heaven, whom it is most just we should honour, as all the other daemons and gods do, and pray pre-eminently to it. For all of us would confess that it is the cause of all good things to us. And we assert to boot that it has given us number, and will give it us still, if any one is willing to follow us. For if a person will proceed to a right view of it, whether it be the pleasure of any one to call it the World, or Olympus, or Heaven, let him so call it; but let him follow, wherever it assumes a varied form, when it causes the stars in it to revolve along all their courses, and when it imparts the seasons and food for all, and the remaining gift of intellect, as we should say, together with all number, and every other good. Now this is the greatest thing, when any one, receiving from it the gift of number, proceeds through every period. Returning back still a little in our discourse, let us call to mind that we have conceived very correctly, that if we take away number from human nature, we should be intellectual not at all. For the soul of the animal, from whom reason is absent, would scarcely any longer be able to receive every virtue. Now the animal, which does not know two and three, even and odd, and is entirely ignorant of number, would never be able to give a reason respecting those things, of which it alone possesses sensation and memory; but nothing hinders it (from possessing) the other virtues, fortitude and temperance. But he, who is deprived of true reason, will never become wise; and he, to whom wisdom is not present, which is the greatest part of the whole of virtue, would never be perfectly good, nor happy. In this way there is every necessity for number to be laid down as a principle. But why it is necessary, there would be a discourse longer than all that has been spoken. And correctly will the present one have been stated likewise, that of the things, mentioned as belonging to the other arts, which we have gone through, and permitted them all to be arts, not even one would remain, but all perish entirely, when any one takes away the science of numbers. But to some of those, who have looked to the arts, the race of man would appear sufficiently for the sake of some small matters to have no need of number. And yet is it a thing of moment. And if any one looks to what is divine and mortal in generation, in which piety towards the gods and true number are known, he could not mention the person, who knows the whole of number, and of what power it is, when present, the cause; since it is evident that what relates to all music, requires numbered motion and sound; and, what is the greatest, that it (number) is the cause of all good things, but of nothing evil, this must be known well, which would perhaps take place by another road; for the movement, which is without reason, and order, and shape, and rhythm, and harmony, and all such things as partake of any evil, is deficient in nearly all number. And this it is meet for him to conceive in this way, who is about to end his days happily; and no one, except him, who knows the just, the good, the beautiful, and all such things, and has laid hold of a true opinion respecting them, will through number know how with regard to any thing to persuade himself and others at all. Let us then proceed to consider this very thing, how we learnt to number. Say, from whence did it arise that we have understood one and two? Do persons possess from the creator a nature of this kind towards their being able to understand them? Nature, indeed, has not been present to many other animals for this very purpose, so that they are able to learn from their father to number; but the deity has established within us this very thing first, so as to be competent to understand what is shown to us; and afterwards he showed it and is still showing; of which things what can a person see one, as compared with one, more beautiful than the birth of day? and then, when he comes to the portion of night, he will have a sight, from whence every thing will appear to him quite different. And when he ceases not revolving upon these very matters for many days and many nights, (he will see) how Heaven ceases not in teaching men one and two, until even the most hard to learn shall learn sufficiently how to number. For thus each of us, on perceiving these, would understand three and four and many. And amongst these the deity has formed one thing, the Moon; which at one time appearing greater, and at another less, proceeds through (her path), showing continually another day up to fifteen days and nights. And this is a period, if any one is willing to establish the whole circle as one; so that the most indocile animal, so to say, would learn to number, if it were one, to whom the deity had imparted the nature of being able to learn. And up to these points, and in these matters, the whole mass of animals have the power to become skilled in numbers, by considering one thing, itself by itself. But always to reckon up all numbers, when compared with each other, I think is a greater work. And for the sake of this, the deity having formed, as we have said, the Moon, increasing and decreasing, has put together months into the year, and caused us to compare every number with number, with a prosperous fortune. Hence, there are fruits for us, and the earth has become pregnant, so that there is food for all animals; while winds and showers take place, neither out of season nor measure.

But if any thing occurs contrary to this on the side of evil, it is meet
to accuse not the divine, but human, nature, as unjustly distributing
its own life. Now to us, while we were investigating the laws, it
appeared, that the other things, which are nearly the best for man,
are easy for us to know; and that every one would be competent to
understand what was said, and to do it, if he knew what is that,
which is likely to be a benefit, and what is not. But it has appeared,
and now appears still, that all the other pursuits are not very difficult; but in what manner it is meet for men to become good, is very
difficult. And, again, to acquire all the rest of good things, as the
saying is, it is both possible and not difficult; but with respect to
substance, how much is requisite and not requisite, and with respect
to the body, how much is requisite and not requisite, and with
respect to the soul, that it ought to be good, every one agrees with
every one. But in what manner it ought to be good, every one (when
asked) answers, by being just, and temperate, and brave, and this;
but (in what manner) to be wise, or what wisdom is, not one, as we
just now observed, agrees at all with one of the many. Now therefore, besides all the previous kinds of wisdom, we have discovered
one, by no means vile for this very purpose, that he, who has learnt
what we have discussed, will seem to be wise; but whether he, who is
skilled on these points, is wise and good, on this it is requisite to hold
a discussion.

Clinias: How reasonably, guest, did you say, that you are endeavouring to speak greatly about great things!

Athenian: For they are not trifling things, Clinias; and, what is
still more difficult, they are in every respect and entirely true.

Clinias: Very much so, guest; but do not however be faint-
hearted in stating what you mean.

Athenian: Truly so; nor do you in hearing.

Clinias: This shall be; for I will speak to you for both of us.

Athenian: It is well. But it is necessary, as it seems, to speak first
of all from the beginning, especially if we are able to comprehend in
one name what is that, which we consider to be wisdom; but if we
are quite unable, (to consider) in the second place, what and how

many are the (arts) through which he, Who receives them, will, according to our story, be a wise man.

Clinias: Say on.

Athenian: What follows after this will be without blame to the legislator; who, making a conjecture about the gods, speaks more beautifully and better than those, who have spoken before; and who passes his life in making use, as it were, of a beautiful discipline, and honouring the gods, and exalting them with hymns, and felicity, and thus passes through life.

Clinias: Well and beautifully are you speaking, guest; and may the end of your laws be this, that after falling down before the gods, and passing a life the most pure, you may meet with its close the best and the most beautiful.

Athenian: How then shall we speak, Clinias? Does it not seem to you that we honour the gods greatly by hymning them, and by praying that it may come into your minds to say things the most beautiful and the best respecting them? Say you in this way, or how?

Clinias: In this way, wonderfully. But do thou, O godlike man, confiding in the gods, offer up a prayer, and speak the one amongst your beautiful speeches that comes into your mind relating to the gods and goddesses.

Athenian: This shall be, if the deity himself be our leader. Do you only pray with me.

Clinias: Say then what is to follow this.

Athenian: It is necessary then, as it seems, for me, since those, who have gone before, have represented improperly the generation of gods and of animals, to give in the first place, according to our former reasoning, a better representation, by resuming the discourse, which I took in hand against impious assertions, and to assert that there are gods, who have a care for all things both small and great; and that they are not to be softened down by those, who are engaged in unjust acts, if you remember, Clinias; for you took down a memorandum of it; for what was then said was very true. But this was the greatest, that every soul is older than every body. Do you not remember (this)? or this at least perfectly, that what is better, and older, and more divine, is credibly prior to that, which is worse, and younger, and less honourable; and in every way that what governs, is (prior) to what is governed; and that what leads, to what is led. Let us then receive this at least, that soul is older than body. Now if this be the case, it is more credible that, what is first in the generation of the first, would be almost the beginning; and let us lay down that the beginning exists in a more becoming manner than a beginning, and that we have most correctly come upon the greatest (parts) of wisdom, relating to the generation of the gods.

Clinias: Let these things be stated to the best of our power.

Athenian: Come, then, let us assert that an animal is said most truly (to exist) according to nature then, when one combination of soul and body coming together produces one form.

Clinias: Correctly so.

Athenian: A thing of this kind then is most justly called an animal.

Clinias: It is.

Athenian: Now it is requisite, according to a probable account, for five solid bodies to be mentioned, from which a person might model the most beautiful and best of things; but the whole of the other genus possesses one form. For there is nothing else, which can be generated without a body, and possessing in no respect and at no time colour, except the really most divine genus of soul. Now this is nearly that alone, to which it pertains to mould and fabricate ; but it belongs to body, as we call it, to be moulded and produced, and to be visible. But to the other (soul)— for let us say it again, since it is to be said not merely once,— (it pertains) to be in visible, and to know and to be intelligible, and to have a share of memory and of the reasoning power in the changes of even and odd.As there are, therefore, five bodies, it is requisite to say that fire (is the first), and water (the second), and air the third, and earth the fourth, and æther the fifth; and in the do minions of each of these there is produced many an animal and of every kind. Now it is meet to learn this singly, thus. Let us, in the first place, lay down the whole of the things of earth as one, namely, all human beings, and all such animals as are with many feet, or none, and such as can move on, and such as are stationary, as being held down by roots. And it is

requisite to consider the one thing belonging to it as this, that all
these are formed of all those genera, but that the greater part is of
the earth and the nature of solidity. It is, however, requisite to lay
down another kind of animal, which is generated, and, at the same
time, able to be seen. For it consists for the most part of fire; but
contains likewise a small portion of earth and air, and of all the
other things. Hence, it is requisite to assert that animals of every
kind and visible are generated from them. It is necessary likewise to
think that all in the heavens are these genera of animals, which it is
necessary to say is the whole divine race of the stars, consisting of a
most beautiful body, and of a soul the most happy and the best. It is
requisite moreover to impart to them, at least in opinion, one of two
fates. For each of them is either indestructible and immortal, and
altogether, from every necessity, divine, or possesses some long-aged
life of life, sufficient for each, than which there would be never any
need of more. Let us then consider first, that there are, as we have
said, these two kinds of animals; and let us say again that both of
them are visible, the one being, as it would seem, wholly of fire, and
the other of earth, and that the earthy is moved in a disorderly
manner, but the fiery in all order. Now it is meet to consider that,
what is moved without order, is senseless, as the animal, which is
around us, acts for the most part; but that, what has its going in
order and in the heavens, it is meet to make for ourselves as a great
proof of its being intellectual; for it goes on ever according to the
same and in a similar manner; and by doing and suffering it would
afford a sufficient proof of its living intellectually. Now the necessity
of a soul possessing intellect would be by far the greatest of all
necessities. For it lays down laws as governing, and not governed.
But when soul, which is a thing the best, deliberates according to the
best intellect, that, which is not to be changed by turning, comes out
perfect in reality according to intellect; and even adamant would not
be superior to such a soul, and less to be changed by turning. But in
reality the three Fates hold and guard, so as to be perfect, that,
which has been deliberated upon by each of the gods with the best
counsel. It was necessary therefore that there should be to man a
proof that the stars are endued with intellect through the whole of

their progression, because they always do the same things, through
its having been planned of old that they are to do so for some
wondrous length of time, and through a change not taking place in
the plan, by their doing some things at one time, and others at
another, and by wandering up and down and altering their orbit.
Now the very reverse of this has appeared to the majority of us,
that, by their doing the same things and in a similar manner, they
have not a soul. The masses, too, have followed persons so senseless,
as to conceive that the human race is intellectual and vital, as being
moved, but the divine race unintellectual, as remaining in the same
movements. But it is allowable for the man, who places himself on
the side of what is more beautiful, and better, and more agree able
(to the gods), to conceive that he ought, on this very account, to
consider as intellectual that, which does always the same things
according to the same and in a similar manner; and that this is the
nature of the stars, most beautiful to behold, and which by a
progression and dance, the most beautiful and magnificent of all
choirs, completes for all animals what is needful. Now (to show) that
we are justly saying they possess a soul, let us consider first their size.
For they are not in reality so small, as they appear to be; but each of
them is of immense bulk, as is worthy to be believed; for this is
admitted by competent demonstrations. For it is possible to conceive
correctly that the whole Sun is larger than the whole earth, and that
all the stars, which are borne along, possess a wonderful size. Let us
then take into our thoughts what would be the method of any
nature in causing so great a bulk to revolve for ever for the same
time that it revolves at present. Now I assert that a god would be the
cause, and that it could not be possible otherwise. For it would not
otherwise become animated than through a god, as we have shown.
But since a god is able in this respect, to him there has been every
facility for every animal, in the first place, to be produced, and every
body, and every bulk; and next, to cause them to move in that way,
which he conceived to be the best. And now upon all these points
we will make one true assertion. It is impossible for the earth and
heavens and all the stars and all the bulky bodies made from them
to subsist, unless a soul were present to each, or in each, so that they

proceed with such accuracy according to years, and months, and days, and for every good, which is produced, to be produced for us all. But it is requisite that, by how much the more vile is man, (the less) ought he to be seen to trifle, but to assert something clear concerning them. Should then any one assert that certain violent motions of bodies or natures or any thing of this kind are the causes, he will say nothing that is clear. It is however requisite to reconsider seriously what we have said, whether our discourse has a reason for it, or altogether comes after it. In the first place then, (we said,) there are two things, the one, soul, and the other, body, and that many things pertain to each; but that all are different from one another, and each from each; and that there is no other third thing common to any one; and that soul differs from body; and that the former is intellectual, but the latter unintellectual; and that the one rules, but the other is ruled; and that the one is the cause of all (that happens), but the other is not the cause of any accident; so that to assert that the things in heaven were generated by something else, and that the productions of soul and body do not exist in this way, is a great folly and a want of reason. If then it is requisite for the reasons, relating to all such matters, to be victorious, and for all things of this kind to seem confidently to be divine, we must lay down one or the other of these two points; we must either hymn those things most correctly, as being gods themselves, or (we must) consider them, like images, to be resemblances of the gods, the gods themselves having manufactured them. For they (are the works of artificers) neither senseless nor of little worth. But, as we have said, we must lay down one or the other of these points. And what is laid down, we must honour pre-eminently before all statues. For never will there be seen statues more beautiful and more common of all men, or put up in pre-eminent places, and excelling for their purity, and solemnity, and the whole of life, than are these, how they have been generated altogether in this way. Let us then endeavour (to prove) so much, at least, relating to the gods, by perceiving that these are the two visible animals, of which we have spoken, (one) immortal; but the whole of the other has been created of the earth, mortal; (and) let us attempt to speak of the three, which are in the midst of the five [between them], and exist according to reasonable opinion, most clearly. For after fire let us place æther; and let us lay down that from it the soul moulds animals, which possess a power, like some other genera, the greater portions from their own nature, but the smaller portions, for the sake of a link, from other genera; and after the æther that soul moulds from air another genus of animals, and a third from water. And it is probable that soul, after it had fabricated all these, filled the whole of heaven with living matter, by making use, to the best of its power, of all genera, since all of them exist, partakers of life; but that the second and the third, and the fourth and the fifth, beginning their generation from the gods, who are manifest, end in us, who are men. The gods, then, Zeus and Juno, and all the rest, (let any one place) where he pleases, according to the same law; and let him consider this reasoning as fixed. We must call therefore the nature of the stars, and such things as we perceive existing together with the stars, the visible gods, the greatest and the most worthy of honour, and who as seeing on every side the most acutely, are the first in rank. And after them, and under them in due order, it is very meet to honour with prayers the dæmons, for the sake of their silent going to and fro, an aërial genus, that occupies a third and middle seat, and is the cause of interpreting. But of these two kinds of living beings, one (formed) of æther, and the other in due order of air, neither of them is entirely visible; and though present and near at hand, they do not become manifest to us; but let us say that, participating in a wonderful intelligence, as being docile and of a good memory, they know all our thoughts; and that in a wonderful manner they love the honourable and good man amongst us, and hate excessively the wicked, as being himself a sharer in pain; for the deity, who possesses the completion of a divine allot-ment, is (placed) beyond these (two), pleasure and pain, but has had a share in thinking upon and knowing, according to all things. And as the heaven is full of living beings, they interpret to each other and the highest gods all things and in all ways, through the living beings in the middle being carried to earth and through the whole of heaven with a light and rapid motion. But he, who assimilates the fifth genus of living beings, which is from water, to a demigod, will assimilate rightly; and this genus is sometimes visible, and sometimes concealed from view; but when visible, it exhibits a wonder through an obscure vision. Since then there are these five kinds of living beings really existing, in whatever manner any of us meets with them, falling in with them in a dream, in an interpretation of a dream, or spoken by oracles and prophecies to some in hearing, healthy or sick, or being met with at the close of life, and opinions being present privately and publicly, from whence many sacred rites of many have taken place, and some will take place; of all these the legislator, who possesses even the smallest particle of mind, will never dare, by making innovations towards a god-worship, which does not possess something clear, to overturn his own state; nor will he, knowing nothing at all (himself), forbid any portion of what the law of his country has spoken, on the subject of the gods. For it is not possible for human nature to know any thing on points of this kind. And does not the same reason hold good, that those are the worst of men, who do not dare to speak to us of the gods really existing in a manifest form, and to make them manifest, by permitting the other gods to be without sacred rites, and not to receive the honours that are due to them? But now there happens a thing of this kind to take place, as if some one of us had seen the Sun and Moon existing and looking upon all of us; and, although able to speak, had not said that they remained still sharing in no honours; nor was he anxious for his part to bring them into a place of honour, nor to cause festivals and sacrifices to take place for them; nor, through the computed time, to distribute to each of them the seasons of frequently longer and shorter years. Would not such a one, if he were said to be bad both to himself and to any other, who knew him, be justly said to be so?

Clinias: How not, guest, as being the worst (of men)?

Athenian: Know then, friend Clinias, that this very thing has now happened respecting myself.

Clinias: How say you?

Athenian: Know that amongst those, relating to the whole heaven, there are eight powers, sisters to each other, on which I have looked; and yet I have done nothing of consequence; for this is easy even to another person. Of these there are three, one of the Sun, one of the Moon, and one of the not-wandering stars, which I mentioned a little before, and there are five others. With respect to all these, and the (gods) in them, whether they move of themselves, or are carried along in cars, let not one of us all think even that some are gods, and others not; nor yet, that some of them are genuine, but others such as it is not lawful for any of us to mention; but let us all say that they are all of them brothers, and live in fraternal allotments; and let us honour them, not one for a year, and another for a month, nor let us ordain for others any allotment or time, in which (each) proceeds through its revolution, and completes the arrangement, which reason, the most divine of all, has ordained to be visible; (and) which he, who is under a good dæmon, has first wondered at, and then felt a desire to learn, as much as it is possible for a mortal nature, from thinking that he shall thus pass through life in the best and most fortunate manner, and after death arrive at places adapted to virtue; and being thus truly initiated and in reality participating in prudence, one in one, will pass the rest of his time as a holy spectator of things the most beautiful, as far as sight is concerned. It now remains for us to state after this how many and what they are. For we shall not be seen to be false. Thus far at least I firmly insist upon. For I say again, that of these there are eight; and that of the eight, three have been already spoken of, and there are five still remaining. Now the fourth and fifth onward movement and oblique path are nearly equal in velocity with the Sun, and are neither slower nor swifter. And let us say that he, who possesses intellect, is altogether competent to lead these three; and that these (movements) belong to the Sun, and Lucifer. But the third it is not possible to speak of by name, through its not being known; and the reason of this, that the person, who first saw it, was a Barbarian. For an ancient place was the nurse of those, who first thought of these matters, in consequence of the beauty of the summer season, which Egypt and Syria possess sufficiently, (enabling) persons to look upon all the stars, visible, so to say, perpetually; inasmuch as they dwelt (in a part) of the world at a distance from clouds and rain. Hence to every where else and hither too has reached what has been tested by

the time of thousands of years, and even infinite; and on this
account it is meet with confidence to lay down these matters as laws.
For (to think) that divine (natures) are not to be held in honour, or
that these are not divine, is clearly the province of persons not
endued with intellect. It is necessary however for this to be assigned
as the reason, why they have no names with the masses; for they
have appellations with some divine persons. For Lucifer and Hespe-
rus, being the same, have the appellation almost of Venus, and are
very well suited to a Syrian name-giver. But the star, which revolves
with an equal velocity with the Sun and this (Lucifer), has (the
name) almost of Mercury. And further, let us speak of three onward
movements (of those stars), that take their course to the right hand,
together with the Sun and Moon. But it is requisite to call the eighth
orb one, which a person may most correctly call the upper world,
which proceeds contrary to all those, and draws the others along
with it, as it would appear to persons who know little on these
matters; but what we know sufficiently, it is necessary to speak of,
and we do speak. For wisdom really existing is somehow in this way
apparent to him, who has a share, although a small one, of
consciousness correct and divine. Three stars then remain, one of
which differs from the rest by the slowness of its motion. Some call
it by the name of Phænon [Saturn]; but that, which is after this in
slowness, it is meet to call Phaethon [Jupiter]; and after this follows
Puroeis, [Mars,] which has the reddest colour of all. Of these things
when a person is speaking, it is not difficult to have a notion; but
after learning, it is requisite to think of them, as we have said. This
however it is necessary for every Greek to have in his thoughts, that
we inhabit a spot, Belonging to the Greeks, nearly the best, as
regards virtue. But it is proper to say that it deserves praise for being
situated in the middle of the natural qualities of summer and
winter. But though its nature, as regards summer, falls short of that,
which belongs to the region there, as I have stated, it gave subsequently to them the mental perception relating to these gods of the
world. Let us then admit that, whatever the Greeks have received
from the Barbarians, they work it out to a more beautiful end. And
the very same notion we ought to have with respect to what has

been said now, that it is difficult to discover all matters of this kind
without feeling a doubt. There is however a hope, both much and
glorious, that the Greeks will respect all these divinities in a manner
more beautiful and more just than the tradition, which has come
from the Barbarians, by employing both discipline and the Delphic
oracles and every attention according to the laws. Nor let any Greek
be afraid of this, that mortals ought not to busy themselves about
divine matters; but to think quite the contrary of this, that the deity
is not senseless, nor ignorant of human nature; but knows that,
where he teaches, (man) will follow, and learn what has been taught;
and that he surely knows that he does teach us this very thing, and
that we learn both number and to number. For being ignorant of
this, he would be the most stupid of all beings. For, according to the
saying, he would in reality be ignorant of himself, if he were
annoyed at a person able to learn, and did not rejoice without a
feeling of envy at a person becoming good through a god. Now
there is a reason great and good (for supposing) that, when men had
their first notions about the gods, how they existed, and of what
kind they were, and what actions they took in hand, ideas were then
broached, not to the mind of the moderate, nor agreeable to them,
nor even of those, who were next after them; amongst whom what
relates to fire and water and the other bodies, was said to be the
most ancient; but posterior to them the wonderful soul; and that the
movement, which the body has obtained by lot, is better and of
more value for carrying on both itself (and soul) by the aid of heat
and cold, and all things of that kind; but that the soul could not (do
so) to body and itself. But now, when we say that soul (exists), if it
exists in body, it would be not at all wonderful for it to move and
carry about both the body and itself; nor would, according to any
reason, soul be believed to be unable to carry about a weight. Since
then soul is the cause of the universe, and of all good things being
such, and on the other hand of evil things being such, it is not at all
wonderful that soul should be the cause of every bearing on and
movement; but that the bearing on and movement towards the good
belongs to the best soul, but the bearing on and movement towards
the contrary, to a contrary (soul); and that it is necessary for the

good to have vanquished, and to vanquish still, what are not of this kind. Hence let these be the assertions of us, now thinking in this way; all of which has been stated with reference to Justice, the punisher of the impious. With respect however to that, which has been brought to a test, it is not possible for us to disbelieve, that we ought not to consider the good to be wise. Let us then see, whether to this wisdom, of which we were of old in search, we can direct our mind either by education or art; and being wanting in the knowledge of which we should be ignorant of things just. Being such we seem to me, and we must speak. For after seeking up and down, I will endeavour to make it at the end plain to you in the way it has become very plain to myself. The greatest part of virtue, when it is not practised correctly, becomes the cause (of ignorance), as, from what has been said, the thing itself seems to me to signify forcibly. But let no one persuade us, that there is any (part) of virtue belonging to the race of mortals greater than piety. Now that this does not exist in the best natures through ignorance, we must declare; since the best are those, which are produced with the greatest difficulty, and which, when produced, are of the greatest benefit. For the soul, that receives moderately and mildly what belongs to a nature slow and the reverse, would be of an easy disposition; and admiring fortitude, and being obedient towards temperance, and, what is the greatest in these natures, able to learn, and with a good memory, it would be able to rejoice much in things of this kind, so as to be a lover of learning. For these things are not easy to be produced; and when they are produced, and meet with the nurture and education of which there is a need, they would be able to keep down most correctly the most part of their inferiors, by instructing them to do and say respecting the gods each of the matters that are requisite, and when they are requisite, relating to sacrifices and purifications, connected with gods and men, and not to make use of artifice in outward shows, but to honour virtue in truth, which is of all things of the greatest moment to every state. This part, therefore, we say is naturally the most important; and if there be a person to teach, it is able to be learnt in the most beautiful and best manner possible. But no one can be a teacher unless a god leads the way. If however a person teaches any thing correctly, but does not perform any thing of this kind in a fitting manner, it is better not to learn. However, from what has been said, it is necessary to learn these things, and for me to say that a nature of this kind is the best. Let us then endeavour to go through by a discourse what these are, and of what kind, and how it is requisite to learn them, both according to my ability, who am the speaker, and the ability of those, who are able to hear, in what manner a person may learn some things about god-worship. It is a thing almost absurd for the hearer. But we mention its name, which is, what a person through his ignorance of the subject would not imagine, astronomy. Are you then ignorant that the person, who is truly an astronomer, is necessarily the most wise? Not, indeed, he, who is an astronomer according to Hesiod, and all such, and looks to risings and settings, but he, who (looks to the circle) of the eight orbits, and the seven under the first, while each is going through its own orbit in such a way, that no nature would be competent to contemplate them easily, unless it par took of a wonderful nature, as we have just now said, and say to those, to whom we are stating what it is meet to learn, and how. Let this be mentioned first by us. The Moon goes through its orbit the quickest, and first leads on the month and the full moon. The second it is meet to consider is the Sun, that leads on the solstices through the whole of its orbit, and those that describe their course together with it. But that we may not frequently converse in the same way about the same things, the other orbits, which we mentioned before, and which it is not easy to comprehend, We ought to contemplate; and for these objects it is requisite to prepare natures, such as can exist, by teaching them many things before-hand, and accustoming the party, while a boy or youth, to labour thoroughly at what is requisite. On this account there would be a need of mathematics; but the greatest and first (need) is of numbers in the abstract, and not of such as are connected with bodies, but of the whole generation and power of the even and the odd, (and) so much as they contribute to the nature of things that exist. Now to him, who learns this, there comes in due order what we call very ridiculously by the name of geometry. But the similitude of numbers, that are naturally not similar to each other, becomes conspicuous, when applied to the properties of plain surfaces; which wonderful thing, not of human but divine origin, will appear very clear to him, who is able to think. And after this, those numbers, that are increased by a triple (ratio), and are similar to the nature of a solid, and those, that are on the other hand dissimilar, and are by another art similar to this, which those, who are conversant with it, call stereometry, (to be considered): which is indeed a thing divine and wonderful to those, who look into it ; that, while the power is ever revolving about the double, and that which is from the opposite to this, according to each analogy does every nature fashion out for itself a species and genus. Now the first power of the double, according to number, proceeds, according to proportion through one to two, possessing a double by power. But that, which, as regards the solid and tangible, is again a double, proceeds from one to eight. But that of the double quantity to the middle, and perhaps, what is more than the less, and less than the greater; while the other by the same part surpasses, and is surpassed by the extremes. But in the middle of six to twelve, there is found the sesquialter and sesquitertian proportions. And in the middle of these, a power, turned to both, has distributed to men a use, where voice and measure are combined, for the sake of sports, rhythm, and harmony, after having been granted to the happy dancing of the Muses. Let all these then be held to take place in this way, and let them exist. But as regards the finish to this, let us proceed to the divine generation and the most beautiful and divine nature of things visible, as far as a deity has granted to man to look upon them; which nature, no one, after having beheld, will boast of having received with facility without the particulars mentioned above. Besides this, in our several intercourse we must refer every individual thing to its species, (and all things to one,) by asking questions and disproving what has been not correctly asserted. For this is truly a touch stone the most beautiful and thoroughly the first amongst men; but in the case of such, as are not (touchstones), and only pretend to be, there is a labour the most vain of all. Further still, the accuracy of time must be considered by us, and how exactly it completes all that takes place in heaven; so that he, who believes the assertion to be true, that soul is a thing older and more divine than body, would also conceive it has been very beautifully and sufficiently said, that all things are full of gods; and that we have never been neglected through the forgetfulness or carelessness of superior beings. But as regards all such things as these, we should bear this in mind, that, if any one apprehends correctly each of these matters, there will be a great benefit to him, who has apprehended them; but if not, that it will be better for him to be ever calling upon a god, according to method. And let this be the method for it is necessary to say so much at least as this Every diagram, system of number, and composition of harmony, together with the one agreement of all the stars in their revolutions, ought to be apparent to him, who learns in a proper manner. And that, of which we are speaking, will become apparent, if a person rightly learns, looking to one thing. For to those, who think upon the matter, there will appear to be naturally one bond to all of these. But if a person will take the matter in hand in any other way, he must, as we have said, call upon fortune. For, without these, no nature will become lucky in states. But this is the method, (and) this the nurture, and through these subjects of instruction we must proceed, whether they are difficult or easy. Nor is it lawful to neglect the gods; since the happy report, relating to all of them, has, according to a manner, become apparent. And I call him, who thus apprehends all these points, the man the most truly wise; who, I stoutly affirm, both in jest and earnest, will, when he shall have filled up by death his allotted portion in things of this kind, if he be still almost dying, neither share any longer in many of his senses then, as at present; and he will, after being a partaker of one destiny alone, and becoming one out of many, be fortunate, and, at the same time, most wise and blessed; whether any one lives blessed on the continent, or in islands; and that he will participate in a fortune, which ever happens to be of this kind; and that, whether any one studies these questions, living a public or a private life, he will meet with the same fate and in a similar manner from the gods. But what we said at the beginning, the same assertion appears even now to be really true; that it is not possible for men to be perfectly blessed and happy, except a few. And this is rightly asserted by us. For such as are divine and at the same time prudent men, and naturally participate in the rest of virtue, and in addition have acquired all, that is closely connected with a blessed instruction, and such things as we have mentioned, to these alone have the gifts of fortune fallen by lot, and are in a sufficient state. To those then, who have laboured in this way upon such points, we say privately and lay down publicly as a law, that the greatest offices ought to be given to those, who have arrived at the period of an old man: and that all the others ought to follow them, and with good words hymn all the gods and goddesses; and lastly, that all of us, after having known and sufficiently examined the nocturnal assembly, most correctly exhort it to this wisdom.

Theages

Persons of the Dialogue: Demodocus, his son Theages, and
Socrates.

Scene: The Stoa of Zeus near the agora in Athens.

DEMODOCUS: I WANT, SOCRATES, TO SPEAK WITH YOU IN PRIVATE
about some matters, if you are at leisure; and if your want of leisure
be not very great, for my sake however make leisure.

Socrates: Nay, I am at leisure in other respects, and on your
account very much so. If then you wish to say anything it is in your
power to do so.

Demodocus: Are you willing then for us to retire out of the way,
to the portico of Zeus Eleutherius hard by?

Socrates: If it seems good to you.

Demodocus: Let us go then, Socrates. All natural productions,
growing out of the earth, and other animals as well as man, appear
to subsist in nearly the same manner. For to such of us as cultivate

the ground it is a thing the most easy in the case of plants, to prepare everything prior to planting, and even the planting itself. But when what has been planted is in a living state, the care of it becomes great and painful, and difficult. The same thing appears to take place with respect to human beings likewise. I form this conjecture as regards other things from my own affairs. For of this my son, whether one must call it the planting, or the procreating, it is the easiest of all things; but his education is difficult, and I am continually in fear about him. On other points much might be said; but the desire which now possesses him alarms me very much. It is not indeed an ignoble one, but it is dangerous. For he desires, Socrates, as he says, to become a wise man. I suspect that certain youths of his own age, and of the same ward, have been going down to the city, and repeating certain discourses, and disturbed his mind very much. Of these he is emulous; and for a long time is giving me great trouble, thinking it fit that I should pay attention to him, and pay money to some of the sophists, who might make him a wise man. For the money indeed I care less than nothing, but think that, in going whither he is hastening, he is running into no small danger. Hitherto I have by soothing restrained him; but as I am no longer able to do so, I think it best to yield to him, lest by frequently associating with others without me, he should be corrupted. Hence I am come for this very purpose, that I may place him with some one of those, who are considered to be sophists. Opportunely then for us have you appeared, with whom, as I am about to engage in affairs of this kind, I wished very much to consult. If then you have any advice to give respecting what you have heard from me, it is both lawful and needful to do so.

Socrates: Counsel, Demodocus, is said to be a sacred thing. If then any other consultation is sacred, this is so, about which you are now considering. For there is not a thing, about which a person may consult, more divine, than about the instruction of himself and of those related to him. In the first place then, let you and I agree together as to what we think that thing is, about which we are consulting; lest I may not perchance take it to be one thing, and you another; and we afterwards perceive, when the conference has proceeded far, that we are an object of ridicule, both I who give, and you who request, advice, in not thinking the same upon anything.

Demodocus: You appear to me, Socrates, to speak correctly; and it is meet so to do.

Socrates: And speak I do correctly, but not entirely so; since I make a trifling alteration. For I am thinking, that perhaps this youth may not desire that, which we think he desires, but something else; and in that case we shall be still more absurd in consulting about something different. It appears, therefore, to me to be the most correct to begin by inquiring of him what the thing is, which he desires.

Demodocus: It appears very nearly to be the best to do as you say.

Socrates: Tell me then what is the name of this handsome youth? what must we call him?

Demodocus: His name, Socrates, is Theages.

Socrates: You have given your son, Demodocus, a beautiful and sacred-like name. Tell us, Theages, do you say that you desire to become a wise man? And do you think it fit for this your father to find out the acquaintance of such a person as may make you wise?

Theages: Yes.

Socrates: Do you call those men wise, who are skilled in that, respecting which they have a knowledge, or those, who have not?

Theages: Those, who have a knowledge.

Socrates: What then, has not your father caused you to be instructed, or taught you himself, what others are taught, who are the sons of fathers good and honourable; for instance, letters, to play on the harp, to wrestle, and other exercises?

Theages: Yes, myself.

Socrates: Do you think then there is still a want of some knowledge, to which it is proper for your father to pay attention for your sake?

Theages: I do.

Socrates: What is it? Tell us it, that we may gratify you.

Theages: My father knows it, Socrates; for I have often mentioned it to him. But he designedly says this to you, as if truly he did not know what I desire; for in this and other matters likewise he opposes me, and is unwilling to place me with any one.

Socrates: But all that you have hitherto said to him, has been said, as it were, without witnesses. Now therefore make me a witness and state before me what is the wisdom you desire. For come now, if you should desire that wisdom, by which men steer ships, and I should happen to ask you — What is the wisdom, Theages, of which being in want you blame your father, because he is unwilling to place you with a man, through whom you might become wise? What answer would you give me? What would you say this wisdom is? Is it not the pilot's art?

Theages: Yes.

Socrates: And if you desired to be wise in that wisdom, by which persons direct chariots, and afterwards blamed your father, on my asking you what this wisdom is, what answer would you give me? Would you not say it is the charioteer's art?

Theages: Yes.

Socrates: But is the wisdom, of which you have now a desire, nameless, or has it a name?

Theages: I think it has a name.

Socrates: Whether then do you know it, but not its name? Or its name likewise?

Theages: Its name likewise.

Socrates: Say then what it is.

Theages: What other name, Socrates, can one say it has, than that of wisdom?

Socrates: Is not then the charioteer's art wisdom likewise? Or does it appear to you to be ignorance?

Theages: It does not.

Socrates: But wisdom?

Theages: Yes.

Socrates: For what do we use it? Is it not for that, by which we know how to manage horses when yoked?

Theages: Yes.

Socrates: Is not then the pilot's art wisdom likewise?

Theages: To me at least it appears so.

Socrates: Is it not that, by which we know how to manage?

Theages: It is.

Socrates: But what is the wisdom of which you are desirous? What by it do we know how to govern?

Theages: By it we know, it seems to me, how to govern men.

Socrates: What, sick men?

Theages: No.

Socrates: For that wisdom is the physician's art. Is it not?

Theages: Yes.

Socrates: Is it that then, by which we know how to regulate singers in choirs?

Theages: It is not.

Socrates: For this is the musician's art.

Theages: Certainly.

Socrates: But is it that, by which we know how to regulate those, who are engaged in gymnastic exercises?

Theages: No.

Socrates: For this is the gymnast's art.

Theages: It is.

Socrates: Is it that of those, who do what? Be ready to state it to myself, as I have the preceding to you.

Theages: It is that, by which persons do something in the city.

Socrates: Are there not then in a city persons who are sick?

Theages: Yes. But I am not speaking of these only, but also of the others in the city.

Socrates: Do I then understand the art of which you are speaking? For you appear to me to say it is not that, by which we know how to govern mowers, and grape-gatherers, and planters, and sowers, and threshers; for it is the husbandman's art, by which we govern these. Is it not?

Theages: Yes.

Socrates: Nor are you speaking of that, by which we govern sawyers, and planers, and turners; for does not this belong to the carpenter's art?

Theages: Yes.

Socrates: But perhaps you are speaking of that wisdom, by which we govern all these, and husbandmen, and carpenters, and all artificers skilled and unskilled, and men and women.

Theages: Of this wisdom, Socrates, I have for a long while ago been wishing to speak.

Socrates: Can you say, that Aegisthus, who slew Agamemnon at Argos, had dominion over what you have mentioned, artificers skilled and unskilled, and men and women, all taken together, or over some other things?

Theages: No; but over these.

Socrates: What then, did not Peleus, the son of Aeacus, have dominion over those very kind of persons in Phthia?

Theages: Yes.

Socrates: And you have heard that Periander, the son of Cypselus, was a ruler in Corinth.

Theages: Yes.

Socrates: And did he not rule over the very kind of persons in his city?

Theages: Yes.

Socrates: What then, do you not think that Archelaus, the son of Perdiccas, who was lately the ruler in Macedonia, had dominion over the same kind of persons?

Theages: I do.

Socrates: And over whom do you think that Hippias, the son of Pisistratus, ruled in this city? was it not over these kind of persons?

Theages: How not?

Socrates: Can you tell me then, what appellation Bacis, and the Sibyl, and our countryman Amphilytus, bore?

Theages: What else, Socrates, than oracle-chaunters?

Socrates: You speak correctly. But endeavour to give me an answer as to what appellation Hippias and Periander bore through the same kind of dominion?

Theages: Tyrants, I think; for what else could it be?

Socrates: Whoever then desires to have dominion over all the men together in the city, desires this very same dominion, the tyrannic, and to be a tyrant.

Theages: So it appears.

Socrates: Do you then say that you desire this dominion?

Theages: It seems so from what I have said.

Socrates: O you wicked youth! Do you desire to tyrannize over us? And have you for a long time blamed your father, because he did not send you to the school of some tyrant-teacher? And are not you, Demodocus, ashamed of yourself? Who, having known a long time ago what this youth desired, and having likewise the power of sending him, where you might have made him that skilful artist in wisdom, of which he is desirous, have, notwithstanding, begrudged him this, and are unwilling to send him? But now, you see — since he has spoken against you before me — let us consult in common, you and I, to whose school we may send him; and through associating with whom he may become a wise tyrant.

Demodocus: Let us, by Zeus, then, Socrates, consult; for it appears to me that there is need of no despicable counsel in this affair.

Socrates: Permit us first, thou good man, to interrogate him sufficiently.

Demodocus: Interrogate him.

Socrates: What then, Theages, if we should make use of Euripides? For he somewhere says,

Tyrants are wise, by converse with the wise.

If then someone should ask Euripides — In what say you, Euripides, do tyrants become wise by the conversation of the wise? just as if he had said,

Farmers are wise, by converse with the wise —

and we had asked him — In what are they wise? What would he have answered? Would he reply that they are wise in anything else than in things pertaining to agriculture?

Theages: In nothing else but those.

Socrates: But what, if he had said,

Cooks become wise, by converse with the wise —

and we had asked him — In what are they wise? What would he

have answered? Would it not have been — In things pertaining to cooking?

Theages: Yes.

Socrates: Again, if he had said,

Wrestlers are wise, by converse with the wise —

and we had asked him — In what are they wise? Would he not have said — In things pertaining to wrestling?

Theages: Yes.

Socrates: But since he says,

Tyrants are wise, by converse with the wise —

upon our asking him — In what say you, Euripides, are they wise? What would be his answer?

Theages: By Zeus, I do not know.

Socrates: Are you willing then for me to tell you?

Theages: If you are willing.

Socrates: It is that, which Anacreon says Callicrete knew. Or do you not know the song?

Theages: I do.

Socrates: What then, do you also desire the conversation of a man, who happens to be a fellow-artist with Callicrete the daughter of Cyane, and who knows the art of a tyrant, as the poet says she did, in order that you may become a tyrant over us and the city?

Theages: You have for some time, Socrates, been laughing at and playing with me.

Socrates: What then, do you say that you do not desire this wisdom, by which you may rule over all the citizens? And doing this, would you be anything else but a tyrant?

Theages: I would pray, indeed, I fancy, to be a tyrant over all men, or, if not of all, of the greatest part; and I think that you, and all other men, would do the same, and perhaps still more, to be a god. But I did not say that I desired this.

Socrates: But what then, after all, is this which you desire? Do you not say that you desire to rule over the citizens?

Theages: Not by violence, nor as tyrants do; but I desire to rule over the willing, in the same manner as other men of note in the city.

Socrates: Do you mean, as Themistocles, and Pericles, and Cimon, and such as were skilled in state affairs?

Theages: By Zeus, I mean those.

Socrates: What then, if you happened to be desirous of becoming wise in horsemanship, by going to whom do you think you would become a skilful horseman? Would it be by going to others than those skilled in horses?

Theages: By Zeus, not I.

Socrates: But you would go to those very men, who are skilled in these matters, and who possess horses, and who continually use both their own and many that are the property of others.

Theages: It is evident I should.

Socrates: What then, if you wished to become wise in the throwing of darts, think you not that you would become skilled by going to those engaged in the art of dart-throwing, and who possess darts, and continually use many darts, both their own and those belonging to others?

Theages: It appears so to me.

Socrates: Tell me then, since you wish to become wise in state affairs, think you that you will become wise by going to any others than those statesmen, who are skilled in state affairs themselves, and who continually make use of their own state and many others, and have an intercourse both with the Greek and Barbarian states? Or do you think, that by associating with certain other persons, but not with these, you will become wise in those things, in which they are wise?

Theages: I have heard the discourses, Socrates, which persons say you have spoken, how that the sons of those very statesmen were in no respect better than the sons of shoemakers: and you appear to me to have spoken most truly, from what I am able to perceive. I should be senseless then, if I thought that anyone of these could impart to me his wisdom, when he could not in any respect benefit his own son; if indeed he were able on these points to benefit any person whatever.

Socrates: What then, O best of men, would you do, if you had a son, who should give you trouble of this kind, and say that he desired to become a good painter, and blame you, his father, because you were not willing to expend money for the sake of these things, while he was despising painters, the artists in this very matter, and unwilling to learn from them; or if, being desirous to become a piper or harper, he should act in this manner towards pipers or harpers? In what way would you treat him, and whither would you send him, when thus unwilling to learn from those persons?

Theages: By Zeus, I do not know.

Socrates: Now then, as you are doing these very things to your father, do you wonder at and blame him, if he is in doubt how he shall treat you, and whither send you? For we will place you with whomever of the Athenians you wish, the most skilled in state affairs, and who will be with you gratuitously; and at the same time you will not lose your money, and likewise be in greater repute with the many than by associating with anyone else.

Theages: What then, Socrates, are not you one of the excellent men? For if you are willing to associate with me, it is sufficient, and I seek no other.

Socrates: Why say you this, Theages?

Demodocus: He does not, Socrates, speak badly; and at the same time by doing this you will gratify me. Since there is nothing I should consider a greater piece of good luck than for my son to be pleased with your society, and for you to be willing to associate with him. And indeed I am ashamed to say how very much I wish it. I entreat both of you, therefore, you, Socrates, to be willing to associate with him, and you, my son, not to seek to associate with any other than Socrates; and you will thus release me from many and dreadful cares. For I now very much fear for him, lest he should meet with some other person able to corrupt him.

Theages: Do not, father, feel any longer any fear for me, if you can but persuade Socrates to permit me to associate with him.

Demodocus: You speak very well. And after this, the conversation, Socrates, will be directed to you. For I am ready, so to say in few words, to give up to you both me and mine, and the nearest related, whatever, in short, you may require, if you will take this youth to your bosom, and benefit him as far as you can.

Socrates: O Demodocus, I do not wonder that you are so impor-
tunate, if you think that your son can be especially benefited by me.
For I do not know anything about which he, who is endowed with
intellect, ought to be more anxious, than how his son may become
the best of men. But from whence it has appeared to you that I am
more able to benefit your son towards his becoming a good citizen,
than you are yourself, and from whence he has thought that I can
benefit him more than you, I very much wonder. For, in the first
place, you are older than I am; and in the next place, you have held
many offices, and those the greatest among the Athenians; and you
are honoured by the people of the Anagyrusian ward, by much the
most, and no less so by the rest of the city. But neither of you can
see any one of these things in me; and next, if Theages here
despises the society of statesmen, and seeks after certain others who
profess themselves able to instruct young men, there is Prodicus of
Ceos, and Gorgias the Leontine, and Polus the Agrigentine, and
many others, who are so wise, that they go to cities and persuade the
noblest and wealthiest of the young men, who are permitted to
associate gratuitously with any one of the citizens they please, —
they persuade, I say, these to give up those of their own city, and to
associate with them, and to put down moreover a considerable sum
of money, and, as a remuneration, to give them thanks besides. Of
these, then, it is reasonable for your son and yourself to select someone; but to select me it is not reasonable; for I know none of that
blessed and beautiful learning, although I wish I did; but I am
always somehow asserting that I happen to know, I may say, nothing
but a mere trifle relating to matters of love. But in that kind of
learning I lay claim to being more skilled than any one man of the
past or present time.

Theages: See you, father, how Socrates does not appear to me to
be very willing to pass the time with me. For, as to myself, I am
ready, if he is willing. But he says this, playing with us. For I know
some of the same age with myself, and others a little older, who,
before they associated with him, were worth nothing; but when they
had been with him, in a very little time they appeared to be better
than all, to whom they were previously inferior.

Socrates: Do you know then, son of Demodocus, how this is?

Theages: Yes, by Zeus, I do; and that, if you are willing, I too shall be able to become such as they are.

Socrates: Not so, thou excellent youth; but you are not conscious how this occurs; and I will tell you. There is, by a divine allotment, a certain daemon that has followed me, beginning from childhood. This is a voice, which, when it exists, always signifies to me the abandonment of what I am about to do; but it never at any time incites me. And, if any one of my friends communicates anything to me, and there is the voice, it dissuades me from that very thing, and it does not suffer me to do it. Of this I will produce you witnesses. You know the beautiful Charmides, the son of Glauco. He once happened to communicate to me that he was about to contend for the stadium at Nemea; and immediately, on his beginning to say, that he meant to contend, there was the voice. And I forbade him, and said, While you were speaking to me, there was the voice of the daimon; do not, therefore, contend. Perhaps, said he, the voice signified to you, that I should not conquer; but, though I should not be victorious, yet, by exercising myself at this time, I shall be benefited. Having thus spoken, he engaged in the contest. It is worth while, therefore, to inquire of him, what happened to him after this very act of contending. And if you are willing to inquire of Clitomachus, the brother of Timarchus, what Timarchus said to him, when, being about to die, he went right against the daemon, both he and Euathlus, the runner in the stadium, who received Timarchus when he was an exile, will tell you what he then said.

Theages: What did he say?

Socrates: O Clitomachus, said he, I indeed am now going to die, because I was unwilling to be persuaded by Socrates. But why Timarchus said this, I will tell you. When Timarchus rose from the banquet, together with Philemon the son of Philemonides, with the view of murdering Nicias the son of Heroscomander, they two alone were cognizant of the plot; and Timarchus, as he rose, said to me, What do you say, Socrates? Do you continue drinking; but I must rise up and go somewhere. I will, however, return shortly, if I am successful. And there was the voice. And I said to him. By no

means, said I, rise up; for there has been to me the usual daemon
signal. Upon this he stayed. And after a slight interval, he was again
going away, and said — Socrates, I am going. And there was again
the voice. Again, therefore, I compelled him to stay. The third time,
wishing to escape me unnoticed, he rose up without saying anything
to me, and escaped unnoticed, having watched me, while I had my
attention otherwise engaged; and thus departing he perpetrated the
acts, through which he went away about to die. Hence he told his
brother, what I have now told you, that he was going to die, through
his not believing in me. Further still, you will hear from many
respecting the events in Sicily, what I said concerning the destruction of the army. And the things that are past, you may hear from
those that know them; but you may now make trial of the daemon
signal, if it says anything to the purpose. For on the departure of
Sannio the beautiful for the army, there came to me the signal; and
he is now gone with Thrasyllus, to carry on the campaign right
through Ephesus and Ionia. And I think that he will either die, or
that he will meet with an end something near to it. And I very much
fear for the rest of the enterprise. All these things have I said to you,
because this power of this daemon is able to effect everything with
respect to the intercourse of those, who pass their time with me. For
it is opposed to many; and it is not possible for those to be benefited
by passing their time with me, so that it is not possible for me to live
with them. With many, however, it does not prevent me from
conversing; and yet they are not at all benefited by being with me.
But they, whom the power of the daemon assists to the intercourse,
are those whom you have noticed; for in a short time they make a
proficiency. And of those, who make a proficiency, some have the
benefit firm and lasting; but many, as long as they are with me,
advance in a wonderful manner; but when they separate themselves
from me, they again differ in no respect from any person whatever.
This did Aristides, the son of Lysimachus and grandson of Aristides, suffer; for, while passing his time with me, he made a very
great proficiency in a short period; but afterwards an expedition
took place, and he went away, sailing with it. On his return he found
Thucydides, the son of Melesias and grandson of Thucydides,

passing his time with me. Now this Thucydides, the day before, had felt some ill against me during a conversation. Aristides, therefore, after he had seen and saluted me, and other matters had been talked of, observed — I hear, Socrates, that Thucydides thinks highly of himself, on some points, and is angry with you, as if he were really something. It is so, said I. What then, said he, does he not know what a slave he was before he associated with you? By the gods, said I, it does not seem that he does. But I too, said he, am in a ridiculous situation, Socrates. What is it? said I. It is, said he, that, before I sailed away, I was able to converse with any man whatever, and not to appear inferior to any one in argument, so that I sought the society of men the most elegant; but now, on the contrary, I shun any one, whom I perceive to be instructed, so ashamed am I of my own littleness. But, said I, whether did this power leave you suddenly or by degrees? By degrees, he replied. When was it present with you, said I? Was it present while you were learning something from me, or was it in some other way? I will tell you, said he, Socrates, a thing incredible indeed, by the gods, but true. I never, at any time, learnt anything from you, as you know. I made, however, a proficiency when I associated with you, even if I was only in the same house, though not in the same room; but more so when I was in the same room with you; and I seemed to myself to improve much more when, being in the, same room, I looked at you, when you were speaking, than when I looked another way. But I made by far the greatest proficiency, when I sat near you and touched you. Now, however, said he, all that habit has entirely oozed away. Of such kind then is, Theages, the intercourse with myself; for, if it is pleasing to the god, you will make a very great and rapid proficiency; but if not, not. See, then, whether it is not safer for you to be instructed by some one of those, who have a power over the benefit, with which they benefit men, than by me, who have the power to do only whatever may happen.

Theages: It appears to me, Socrates, that we should act in this manner, namely, to make a trial of this daemon by associating together. And, if he is favourable to us, this will be the best; but if not, then let us immediately consult what we shall do, whether we shall associate with some other person, or endeavour to appease the divine power, that is present with you, by prayers and sacrifices, or any other method that the diviners may explain.

Demodocus: Do not, Socrates, oppose the lad any longer on these points; for Theages speaks well.

Socrates: If it appears proper so to act, let us act so.

Erastai, or Lovers

I ENTERED THE SCHOOL OF DIONYSIUS, THE TEACHER OF GRAMMAR, and I saw there those of the young men, who were deemed to be the most remarkable for their personal appearance and the good repute of their fathers, and their admirers likewise. Two of the youths happened to be disputing, but about what I did not very well hear. They appeared however to be disputing about Anaxagoras, or Oenopides; as they were describing circles, and imitating by their hands certain inclinations, with great earnestness. And, for I was sitting near an admirer of one of the young persons, nudged him with my elbow, and asked — On what were the two youths so earnestly engaged? and I said, Surely it is a subject important and beautiful, on which they have bestowed so serious an attention. — What call you important and beautiful? said he. They are prating about things above in the sky, and trifling away their time in philoso-phizing. — And I, in wonder at such an answer, said — Do you think it, young man, to be a disgraceful thing to philosophize? or why do you speak so harshly? — But another person, who was a rival admirer of the youths, and happened to be sitting near, on hearing me asking the question, and the answer, said — It is not for you, Socrates, to ask this man, whether he thinks it disgraceful to philosophize. Know you not that he has spent all his time in being throstled, and cramming himself, and sleeping? so that what other answer think you he would give, but that it is disgraceful to philosophize? — Now this person had employed his whole time in mental cultivation, but the other, whom he abused, in bodily exercises. It seemed then to me that I ought to dismiss the one, who had been interrogated, for he did not pretend even to be skilled in words, but in deeds; and to interrogate thoroughly the other, who pretended to be rather clever, in order that I might, if I could, be benefited by him in knowledge. I said therefore to him, that I had proposed my question in common for all; but if you think you will give a better answer, I put the same question to you as I did to him, Whether you think it honourable to philosophize or not? — Just as we were conversing thus, the two youths, overhearing us, became silent; and ceasing from the dispute, became listeners. Now, what their admirers suffered, I know not; but I was struck with astonishment. For I am always struck so in the case of the young and handsome. One of them, however, seemed to me in no less an agony than myself; and he answered with the air of a person eager for honour. — Should I ever, Socrates, said he, consider it disgraceful to philosophize, I should no longer deem myself a human being nor, indeed, anyone else, so disposed, pointing to his rival, and speaking with a loud voice, so that the objects of their admiration might hear. — To you, then, said I, it seems honourable to philosophize. — Most highly, replied he. — What then, said I; does it seem to you possible for a man to know anything whatever, whether it is disgraceful or honourable, who does not know at all what that thing is? — No, said he. — Know you then, said I, what it is to philosophize? — Perfectly, said he. — What is it then? said I. — What else, said he, than according to the sentiment of Solon? For Solon says somewhere, "*Even as I grow old, still much I learn*".

And it appears to me that the man, who would philosophize, ought to be always learning some one thing at least, when he is either young or old, in order that he may during life learn the greatest number of things. — At first it seemed to me that he had said something to the purpose; but afterwards, on thinking thrice, I

asked him, whether he considered philosophy to be much learning?
— Completely so, said he. — And do you consider, said I, that
philosophy is only honourable? or good likewise? — It is likewise
very good, said he. — Do you perceive this to be something peculiar
to philosophy? or does it seem to you to be the case in other things
likewise? For instance, do you consider a love of gymnastic exercises
to be not only honourable but good likewise, or not? — To this he
said very ironically two things. To this man let it be said, that it is
neither; but to you, Socrates, I acknowledge it to be both
honourable and good. — I then asked him, Do you think that in
these exercises the undergoing much toil is a love of exercise? — By
all means, said he; just as in philosophizing, I consider that much
learning is philosophy. — Do you think then, said I, that the lovers
of those exercises desire anything else than that, which will cause
the body to be in a good state? — That very thing, he replied. —
Do then, said I, many labours, cause the body to be in a good state?
— Certainly, said he; for how should a person have, from little
labour, his body in a good state? — Here I thought it best to call
upon the lover of gymnastics, in order that he might assist me
through his knowledge of the gymnastic art. And I asked him, Why
are you silent, O best of men, while this person is talking thus? Or
to you likewise do persons seem to have their bodies in a good state
from much labour or little? For my part, Socrates, said he, I thought
he had known the saying, that moderate labour is best for the body.
How so? said I. — I speak not of a man sleepless, and foodless, and
having his neck not worn down and attenuated by care. On his
saying this the youths were delighted, and burst into a laugh; but the
other party blushed. — I then said, What then, do you now concede
that neither much nor little labour causes human beings to have
their bodies in a good state, but only what is moderate? Or will you
contest with us two? — Against him, said he, I would enter the lists
with much pleasure, and I know well that I should be competent to
support the proposition I have laid down, if I had laid down one
weaker than this; for he is nothing. But against you I beg not to
contend in favour of a paradox; and I admit, that not many, but
moderate exercises procure for men a good habit of body. And what

in the case of food? said I. Is it the moderate, or much? — He
admitted it in the case of food. And thus I compelled him to confess
that, in the case of all the other things relating to the body, the
moderate is the most beneficial, and not the much or little. And he
confessed the moderate and all this he granted me. — What then,
said I, as regards the soul? Of the things applied to it do the
moderate or the immoderate benefit it? — The moderate, said he.
— Is not learning one of the things applied to the soul? — He
admitted it. — Of learning then, the moderate quantity benefits,
but not the great. — He assented. — Of whom then, making an
inquiry, should we justly inquire what kind of exercise and of food
are moderate for the body? We all three agreed that it is a physician
or a master of exercise. And of whom shall we inquire about the
sowing of seeds? About this, we confessed the husbandman. But
inquiring of whom, should we justly inquire respecting the planting
and sowing of learning in the soul, how many, and of what kinds of
it are moderate? We were here all full of difficulty. Upon which I
said, by way of a joke, Since we are all at a loss, are you willing for
us to ask these youths here? Or perhaps we are ashamed, as Homer
says the suitors were, who deemed that no one else was fit to stretch
the bow.

Since then they now seemed to be dispirited on the question, I
endeavoured to view it in another light, and I said — What kinds of
learning do we best conjecture those are, which a philosopher ought
to learn? Since they are not all or many. Whereupon the wiser
person, taking up the discourse, observed that the most beautiful
kinds of learning, and the most becoming, are those by which a
person would obtain the highest reputation for philosophy; and that
he would obtain the highest, if he seemed to be skilled in all arts
and, if not all, at least in as many as possible, and especially those of
the greatest account, after having learnt such of them as are fitting
for freemen to learn, and are connected with intellect, and not with
a handicraft merely. — Do you mean in the same way, said I, as in
carpentry? For there you may purchase a tip-top carpenter for five
or six minas but you could not buy an architect even for ten thousand drachmas; so few of these are to be found amongst all the

Greeks. Are you speaking of some such thing? — And he, on hearing, admitted that he was speaking of such a thing. — I then asked
him, if it was not impossible for one person to learn thus only two
arts, much less, many and great. — Do not understand me,
Socrates, said he, as if I were saying that a philosopher ought to
know each of the arts accurately, as he does, who makes it his
profession; but to be able, as becomes a person of a liberal education, to follow better than the persons present, what is said by the
handicraftsman; and to give his opinion so as to appear, in what is
said and done relating to the arts, to have a finer taste, and more
knowledge, than those who happen to be present. — Then I — for I
was still doubtful what he meant by his speech — said to him, Do I
conceive rightly what kind of person you call a philosopher? For you
seem to me to speak of a person, such as are the competitors in five
kinds of contest, compared with the runner, or the wrestlers. For the
former fall short of the latter, as regards the contests of the latter,
and are second to them but of all the other competitors, they are the
first, and are the victors. Some such thing you mean perhaps that
the study of philosophy effects in those, who pursue it, in that in the
intellect relating to the arts, but in attaining the second, they are
superior to all the rest; so that he, who has studied philosophy,
becomes in everything a person under the tip-top man. Somesuch
person you seem to me to point out. — You appear to me, Socrates,
said he, to understand correctly what relates to a philosopher, in
likening him to a competitor in five contests. For he is really such a
man, as not to be a slave to anything nor has he laboured upon any
one thing with such accuracy, as, through his attention to that one
thing, to be deficient in all the rest, as are handicraftsmen, but he
has touched moderately upon all.

After this reply, I was anxious to know clearly what he meant,
and I inquired of him, whether he considered good persons to be
useful or useless. — Useful, surely, Socrates, said he. — If then the
good are useful, are not the bad useless? — He agreed. — Well
then, said I, do you deem philosophers to be useful, or not? — He
acknowledged they were useful; and moreover he said, that he
deemed them the most useful of all persons. — Come now, said I,

let us see whether you say what is true. How can these second-rate men be of any use to us? For it is plain that the philosopher is inferior to each of those who possess their respective arts. — He acknowledged it. — Come then, said I, if either yourself were unwell, or any of your friends, for whom you have a great regard, would you, being desirous to recover health, introduce that second-rate person, the philosopher, to your family; or take a physician. — Both of them, said he. — Do not say both, I replied; but which in preference, and the first? — No man, said he, would hesitate about this, that I would take the physician in preference and first. — What then, in a vessel tossed in a storm? To whom would you rather intrust yourself and your property? To a pilot, or to a philosopher? — To a pilot, for my part, said he. — And so, too, in all other affairs; so long as there is a person of skill in a profession, the philosopher is of no use. — It appears so, said he. — The philosopher, therefore, said I, is some useless person; for there are surely persons of skill in all professions. But we have agreed that the good are useful, and the wicked useless. — He was forced to own it.

What then, said I, shall I ask you about what comes after this? Or is it not rather rude to put a question? — Ask what you please, said he. — I desire nothing else, said I, than to repeat the concessions already made. Now the matter stands thus. We have conceded that philosophy is an honourable thing, and that we are ourselves philosophers and that philosophers are good; and that the good are useful, and the wicked useless. Again, on the other hand, we have conceded that philosophers are useless, as long as there are persons of skill in any particular profession; and that such persons are existing at all times. For was not all this conceded? — Certainly, said he. — We concede, therefore, agreeably to your own reasoning, that if it be philosophy to be skilled in arts in the manner you state, such persons are wicked and useless as long as there are artists. But see, my friend, if the case be so, and that to philosophize is not to attend to arts, nor to busy oneself about many things, nor to be living like a workman, bending over his work, nor to be learning many things, but something else? Since I thought, it was a reproach for persons, much occupied in arts, to be called artisans.

But we shall know more clearly by this means, whether I am speaking truly, if you will answer me this. Who know how to punish horses correctly? Whether they, who make them better, or others? — They who make them better. Well then, do not they, who know how to make dogs better, know how to chastise dogs properly? — Yes. — The same art then makes better, and chastises properly. — I agree, said he. Well then, is the art, which makes better and chastises properly, the same as that which knows the good and the vicious, or is it a different one? — It is, said he, the same. — Are you then willing, said I, to concede this, in the case of human beings likewise, that the art, which makes men better, is that, which chastises properly, and knows the good and the bad? By all means, said he. — Does not then the art which applies to one apply to many too, and that which applies to many apply to one likewise? And so too as regards horses and all other things? — I confess it, said he. — What then is the science, which chastises properly the licentious and the lawless in civil states? Is it not the judicial science? — Yes. — Do you mean by justice any other science than this? — No other. — Do not then men know the good and the bad by that science, by which they chastise properly? — By that. — And he, who knows one, will know many? — Yes. — And whoever does not know many, will not know one. — I confess it. — If then a horse, as being but a horse, knows not good and bad horses, he would not know of which kind he is himself? — I admit it. — And if an ox, being but an ox, knows not good and bad oxen, he would not know of which kind he is himself? — True, said he. — And so too, in the case of a dog? — He admitted it. — What then, if a man knows not the good men and the bad, would he not be ignorant whether he is good or bad, inasmuch as he too is a man? — He agreed. — Now to be ignorant of oneself, is it to be of sound mind, or not sound? — Not sound. — To know then oneself, is to be of sound mind. — I admit it, said he. — To this then, as it seems, the Delphic inscription exhorts, namely, to exercise a sound mind, and justice. — It seems so. — And by the very same science we know too how to chastise properly. — I admit it, said he. — Is not then justice that, by which we know how to chastise properly? but soundness of mind that, by which we have the skill to know ourselves and others? — It seems so, said he. — Justice then, said I, and soundness of mind are the same thing. — It appears so.

In this way, said I, states are well governed, when they, who do wrong, suffer punishment. — You speak the truth. — The same science too, said I, is that of the statesman. — He assented. — What then, when a single man administers correctly the affairs of a state, he is not a tyrant, and a king? — I admit it. — Does he not administer affairs by the art of the king? or the tyrant? — Just so. — These arts then are the same with those. — They appear so. — Well then, when one man administers the affairs of a household correctly, what is his name? Is it not steward, or master? — Yes. — Whether by justice would he administer the affairs of a household correctly? or by any other art? — By justice. — The same kind of person then, it seems, is a king, a tyrant, a statesman, a steward, a master, a man of sound mind, and a just man; and one is the art of the king, of the tyrant, of the statesman, of the master, of the steward, of the just man, and the man of sound mind. — So it appears, said he.

Is it not then disgraceful for a philosopher, when the physician is speaking about persons who are ill, not to be able to follow what is said, nor to give an opinion on what is said or done, and similarly, when any one skilled artisan is speaking? And when a judge, or a king, or anyone else of those whom we have just now enumerated, is speaking of things belonging to his office, is it not disgraceful for a philosopher not to follow what they say or do, nor to be able to give an opinion respecting them? How, Socrates, said he, is it not disgraceful for him, to be able to give no opinion on subjects so important? — Shall we assert then, said I, that on these points the philosopher must be a competitor in five contests, and be second-rate, having the second prize after all, and be useless, so long as there exists any of the first-rate? Or must he in the first place not commit his household to another person, nor have the second place in that business; but ought himself to chastise after being the judge, if his household is about to be administered correctly. — In this he agreed with me. And then, said I, should his friends submit an award to him, or the state order him to decide upon anything, or to act the judge, would it not, my friend, be disgraceful for him to appear in such cases to be second or third, and not to take the lead? — So it seems to me. To philosophize therefore, thou best of men, wants much of being great in learning, or the busying oneself about arts. — On my saying this, the wise man, ashamed of what he had before asserted, was silent; but the illiterate person said, it was in that way, and the rest approved of what had been stated.

Hipparchus

Persons of the Dialogue: Socrates and an Anonymous Friend.

SOCRATES: WHAT IS THE LOVE OF GAIN, AND WHO ARE ITS LOVERS?

Friend: They seem to me to be those, who think it worth while to make a gain from what is nothing worth.

Socrates: Whether then do they seem to you to do so, while knowing that the things are of no worth, or not knowing? For if they do so not knowing, you call the lovers of gain senseless.

Friend: Nay, I do not call them senseless, but thorough knaves and villains, the slaves of gain, and who know indeed that the things are worthless, from which they dare to make a gain, but yet through their shamelessness they dare to have a love of gain.

Socrates: Do you then call a person of this kind a lover of gain? For instance, should a husbandman, while planting, and knowing the plant to be worthless, nevertheless think to make a gain from it when grown up, do you call such a person a lover of gain?

Friend: The lover of gain, Socrates, thinks he ought to make a gain from everything.

Socrates: Do not thus answer me at random, like a person injured by someone, but, giving your mind, answer me, as if I were questioning you again from the beginning. Do you not agree with me, that a lover of gain knows the value of that, from which he thinks it worth while to make a gain?

Friend: I do.

Socrates: Who then is he, that knows the value of plants, and in what time and place it is worth while to plant them? That we also may introduce something from the words of the wise, which the clever in law-suits employ for the sake of elegance.

Friend: A husbandman, I think.

Socrates: Do you then mean by the expression — It is worth while to make a gain — anything else than to think that one ought to make a gain?

Friend: I mean this.

Socrates: Now do not you, who are so young, endeavour to deceive me, your elder, by answering as you do at present, what you do not think but tell me truly, do you think that a husbandman exists, who knows it is not worth while to plant a certain plant, and yet fancies he will make a gain by such a plant?

Friend: By Zeus, not I.

Socrates: What then, think you that a horsedealer, who knows that the food which he gives a horse, is of no worth, does not know that it destroys the horse?

Friend: I do not.

Socrates: He does not think then that from such worthless food he will make a gain.

Friend: He does not.

Socrates: What then, do you think that a pilot, who has furnished his ship with sails and a rudder of no worth, does not know that he will sustain a damage, and be in danger of perishing himself, and of losing the ship and all it carries?

Friend: I do not.

Socrates: He will not think then that he will make a gain by worthless articles.

Friend: He will not.

Socrates: But does the general, who knows that his army carries worthless arms, think he will make a gain, or that he is worthy to make a gain by them?

Friend: By no means.

Socrates: But if a hautboy-player possesses a worthless hautboy, or a lyre-player a lyre, or a bowman a bow, or, in short, any other artist or skilled person possesses instruments or any other apparatus of no value, does he think he will make a gain by these?

Friend: It appears he will not.

Socrates: Whom then do you call lovers of gain? For surely they are not those, whom we have already mentioned, who, knowing what are things of no value, think they must make a gain by them. And thus, O wonderful man, according to what you say, no one is a lover of gain.

Friend: But, Socrates, I mean to say, that those are lovers of gain, who, through insatiable avidity, are perpetually and beyond all measure, greedy after things that are small and worth little or nothing, and thus have a love of gain.

Socrates: But surely, thou best of men, they do not know this, that they are worthless; for we have proved against ourselves, that this is impossible.

Friend: So it seems to me.

Socrates: If then they do so not knowing it, it is evident that, not knowing it, they fancy things of no worth to be of great value.

Friend: It appears so.

Socrates: Do not the lovers of gain love gain?

Friend: Yes.

Socrates: But do you say that gain is contrary to loss?

Friend: I do.

Socrates: Is it therefore a good to anyone to suffer a loss?

Friend: To no one.

Socrates: But it is an evil?

Friend: Yes.

Socrates: Are men then injured by a damage?

Friend: They are injured.

Socrates: Is then damage an evil?

Friend: It is.

Socrates: But gain is contrary to damage?

Friend: Contrary.

Socrates: Gain is therefore a good?

Friend: It is.

Socrates: Do you then call those, who love a good, lovers of gain?

Friend: It seems so.

Socrates: You do not then, my friend, call the lovers of gain mad-men. But do you yourself love what is a good, or not love it?

Friend: I do.

Socrates: Is there a good which you do not love, but an evil which you do?

Friend: By Zeus, there is not.

Socrates: But you love all good things equally?

Friend: I do.

Socrates: Ask me, if I also do not. For I also shall acknowledge to you, that I love good things. But besides I and you, do not all the rest of men appear to you to love good things, and to hate evil?

Friend: To me it appears so.

Socrates: But have we not acknowledged that gain is a good?

Friend: Yes.

Socrates: In this way then, all appear to be lovers of gain; but that, in which we before mentioned, no one was a lover of gain. By employing then which assertion, would a person not err?

Friend: Should, Socrates, one rightly apprehend what a lover of gain is, I think it is right to consider him a lover of gain who earnestly applies himself to, and thinks it worthwhile to make a gain from those things, from which the good do not dare to make a gain.

Socrates: But do you not see, O sweetest of men, that we just now acknowledged that to make a gain is to be benefited?

Friend: What then?

Socrates: Because this also we previously admitted, that all men always wished for good things.

Friend: We did.

Socrates: Do not, then, good men wish to possess everything gainful, since such things are good?

Friend: But not the things, Socrates, by which they are about to be hurt.

Socrates: By "to be hurt" do you mean "to be damaged"? Or something else?

Friend: No, but I mean "to be damaged."

Socrates: Are persons damaged by gain, or by damage?

Friend: Through both. For they are damaged by damage, and through iniquitous gain.

Socrates: Does it then appear to you that anything useful and good is iniquitous?

Friend: To me it does not.

Socrates: Did we not then a little before acknowledge that gain is contrary to damage, which is an evil?

Friend: We did.

Socrates: And that being contrary to evil, it is a good?

Friend: We granted this.

Socrates: You endeavour then, you see, to deceive me, by designedly asserting the contrary to what we just now granted.

Friend: By Zeus, I do not, Socrates; but you, on the contrary, are deceiving me; and I know not how, in your reasonings you turn things topsy-turvy.

Socrates: Speak fair words. For I should not act correctly, if I were not persuaded by a man good and wise.

Friend: Who is he? And why particularly say you this?

Socrates: My fellow-citizen, and likewise yours, Hipparchus, the son of Pisistratus, one of the Philaidae, and the eldest and wisest of the sons of Pisistratus; who exhibited many other illustrious acts of wisdom, and was the first who introduced into this land the poems of Homer, and compelled the rhapsodists during the Panathenaea to go through them successively and in order, just as you know they do at present; and having sent for Anacreon, the Teian, a ship of fifty oars, brought him to this city, and always had about him Simonides of Ceos, having induced him to stay by great rewards and gifts. And this he did, wishing to instruct the citizens, in order that he might rule over them being the best of men nor thinking, that he ought to begrudge wisdom to any man, as being himself a highly educated person. And when such of the citizens as were living around the town had been educated well, and admired him for his wisdom, he likewise laid down a plan to instruct those in the country; and he set up for them statues of Hermes along the roads, in the middle of the city and of each of the wards; and afterwards selecting from his wisdom, on points he had partly learned, and partly discovered himself, what he deemed to be the cleverest idea, he put them into elegiac verses, and engraved them on the Hermae as his poems, and specimens of wisdom; in order that in the first place the citizens might not wonder at those wise inscriptions on the temple at Delphi, "Know thyself," and "Nothing too much," and the rest of that kind, but that they might deem the words of Hipparchus still wiser; and, in the next place, that passing by them, up and down, they might read them, and have a taste of his wisdom, and come from the fields and be instructed in the remaining branches of learning. And there are two epigrams. In some upon the left-hand sides of each of the Hermae there is sculptured a Hermes, saying that he was standing midway between the city and the ward; and in others upon the right-hand sides he says: — "This is the memorial of Hipparchus. Go on, having just thoughts." There are also many other beautiful poetical descriptions on other Hermae; and there is this in the Steiriac road, in which he says — "This is the memorial of Hipparchus. Do not deceive your friend." I would not then have dared to deceive you, being my friend, and disobey so great a man; after whose death, the Athenians were tyrannized over by his brother Hippias; and you have heard from all the old men, that only during those years did there exist a tyranny at Athens, and that during all the other period, the Athenians lived nearly as when Saturn reigned. But it is said by rather clever persons, that he did not die in the way which the multitude have thought, through the dishonour done to the sister of Harmodius respecting the carrying the sacred basket — for that is a silly reason — but that Harmodius was the bosom friend and pupil of Aristogeiton, who valued himself highly upon instructing a man, and fancied that Hipparchus would be his rival. But at that time it happened that Harmodius was the lover of one of the handsome and nobly-born youths — whose name persons have mentioned, but I do not remember — and that this young person did for a time admire Harmodius and Aristogeiton, as wise men; but afterwards associating with Hipparchus, he despised them; and that they, being very much annoyed at the dishonour, slew Hipparchus.

Friend: You run the risk, Socrates, of either not considering me a friend; or, if you do think me a friend, of not being persuaded by Hipparchus: for I cannot be persuaded that you have not deceived me in I know not what manner, during the discourse.

Socrates: But indeed, just as in the game of backgammon, I am willing to put back whatever part you please of the assertions already made, in order that you may not think you have been deceived. Whether therefore shall I retract this assertion for you, that all men desire good?

Friend: Not for me.

Socrates: But that to be damaged, and damage itself, is not an evil?

Friend: Not for me.

Socrates: But that gain, and to make a gain; are not contrary to damage, and to be damaged?

Friend: Nor this neither.

Socrates: But that to make a gain, as being contrary to evil, is not a good?

Friend: Retract nothing of this kind at all for me.

Socrates: It appears to you then, as it seems, that of gain one part is a good, and another an evil.

Friend: Yes, to me.

Socrates: I retract therefore this for you. For let it be, that one kind of gain is a good, and another kind an evil; but that gain itself is not more good than evil. Is it not so?

Friend: Why do you ask me?

Socrates: I will tell you. Is there food good, and bad?

Friend: Yes.

Socrates: Is therefore one of them more food than the other? Or are both of them similarly food? And does the one differ in no respect from the other, so far as each is food, but so far as one is good, and the other bad?

Friend: Just so.

Socrates: And is it not as regards drink, and all other things which are parts of things existing, that some at least are so circumstanced as to be bad, and others, good; and that they differ not at all from each other, in that they are the same just as one man is good, and another bad?

Friend: Yes.

Socrates: But one man is, I suppose, neither more nor less a man than another, neither the good than the bad, nor the bad than the good.

Friend: You speak the truth.

Socrates: Shall we not then think in like manner respecting gain, that both the good and the bad are similarly gain?

Friend: It is necessary.

Socrates: He, therefore, who has a good gain, does not in any respect make a gain more than he, who has a bad gain: for neither of these, as we have granted, appears to be more a gain than the other.

Friend: True.

Socrates: For to neither of them is the more or the less present.

Friend: It is not.

Socrates: But in a thing of this kind, to which neither of these accidents is present, how can any one do, or suffer, more or less?

Friend: It is impossible.

Socrates: Since, then, both are similarly gain and gainful, it is requisite that we should still further consider this — why do you call both of them gain? And what do you see to be in both the same? Just as if you had asked me about the recent question, why I called both good and bad food similarly food, I would have said — Because each is a dry aliment of the body, on this account I called them so. For that this is food, you would surely acknowledge; would you not?

Friend: I would.

Socrates: And there will be the same manner of answering respecting drink; that for the moist aliment of the body, whether it is good or bad, the name is drink; and for the rest of things, in like manner. Do you therefore endeavour to imitate me, by answering thus. When you speak of good gain and bad gain, as being both of them gain, what same thing do you perceive in them, that this too is gain? But if you are not able to answer me in this way, reflect, while I am speaking. Do you call a gain every acquisition that a person obtains, when he either spends nothing, or when, after spending less, he receives more?

Friend: I seem to myself to call the latter gain.

Socrates: Are you therefore speaking of such things as these? If a person after having been feasted and spending nothing, and indulging in good living, should become diseased?

Friend: Not I, by Zeus.

Socrates: But if he should obtain health after feasting, would he obtain a gain or damage?

Friend: Gain.

Socrates: This then is not a gain, to obtain any acquisition whatever.

Friend: It is not.

Socrates: Whether will he, who obtains what is an evil, or at least what is not a good, not obtain a gain?

Friend: It appears so, at least if it be a good.

Socrates: But if he obtains an evil, will he not obtain a damage?

Friend: To me it appears so.

Socrates: See then how you are again running round to the same point? For gain appears to be a good, but damage an evil.

Friend: I really am at a loss what to say.

Socrates: Nor unjustly are you at a loss. But, answer me still further this. If any one after having spent less, obtains more, do you say this is a gain?

Friend: I do not say it is an evil, but if after having spent less of gold or silver money, he receives more.

Socrates: I too am about to ask you this. For come, tell me, should a person spending half a pound of gold, receive double this weight of silver, would he obtain a gain or a damage?

Friend: A damage surely, Socrates; for, instead of a value twelve times as much, the silver is only twice as much.

Socrates: But yet he has received more. Or is not double more than half?

Friend: But silver is not of the same value as gold.

Socrates: It is requisite then, as it seems, that this, namely, value, be added to gain; for in this case do you not say that the silver, although being more than the gold, is not of equal value? The gold, although being less, you say, is of equal value.

Friend: Very much so: for such is the fact.

Socrates: Value, therefore, is gainful, whether it is small or great; but that which is valueless is gainless.

Friend: Yes

Socrates: By "value," do you mean any thing else than what it is worthy to acquire?

Friend: I do not.

Socrates: But by the expression "it is worthy to acquire," do you mean the useless, or the useful?

Friend: The useful, certainly.

Socrates: The useful, therefore, is a good.

Friend: Yes.

Socrates: Hence, thou most manly of all men, has not the lucrative come to us again a third or a fourth time, as being an acknowledged good?

Friend: So it seems.

Socrates: Do you remember, then, from whence this discourse of ours originated?

Friend: I think I do.

Socrates: If you do not, I will remind you. You contended that good men are not willing to make every kind of gain, but of gains the good alone but not the iniquitous.

Friend: It did originate from this.

Socrates: But has not reason forced us to acknowledge, that all kinds of gain, both small and great, are good?

Friend: It has forced me, Socrates, rather than persuaded.

Socrates: But perhaps after this it will also persuade you. Now, however, whether you are persuaded, or in whatever manner you may be affected, you agree at least with us, that all kinds of gain are good, both small and great?

Friend: I do agree.

Socrates: And do you agree with me, or not, that all good men wish for all things that are good?

Friend: I do.

Socrates: But you said that bad men love gain of every kind, both small and great.

Friend: I did say so.

Socrates: According to your assertion, then, all men, both good and bad, would be lovers of gain.

Friend: It appears so.

Socrates: If then any person reproaches another with being a lover of gain, he does not correctly reproach him; for the very person so reproaching happens to be such a character himself.

Minos

Persons of the Dialogue: Socrates and a Friend.

SOCRATES: WHAT THING IS LAW WITH US?

Friend: Of what kind is the law are you asking about?

Socrates: What, is it that law differs from law, according to this very thing, in being law? For consider what I happen to be asking you. For I am asking, as if I should inquire what is gold? and if you should in a similar manner ask me, about what kind of gold am I speaking, I should think you would not rightly ask. For neither does gold differ in anything from gold, so far as it is gold, nor a stone from a stone, so far as it is a stone. And in like manner, neither does law differ in anything from law; but all laws are as laws the same. For each of them exists similarly as law; nor is one more, and another less so. I ask you, therefore, this very thing as a whole, what is law? and if you have an answer at hand, state it.

Friend: What else, Socrates, can law be, than the things established by law?

Socrates: Does speech too appear to you to be the things which are spoken? or sight, the things which are seen? or hearing, the things which are heard? Or is not speech one thing, and the things spoken another? Is not sight one thing, and the things seen another? Is not hearing one thing, and the things heard another? And is not law one thing, and the things established by law another? Does it appear to you in this way? Or how?

Friend: It now appears to be another thing.

Socrates: Law therefore is not the things established by law.

Friend: It does not appear to me that it is.

Socrates: What then can law be? Let us consider it thus. If some one had asked us respecting the things just now spoken of — Since you say that things seen are seen by the sight, by the sight being what, are they seen? we should have answered — by that sense, which through the eyes manifests colours to us. And if he had asked us again — Since things heard are heard by hearing, by the hearing being what, are they heard? we should have answered — by a sense, which through the ears manifests sounds to us. In like manner, if he had asked us, — Since things are established by law, by the law being what, are they thus established? Is it by a certain sense, or manifestation, in the same manner as things learnt are learnt by some art rendering them manifest through some discovery? just as things discovered are discovered; as, for instance, things salubrious and noxious are discovered through the medical art; and what the gods have in their thoughts, as the diviners say, through the divining art. For art is with us the discovery of things: or is it not?

Friend: Entirely so.

Socrates: Which of these then may we especially understand law to be?

Friend: Decrees and votes, as it seems to me. For what else can any one say law is? So that it nearly appears that law, about which you were asking, is, taken as a whole, the decree of a state.

Socrates: You call, as it seems, law, a state-opinion.

Friend: I do.

Socrates: And perhaps you speak well; but perhaps we shall know better in the following manner. You call some persons wise?

Friend: I do.

Socrates: Are not then the wise, wise by wisdom?
Friend: Yes.
Socrates: But what, are the just, just by justice?
Friend: Entirely so.
Socrates: Are not then the lawful, lawful by law?
Friend: Yes.
Socrates: And the lawless, lawless by an absence of law?
Friend: Yes.
Socrates: And the lawful are just?
Friend: Yes.
Socrates: But the lawless unjust?
Friend: Unjust.
Socrates: Are not justice and law therefore things most beautiful?
Friend: They are.
Socrates: And are not injustice and lawlessness the least beautiful?
Friend: Yes.
Socrates: And does not the former preserve cities and everything else, but the latter destroy and overturn them?
Friend: Yes.
Socrates: It is necessary then to consider the law as something beautiful, and to seek it as a good.
Friend: How not?
Socrates: Now have we not said that law is a decree of the city?
Friend: We have said so.
Socrates: What then, are not some decrees good, and some evil?
Friend: They are.
Socrates: Law however is not evil.
Friend: It is not.
Socrates: It is not correct then to answer thus simply, that law is a decree of the city.
Friend: It appears to me it is not.
Socrates: Nor is it suited to reason for an evil decree to be law.
Friend: Certainly not.
Socrates: Law however appears to me too to be a certain opin-

ion. And since an opinion is not evil, is not this evident, that it is a good one, if law is opinion?

Friend: Yes.

Socrates: But what is a good opinion? Is it not a true one?

Friend: Yes.

Socrates: Is then a true opinion the discovery of that which is?

Friend: It is.

Socrates: Law therefore would be the discovery of that which is.

Friend: How then, Socrates, if law is the discovery of that which is, do we not always use the same laws about the same things? since things that are have been discovered by us.

Socrates: The law nevertheless would be the discovery of that which is. But if men do not always, as we think, use the same laws, they are not always able to discover that which law wishes, namely, that which is. But come, let us see if it will hence become evident to us, whether we always use the same laws, or some at one time, and others at another; and if all use the same laws, or different persons different laws.

Friend: But this, Socrates, it is not difficult to know, that neither do the same persons always use the same laws, nor different persons always different laws. Thus, for example, it is not a law with us to sacrifice human beings, but it is an unholy act; but the Carthaginians sacrifice them, as being a holy and a lawful act with them; so that some of them sacrifice their sons to Kronos, as perhaps you too have heard; and not only do Barbarians use laws different from ours, but also those fellows in Lycea, and the progeny of Athamas, what sacrifices do they perform, although they are Greeks! In like manner you surely know by hearsay yourself what laws we formerly used concerning the dead, by cutting the throats of the victims before the dead body was carried out, and sending for the women who collect the bones of the dead in jars and those, who still, antecedent to them, buried the dead at home; but we do none of these things. Ten thousand instances of this kind one might mention; for wide is the field of demonstration, that neither do we always have customs in the same manner amongst ourselves, nor do men amongst each other.

Socrates: It is by no means wonderful, O best of men, if you are speaking correctly, this has lain hid from me. But as long as you by yourself declare what appears to you in a long discourse, and I again do the same, we shall never, as I think, come to an agreement. But if the inquiry be laid down in common, we shall perhaps think alike. If then you are willing, ask me some question, and consider with me in common. Or, if you wish it, give an answer.

Friend: Nay, I am willing, Socrates, to answer whatever you choose to ask.

Socrates: Come then, do you think that what is just is unjust, and what is unjust is just? Or that what is just is just, and what is unjust is unjust?

Friend: I indeed think that what is just is just, and what is unjust is unjust.

Socrates: Is it not so held by all persons as it is here?

Friend: Yes.

Socrates: Among the Persians also?

Friend: And among the Persians too.

Socrates: But is it really always so?

Friend: Always.

Socrates: Whether are things, that draw the greater weight, thought by us here to be the heavier, but those that draw the less, lighter? or the contrary?

Friend: No; but those that draw the greater weight, are the heavier, and those that draw the less, are lighter.

Socrates: Is this the case, therefore, in Carthage and in Lycia?

Friend: Yes.

Socrates: Things beautiful, as it seems, are everywhere held to be beautiful, and things ugly to be ugly; but things ugly are not thought to be beautiful, nor things beautiful to be ugly.

Friend: It is so.

Socrates: In the case of all things, so to say, the things that exist are held to be, not the things that do not exist, both with us and with all others.

Friend: It appears so to me.

Socrates: He, therefore, who errs in that which is, errs in that which is lawful.

Friend: Thus, Socrates, as you say, the same things always appear lawful both to us and to others. But when I consider, that we never cease altering the laws up and down, I cannot be persuaded.

Socrates: For perhaps you do not bear in mind that these things, being put into a changed place, are the same. But look at them thus with me. Have you ever met with any book relating to the health of the sick?

Friend: I have.

Socrates: Do you know then to what art that book belongs?

Friend: I know it belongs to the medical art.

Socrates: Do you then not call those skilled in these matters physicians?

Friend: I do.

Socrates: Do then the skilled think the same about the same, or do some think one thing and others another?

Friend: They seem to me to think the same.

Socrates: Do then Greeks alone think the same with Greeks about things of which they know? or do Barbarians likewise do so with each other, and with Greeks?

Friend: There is a great necessity for both Greeks and Barbarians, who know, to think the same with themselves and each other.

Socrates: You have answered correctly. Do they not then always do so?

Friend: Yes, always.

Socrates: Do not physicians also write about health what they think to be true?

Friend: Yes.

Socrates: Things relating to medicine and medical laws are the writings of physicians.

Friend: Things relating to medicine, certainly.

Socrates: Are not then the writings relating to agriculture agricultural laws?

Friend: Yes.

Socrates: Of whom then are the writings and institutes relating to gardening?

Friend: Of gardeners.

Socrates: These then are the laws about gardening.

Friend: Yes.

Socrates: Of those, who know how to manage gardens?

Friend: How not?

Socrates: But gardeners possess this knowledge.

Friend: Yes.

Socrates: And of whom are the writings and institutes relating to the dressing of savoury food?

Friend: Of cooks.

Socrates: These, therefore, are the laws of cookery.

Friend: Of cookery.

Socrates: Of those, as it seems, who know how to manage the dressing of savoury food.

Friend: Yes.

Socrates: But cooks, as they say, know.

Friend: They do know.

Socrates: Be it so. And of whom are the writings and institutes concerning the administration of a state? Are they not of those, who know how to govern states?

Friend: It appears so to me.

Socrates: But do any others than statesmen and kings know?

Friend: They alone.

Socrates: Those writings then relating to a state, which men call laws, are the writings of kings and good men.

Friend: You speak the truth.

Socrates: Will then they, who know, write one thing at one time, and another at another, about the same things?

Friend: Certainly not.

Socrates: If then we see certain persons doing this at any place whatever, shall we say that those, who do so, are skilled or unskilled?

Friend: Unskilled.

Socrates: Shall we then say that what is right is in each case lawful, whether it relate to medicine, or cooking, or gardening?

Friend: Yes.

Socrates: But that, which is not right, we shall no longer assert to be lawful.

Friend: No longer.

Socrates: It therefore becomes lawless.

Friend: Necessarily so.

Socrates: Hence, in writings concerning things just and unjust, and, in short, concerning the orderly arrangement of a city, and the manner in which one ought to administer it, that, which is right, is a royal law; but that, which is not right, is not a royal law, because science is wanting : for it is lawless.

Friend: Yes.

Socrates: We have rightly therefore acknowledged that the law is the invention of that which is.

Friend: So it appears.

Socrates: Let us still further consider it in this way likewise. Who is skilled in distributing the seeds to the earth?

Friend: The husbandman.

Socrates: Does he then distribute seeds proper for each soil?

Friend: Yes.

Socrates: The husbandman therefore is a good distributer of these things, and his laws and distributions in these particulars are right.

Friend: Yes.

Socrates: And who is a good distributer of pulsations for tunes, and distributes such as are proper? And whose laws are right?

Friend: Those of the piper and the harper.

Socrates: He then, who acts most according to law in these things, is, in the greatest degree, a piper.

Friend: Yes.

Socrates: But who is the best to distribute nutriment to the bodies of men? Is it not he, who distributes the proper?

Friend: Yes.

Socrates: The distributions therefore and the laws of this man are the best; and he, who acts the most according to law in these things, is the best distributer.

Friend: Entirely so.

Socrates: Who is he?

Friend: The training-master.

Socrates: Does he know how to feed the flock of the human body in the best manner?

Friend: Yes.

Socrates: And who is the best to tend a flock of sheep? What is his name?

Friend: Shepherd.

Socrates: The laws therefore of the shepherd are the best for the sheep.

Friend: Yes.

Socrates: And those of the herdsman for oxen.

Friend: Yes.

Socrates: And whose laws are the best for the minds of men? Are they not those of a king? Tell me.

Friend: I say so.

Socrates: You speak well. Can you therefore tell me, who among the ancients was a good maker of the laws relating to pipes? Perhaps you have him not in your thoughts. Are you then willing that I should remind you?

Friend: By all means.

Socrates: Was not Marsyas said to be so, and his loved Olympus the Phrygian.

Friend: True.

Socrates: The pipe-playing of these men is most divine, and alone excites and shows forth those who are in need of the gods; and it alone remains to the present time as being divine.

Friend: Such is the case.

Socrates: And who amongst the ancient kings is said to have been a good lawmaker, and whose institutions remain even now as being divine?

Friend: I do not recollect.

Socrates: Do you not know, which of the Greeks are making use of laws the most ancient?

Friend: Are you speaking of the Lacedaemonians, and of Lycurgus the law-giver?

Socrates: These institutions, however, are perhaps not three hundred years old, or a little more. But do you know from whence came the best of their laws?

Friend: They say, from Crete.

Socrates: Do not they of all the Greeks make use of laws the most ancient?

Friend: Yes.

Socrates: Do you know then who among these were good kings? Were they not Minos and Rhadamanthus, the sons of Zeus and Europa, by whom those laws were made?

Friend: They say, Socrates, that Rhadamanthus was a just man, but that Minos was rustic, morose, and unjust.

Socrates: You are telling, O best of men, a tale of Attica, and of tragedy.

Friend: What, are not such things told of Minos?

Socrates: Not by Homer, at least, and Hesiod; and they are more trust-worthy than all the tragic poets, from whom you have heard what you are saying.

Friend: But what do they say about Minos?

Socrates: I will tell you, that you may not, like the many, be guilty of impiety. For there is not anything more impious than this, nor of what we ought to be more cautious, than of sinning against the gods, either in word or in deed; and next, against divine men. But you ought to take ever a very great care, when you are about to praise or blame any man, that you speak correctly; and for the sake of this, it is meet to learn how to distinguish good and bad men. For the deity feels indignant when anyone blames a person similar to himself, or praises one dissimilar; for this is the good man. For think not that stones, and wood, and birds, and serpents are sacred, but that men are not so; for a good man is the most sacred, and a depraved man the most defiled of all things. Now then, since Homer and Hesiod pass an encomium on Minos, on this account I will speak, in order that you, being a man sprung from a man, may not sin in word against a hero the son of Jupiter.

For Homer, speaking of Crete, says, there are many men, and ninety cities in it;

> Amongst them Knossus, a great city, where
> Reign'd Minos, who each ninth year converse held
> With mighty Zeus.

This then is Homer's praise of Minos, expressed in few words, such as he has not given to even one of his heroes. For that Zeus is a sophist, and that the art itself is all-beautiful, he shows in many other places, and here likewise. For he says that Minos conversed in the ninth year with Zeus, and went to be instructed by him, as if Zeus were a sophist. That Homer, then, does not bestow the honour of being instructed by Zeus upon any other hero than Minos, is praise indeed to be wondered at. In the scene of the Odyssey, too, relating to the Dead, Homer has represented Minos as a judge, and holding a golden sceptre; but not Rhadamanthus as judging there, or conversing with Zeus anywhere. On this account I say that Minos is extolled by Homer beyond all other heroes. For to have been instructed merely by Zeus, when he was the son of Zeus, carries with it no excess of praise. For the verse — He reigned, and each ninth year conversed with Zeus — means that he was the associate of Zeus. Hence at each ninth year, Minos went to the cavern of Zeus, to learn some things, and to show forth others which, during the preceding period of nine years, he had learnt from Zeus. There are, however, some who understand by "oaristes" the "associate" of Zeus in drinking and sport; although anyone may make use of this as a proof to show that they, who thus understand the word, say nothing to the purpose; for although both the Greeks and Barbarians are numerous, there are none, who abstain from banquets, and the sport to which wine belongs, except the Cretans, and next the Lacedaemonians, who were instructed by the Cretans. But in Crete this is one of the other laws, which Minos laid down, "not to drink with each other to intoxication." And it is evident, that what he deemed to be beautiful institutions, these he laid down for his own citizens. For Minos did not, like a knave, think one thing, and do another, contrary to what he thought; but his intercourse with Zeus was, as I assert, through discourses for the attainment of virtue.

Hence he laid down those laws for his citizens, through which Crete has been for all time prosperous, and Lacedaemon likewise, from the time when it began to make use of those laws, as being divine. But Rhadamanthus was indeed a good man; for he was instructed by Minos. He did not however learn the whole of the royal art, but that part of it, which ministers to the royal, as far as presiding over courts of justice from whence he was said to be a good judge. For Minos employed him as a guardian of the laws in the city; but Talus for those through the rest of Crete. For Talus thrice every year went through the villages in order to preserve the laws in them, and carried with him the laws written in tables of brass; from whence he was called "brazen." Hesiod too asserts respecting Minos, what is closely related to this. For, having mentioned his name, he says,

Most regal was he of all mortal kings,
And o'er the most of neighbouring people ruled,
Of Zeus the sceptre holding, king like him;

and he too means by the sceptre of Zeus, nothing else than the instruction of Zeus, by which he regulated Crete.

Friend: On what account then, Socrates, was the report spread against Minos, of his being an unlearned and morose man?

Socrates: On that account, through which you, O best of men, if you are prudent, and every other person to whom it is a care to be in good repute, will be cautious never to incur the anger of a poet. For poets are able to effect much as regards reputation, in whatever way they may represent acts, by praising men and blaming them. On which ground Minos erred, when he made war upon this city; where there is much of other wisdom, and poets in every other kind of poetry, and in tragedy likewise. Now tragedy here is of an old date, not beginning as persons fancy from Thespis, nor from Phrynichus; but, if you are willing to turn your thoughts to it, you will find it is a very ancient invention of this city. Now, of poetry in general, the most pleasing to the vulgar and the most soul-alluring is tragedy; to which we, applying our minds, have revenged ourselves upon Minos, for the tribute he compelled us to pay. In this then Minos erred, by incurring our anger; from whence, in reply to your question, he became in rather bad repute. For that he was a good man, a friend to law, and a good shepherd of the people, as I have before observed, this is the greatest proof, that his laws have been unchanged, in consequence of his having discovered correctly the truth of what is, with reference to the administration of a state.

Friend: You appear to me, Socrates, to have stated a probable reason.

Socrates: If then I am speaking the truth, do not the Cretans, the citizens of Minos and Ehadamanthus, appear to you to have made use of laws the most ancient?

Friend: They appear so.

Socrates: These therefore were the best lawgivers of the ancients, and distributors and shepherds of men; just as Homer likewise says, that a good general is "a shepherd of the people."

Friend: Entirely so.

Socrates: Come then, by Zeus, who presides over friendship, if anyone, who is a good lawgiver and shepherd of the body, should ask us — What are those things, which a person by distributing to the body will make it better? we should well and briefly answer, that they are nutriment and labour, by the former increasing, and by the latter exercising and knitting together the body.

Friend: Right.

Socrates: If then he should after this ask us — What are those things which a good law-giver and shepherd will, by distributing to the soul, make it better? — making what answer, by should we be not ashamed of ourselves, and of our age?

Friend: This I am no longer able to say.

Socrates: It is however disgraceful to the soul of each of us, to seem not to know the things pertaining to them, and in which their good and evil consist, but to have considered those pertaining to the body, and to other things.

Clitopho

Persons of the Dialogue: Socrates and Clitopho.

SOCRATES: A CERTAIN PERSON HAS LATELY TOLD ME THAT CLITOPHO, the son of Aristonymus, has been conversing with Lysias, and blaming the passing the time with Socrates, but been praising immoderately the intercourse with Thrasymachus.

Clitopho: Whoever he was, Socrates, he has not accurately related to you the conversation I had with Lysias about you. For in some things indeed I did not praise you, but in others I did. But since you are evidently blaming me, although you pretend to care nothing about the matter, I will most willingly go through the conversation myself, especially since we happen to be alone, in order that you may the less imagine that I am ill disposed towards you. For now perhaps you have not heard correctly; so that you appear to be more harshly disposed towards me than is fitting. But if you will grant me the liberty of speech I shall most cheerfully accept it, and am willing to speak.

Socrates: Nay it would be disgraceful for myself, when you are willing to benefit me, not to bear with you. For it is evident that, when I know in what respect I am better and worse, I shall pursue some things, and avoid others, to the utmost of my power.

Clitopho: You shall hear then. For while I am with you, Socrates, I am often astonished on hearing you; and you appear to me, as compared with other men, to speak most beautifully, when, reproving men, you exclaim like a god upon a machine —" Whither are ye borne along? And —Are ye ignorant, that ye are doing nothing that ye ought, ye, who make every exertion how ye may get money, but neglect your children, to whom ye are to leave it, and the means whereby they may know how to use it justly; and do not find for them teachers of justice, if indeed it can be taught, and who, if it is to be made the subject of meditation and exercise, may suffi-ciently exercise them in it. Nor yet do ye previously attend to your-selves; but, seeing that both ye and your children have learnt sufficiently grammar, and music, and the gymnastic arts, which ye have considered as the perfect discipline of virtue, yet afterwards that ye become no less depraved with respect to riches, why do ye not despise the present mode of education, and seek after those, who will cause you to cease from this illiberal line of life? And yet it is through this neglect of what is right, and indolence, and not through the foot being out of time with the lyre, that brother himself arrays himself against brother, and states against states, and, out of all measure and harmony, are stirring up strife and war upon each other, and do and suffer the extreme of ill. But ye say, that they, who are unjust, are unjust not through the want of instruction, nor through ignorance, but voluntarily; and again, ye dare to assert that injustice is disgraceful and hateful to the gods. How then can any one voluntarily choose so great an evil? He (does so) ye say, through being conquered by pleasure. Is not this then an involuntary act, since to conquer is a voluntary one? So that reason perfectly convinces us, that to act unjustly is involuntary; and that every man privately, and all cities publicly, ought to pay more attention than they do. at present to their conduct." When therefore, Socrates, I hear you perpetually speaking so, I am greatly delighted with you, and pay you in a wonderful manner the tribute of praise. And when

you say what follows in order upon this, that they, who cultivate
their bodies, but neglect their soul, !do something different of this
kind, in neglecting that which is to govern, but busily attending to
what is to be governed; and when you assert that it is better for him,
who does not know how to use a thing, to leave alone the use of it;
for if a person does not know how to use his eyes or ears, or his
whole body, it is better for him not to hear, nor see, nor to use his
body for any need, than to use it in any way; and in a similar
manner with respect to art. For it is evident (as you say) that he, who
does not know how to use his own lyre, will not (know how to use)
that of his neighbour; nor will he, who (knows not how to use) the
(lyre) of others, (know how to use) his own, nor any other instrument
or chattel whatever; and this your discourse ended beautifully (by
inferring), that for him, who does not know how to use his soul, it is
better to be at rest with respect to his soul, and not to live, than to
live and act according to his own caprice; but, if there is any necessity for such a person to live, that it is better for him to lead the life
of a slave, than of a freeman. For that this is to deliver the rudder of
the mind, like that of a ship, to another, who has learnt the art of
governing men; which, Socrates, you have often called the statesman's art, and said it is the same as that of the judge and justice. To
these, and many other and very beautiful reasonings, in which it is
asserted that virtue can be taught, and that a person ought above all
things to pay attention to himself, I have scarcely at any time said a
word in opposition, nor do I think that I shall ever say. For I deem
them to be very exhortatory and useful, and really awakening us, as
if we were asleep. I have therefore given my mind to them, as one
about to hear what is to follow; and I have asked at first, not yourself, Socrates, but your equals in age, or fellow-thinkers, or friends,
or in whatever name one must call the (party) thus disposed towards
you. For among them, I have first of all asked those, who are
thought by you to be something, by inquiring what would be the
discourse after this; and laying down a subject® after your manner, I
have said to them—How are we to receive for the present, O best of
men, the exhortation of Socrates to virtue? as being merely a word,
but that it is not in our power to follow it up in deed, and to compre-

hend it thoroughly? And will this be our employment through the
whole of life, to exhort those who have not been exhorted as yet?
and for them (to exhort) others? Or is it requisite for us after this to
inquire of Socrates and each other, since we confess that this should
be done, what is to come next? How, say we, ought we to begin the
discipline relating to justice? As if some one had exhorted us to pay
attention to the body, on perceiving that we, like boys, had no notion
that the care of the body belongs to the gymnastic and medical arts,
and afterwards reproached us by saying, that it was disgraceful to
pay every attention to wheat and barley, and vines, and such other
things as we labour to obtain for the sake of the body, but that we
search after no art or device, so that the body may be rendered in
the best condition, and this too when there is such an art. If then we
inquired of the person so exhorting us—Do you say there are such
arts as these? perhaps he would say, There are the gymnastic and
medical arts. And what now, we said, is the art that relates to the
virtue of the soul? Let it be mentioned. But he, who seemed to be of
the greatest strength for giving an answer to these questions, said to
myself, that the very art, which you have heard Socrates mention, is
no other than justice. And on my saying—Tell me not merely the
name of the art, but explain it further in this way. There is an art
called the medical. By this two things are effected; one, that physicians are always forming other physicians in addition to those
already existing; the other, to effect health. Now of these one is no
longer an art, but the work of the art, which teaches and is taught,
which we call health. And in the case of carpentry, there is the
building and the art; one the effect, and the other the teaching. So
too of justice, one part is to make persons just, as each (of the arts
mentioned) above (makes) artists. But what shall we say is the other
work, which a just man is able to do for us? State it. One person has,
I think, said in answer to us, that it is "the conducible;" another, that
it is "the becoming ;" another, that it is "the useful;" and another,
that it is "the profitable." But I rejoined by saying, that these very
names exist in each of the arts, namely, to act rightly, profitably,
usefully, and the like. But that, to which all these tend, each art will
state itself. Thus, the art of carpentry will say, that "the right," "the

beautiful," "the becoming," (tend to this,) that wooden furniture may be (aptly) made; which is not art, (but the work of art) Let in like manner be mentioned the work of justice. At last one of your friends, Socrates, who appeared to speak most elegantly, answered me, that this was the work peculiar to justice, which does not belong to any other science, namely, to cause a friendship amongst states. But he, on the other hand, on being interrogated, said that friendship was a good, and by no means an evil. But on being asked about the friendships of boys and of wild animals, for by that name we call (their attachments), he did not admit that they are friendships; for it happened that such (friendships) of theirs were for the greater part hurtful rather than advantageous; and that those, who call them so, call them falsely; but that friendship existing really and truly was most clearly an union of sentiment. But on being asked whether he meant by an union of sentiment, an agreement in opinion or science, he repudiated the agreement in opinion; for many and hurtful agreements in opinion are compelled to take place amongst men; but he conceded that friendship was entirely a good, and the work of justice; so that he said, an agreement in sentiment was the same as science really existing, but not opinion. But when we were at this part of our discourse, the parties present being in a state of doubt were competent to find fault with him,® and to say, that the reasoning had run round to the point first mooted; and they affirmed that the medical art is a certain agreement in sentiment; and so are all the other arts; and that they are able to state about what they are conversant; but that the art called by you justice, or an agreement in sentiment, it had escaped them as to whither it tends, and that it is not manifest what is its work. At last I inquired of yourself, Socrates, upon these points; and you told me that it is the work of justice to injure enemies, and benefit friends; but afterwards it appeared to you, that the just man will never injure any one, but will act to the advantage of every one in all things. Having endured this not once, nor even twice, but for a length of time, and being urgent with you, Socrates, I was tired out; thinking, indeed, that you effected in the best manner of all men, the exhortation to the study of virtue; but that one of two things (must take place), either that you are able to effect thus much alone, but nothing further—which might happen in the case of any other art—as, for instance, that he who is not a pilot, may exercise himself in praising the pilot's art, as a thing of great value to man; and similarly in the case of other arts —so a person may perhaps apply the same remark on the subject of justice to yourself, as not having a greater knowledge than others of its nature, because you praise it in a beautiful manner. Such however is not my (opinion), but (as I say), one of two things (take place); either that you do not know (what justice is), or that you are unwilling to impart (the knowledge of it) to me. On this account then, I think I shall go to Thrasymachus, and wherever else I can, as being in doubt, (and where I hope I shall be freed from doubts; nor should I betake myself elsewhere,) if you were willing to finish your exhortatory discourses to me. Now, for instance, if I had been exhorted on the subject of the gymnastic art, that I ought not to neglect the body, you would state to me what comes next after the exhortation-speech, what is the nature of my body, and what attention it requires. And let this be done at present. Lay it down then that Clitopho acknowledges it to be ridiculous to pay attention to other things, but to neglect the soul, for the sake of which we labour in other things; and imagine that I have really spoken upon all other points, next in order to those, which I have just now gone through. I beg of you not to act in any respect otherwise, that I may not (hereafter) as at present, partly praise you before Lysias and the rest, and blame you likewise in part. For I will say, Socrates, that you are worth every thing to the man, who is not yet exhorted; but to him who has been exhorted, you are nearly an impediment to his arriving at the end of virtue, and becoming happy.

Epistles / Seventh Letter

Plato to the Kindred and Friends of Dion—Prosperity

YE HAVE WRITTEN TO ME, THAT I OUGHT TO THINK YOUR sentiments are the same as those which Dion held; and, moreover, you exhort me to make a common cause, as far as I can, in word and deed. If ye have the same opinion and desires with him I agree to unite with you; but if not, to take frequent counsel with myself. Now what his sentiments and desires were, I can tell pretty nearly, not by conjecture, but by having known them clearly.

For when I came originally to Syracuse, being then nearly forty years old, Dion was of the age that Hipparinus is now; and the opinion he then held, he has still continued to hold, namely, that the Syracusans ought to be free and live according to the best laws. So that it is by no means wonderful, if some god has caused the latter to agree in the same opinion with the former on the subject of a polity. But what was the method of producing this, is a thing not unworthy for the young [500] and not young to hear; and I will endeavour to relate it to you from the beginning; for the present events offer the opportunity.

When I was a young man, I was affected as the many are. I

thought, if I became quickly my own master, to betake myself immediately to the public affairs of the state. Now some such circumstances as these fell out relating to state affairs. Of the polity existing at that time, when it was abused by many, a change took place; and over the change one and fifty men presided as governors, eleven in the city, and ten in the Piraus; and each of these had a jurisdiction about the Agora, and whatever else it was necessary to regulate in the cities, while thirty of them were invested with supreme authority. Some of these happened to be my relatives and acquaintances; and they forthwith invited me (to attend) to state-affairs, as being a suitable pursuit. And how I was affected is, on account of my youth, not at all wonderful. For I thought that they would, by leading the city from an unjust mode of living to a just one, administer it in the way it was meet; so that I diligently gave my mind to what they did. But when I saw these men proving in a short time that the previous form of government had been (as it were) gold, and that they committed other acts (unjustly), and sent my friend Socrates, advanced in years, whom I am not ashamed to say was nearly the most righteous man of those then living, together with certain others, against one of the citizens, [501] and to bring him by force, in order that he might be executed, so that he (Socrates) might have a share in their deeds, whether he wished it or not, and that he did not comply, but ran the risk of suffering every thing, rather than take any part in their impious acts—all this when I saw, and other similar acts of no trifling kind, I felt indignant, and withdrew myself from the evil men of that period.

Not long after this, the power of the thirty fell by a revolution, together with the whole of the then existing form of government. Again, therefore, but somewhat more slowly, did a desire still drag me on to engage in public and political affairs. Now in these, as being in a troubled state, many things took place, at which any one might be indignant; nor was it wonderful, that in revolutions the punishment of hostile factions should have been rather severe in the case of some; although they who returned acted with considerable clemency. But by some chance some of those in power brought before a court of justice our friend Socrates, laying upon him an

accusation the most unholy, and belonging the least of all to
Socrates. For some brought him to trial, and others gave their vote
against him, and destroyed the man, who had been unwilling to
share in the unholy act of a removal relating to one of his then
exiled friends, when the exiles themselves were unfortunate. On
reflecting then upon these matters, and on the persons who
managed political affairs, and on the laws and customs, the more I
considered them, and I advanced in years, by so much the more
difficult did it appear to me to administer correctly state affairs. For
it is not possible to do so without friends and faithful associates;
whom, existing at that time, it was not easy to find—for our city was
then no longer administered according to the manners and institutions of our fathers and it was impossible to acquire new with any
facility; while the written laws and customs were corrupted, and
(unholiness) was increasing to a degree how wonderful! [502]

So that I, who had been at first full of ardour towards engaging
in affairs of state, did, upon looking at these things and seeing them
carried along in every way and on every side, become giddy; but not
so as to withdraw from considering how at any time something
better might take place respecting these very matters, and likewise
the whole form of government, but to be wisely waiting continually
for opportunities of acting. At last I perceived that all states existing
at present were badly governed. For what relates to their laws is
nearly in an incurable state, without some wonderful arrangement
in conjunction with fortune. I was therefore compelled to say, in
praise of true philosophy, that through it we are enabled to perceive
all that is just as regards the state and individuals; and hence that
the human race will never cease from ills, until the race of those,
who philosophize correctly and truthfully, shall come to political
power, or persons of power in states shall, by a certain divine allotment, philosophize really.

Holding these sentiments I arrived in Italy and Sicily, when I
first came there. But on my arrival, the life, which is there called
happy, pleased me at no time or manner; (a life) full of the tables
prepared by Italiotes and Syracusans; and where one is filled twice a
day; and never lies alone by night, and (has) such other pursuits as

follow a life of this kind. For from these habits, no man under heaven, having such pursuits from his youth, would ever become prudent, not even if he were [503] mixed up with a wondrous nature by some god; but to become temperate it will never be his care. And the same thing may be said respecting the remaining portion of virtue. Nor will any state rest quietly according to any laws whatever, while men conceive that it is proper to waste every thing on excesses, and deem that they ought to be idle in every thing except good living and drinking, and the laboured exertions made for sexual intercourse. But it is necessary for such states never to cease changing their tyrannies, oligarchies, and democracies, and for the powerful in them not to endure even the name of a polity just and with equal laws.

With these and the above-mentioned sentiments I passed over to Syracuse; perhaps through an accident of fortune; at least it seems that by the planning of some superior being a beginning was laid of the doings, that have lately taken place relating to Dion and of those too relating to Syracuse, and, there is a fear, to still more persons, if you do not yield to me, when giving advice a second time. How then do I assert that my journey to Sicily was the beginning of all the then doings? For while associating with Dion, then a young man, and pointing out to him by words that, what seemed good to me would be the best for mankind, and counselling him so to act, I was nearly ignorant that I was unconsciously planning in some manner the dissolution of a tyranny. For Dion being very docile, both with respect to other things, and the reasons urged by me, he heard so quickly and attentively, as not one ever did of the young men whom I had fallen in with; and he was desirous of passing the remainder of his life in a manner superior to the majority of the Italiotes and Siceliotes, by loving virtue rather than pleasure and the rest of luxuries; [504] and hence he lived rather odious to those, who passed their lives according to tyrannical institutions, until the death of Dionysius occurred. Subsequently, however, he perceived that the sentiments, which he held under the influence of correct reasoning, did not exist in him alone, but in some others; not numerous indeed, but amongst some, one of whom he thought would be probably

Dionysius (the younger), if the gods assisted; and should this take place, that both his own life, and that of the other Syracusans, would turn out to be beyond all measure happy. He thought, moreover, that I ought by all means to come as quickly as possible to Syracuse, to take part in these doings; for he remembered how our mutual intercourse had easily worked him up to the desire of a life the most beautiful and best; which if he could but accomplish, as he was attempting to do, in the case of Dionysius, he had great hopes that he could, without slaughter and death, and the evils which have now taken place, make, in the whole of the country, life to be happy and rational.

With these correct sentiments Dion persuaded Dionysius to send for me; and he himself requested me by all means to come as quickly as possible, before certain other persons, associating with Dionysius, should turn him aside to a life different from the best. But it is necessary to relate what he requested, although it is a rather long story. What opportunity, said he, shall we wait for, greater than that through a certain divine fortune? and giving a statement of their command over Italy and Sicily, and of his own power in it, and of the youth of Dionysius, and of the desire he felt so vehemently for philosophy and instruction, and saying how his cousins and kindred were to be easily exhorted to the reasoning and mode of life ever laid down by myself, and that they were most competent to exhort Dionysius, so that now, if ever, all the hope would be fulfilled of the same persons becoming philosophers and rulers of mighty states. Such then and many others of a like kind were his exhortations. But a fear still possessed my mind, as to how, perchance, the conduct of the young men would turn out; for the passions of such persons are hasty, and are often borne along in a direction contrary to themselves. I knew, however, that Dion was naturally of a steady disposition and of a moderate age. Hence, while I was considering and doubting whether I ought to go, or how, the balance inclined that I ought (to go). For if perchance any one should attempt to give effect to my ideas upon laws and a form of government, I ought to attempt it now. For by persuading only one person, I should work out every good. With these ideas and confidence, and not from what some imagined, I set sail from home; feeling for myself the greatest shame, lest I should seem to myself to be altogether mere talk, and never willing to lay hold of any thing to be done; and run the risk of betraying first the hospitality and friendship of Dion, exposed in reality to no small dangers; and should he suffer aught, or, being driven out by Dionysius and his other enemies, fly to us, and, making an inquiry, say—"I am come to you, Plato, an exile; but I am neither in want of cavalry nor of heavy-armed soldiers to ward off my enemies, but of words and persuasion; by which I know you are especially able to turn young persons to what is good and just, and to place them on each occasion on terms of friendship and fellowship with each other; through the want of which on your part I have now left Syracuse, and am present here. What relates to myself indeed will bring upon you less disgrace; but the philosophy, which you are always praising, and which you say is held in dishonour by the rest of mankind, how is it not now betrayed by you together with myself, as far as depends upon you? If, indeed, we had been inhabitants of Megara, you would surely have come to me as an assistant for what I had called you, or I should have considered you the meanest of men. But now, excusing yourself by the length of the journey, and the danger of the voyage, and the greatness of the trouble, think you that you shall avoid perchance the charge of cowardice? It will be far from this."

To language like this, what would have been a becoming answer? There is none. But I came with reason and justice, as much as it is possible for a man, having left my own pursuits, which were not unbecoming, under a tyranny, which was neither suited to my discourses nor myself. But by my coming I liberated myself (from any charge), and exhibited myself to be unreproved by Zeus, who presides over hospitality and the allotment of philosophy, which would have been exposed to reproach, had I acted an effeminate part, and through cowardice shared in disgrace and shame. On my arrival then—for there is no need to be prolix—I found all the affairs of Dionysius full of sedition and calumnies on the part of a tyranny respecting Dion. I defended Dion, therefore, to the utmost of my power; but I was able to do but little. But nearly in the fourth

month after my arrrival, Dionysius accused Dion of plotting against
his power, and putting him on board a small vessel, sent him out
with dishonour. Whereupon all of us, who were the friends of Dion,
were fearful lest he should accuse and punish some one of us as an
accomplice in the plot of Dion. And a report went abroad at Syracuse, that I had been put to death by Dionysius, as being forsooth
the cause of all that happened at that time. But on perceiving that
we were all thus disposed, and dreading lest something of greater
consequence should arise from our fear, he received all of us most
kindly into his favour, consoled me, and exhorted me to be of good
cheer, and requested me by all means to stay; for there would be an
advantage to him from my not flying away, but from my remaining;
and on this account he pretended to make an urgent request. We
know however that the requests of tyrants are mingled with necessity. By a contrivance, therefore, he prevented my sailing-away. For
taking me to the Acropolis, he made me reside there; from whence
no ship-master could carry me off, not through Dionysius forbidding
it merely, but unless Dionysius himself sent a person with an order,
commanding him to lead me out. Nor was there any foreign trader,
nor even one of those having jurisdiction over the departures from
the country, who would have overlooked my going away alone; but
he would immediately have laid hold of me and brought me back
again to Dionysius; especially since it had been already bruited
abroad contrary to what had been done before, that Dionysius was
again holding Plato to his arms in a wonderful manner. And indeed
this was the case, for it is necessary to speak the truth. He did indeed
hold me to his arms, ever as time went on, more (and more) in
respect to the intercourse of my manner and habits. But he wished
me to praise him more than Dion, and to hold him as a friend in a
far greater degree than the other; and for such an end he made
wonderful efforts. But the way by which this might have taken place
in the best manner, if it took place at all, he omitted; for he shrunk
to become familiar and to associate with me, by hearing and
learning discourses on philosophy, through the fear lest, (according)
to the language of calumniators, he should be shackled, and Dion
administer all affairs. However I endured every thing, keeping to the

original sentiments, with which I arrived, if by any means he should come to the desire of a philosophic life. But he, by his pulling in a contrary direction, obtained the victory. In this way then happened to turn out the first period of my sojourning and pursuits in Sicily. After this I went away and came back again, through Dionysius having sent for me with all earnestness. But on what account (I came), and what I did, as being reasonable and just, I will, having first advised you what you ought to do, after what has just now taken place, subsequently relate in detail, for the sake of those who are inquiring with what view I came a second time to Sicily; and that deeds of no moment may not happen to be mentioned as deeds of moment.

I say then something what I ought to say. For the party, who gives advice to a sick man and to one who uses a diet improper for good health, it is especially necessary in the first place to change the mode of living, and to recommend to the patient willing to comply, the other things that are proper; but if he is unwilling, I consider that he, who retires from advising such a person, acts like a man and a physician; but that he, who stays, like a person unmanly and devoid of art. The same is the case of a state, whether its master be one or many. If, while the government is proceeding in a right road according to the constitution, it takes counsel about what is conducive to its interest, it is the part of a man with mind to give to such parties advice; but in the case of those, who are proceeding entirely out of a straightforward polity, and not at all willing to walk in its steps, and who proclaim to the adviser to leave alone the form of government, and not to disturb it since, if he does disturb it, he shall suffer death and at the same time exhort him to minister to their wishes and passions, and to advise in what way these may for all time to come be gratified, I should consider the person, who endures to give such advice, unmanly; but him, who does not endure, a man.

Holding then such sentiments, whenever any one consults with myself about any thing of the greatest moment relating to his life, such as the acquisition of wealth, or the care of his body or soul, I readily advise with him, if he appears to me to live day by day in an orderly manner, or is willing to be persuaded by me when giving advice, nor do I desist, as if I have gone through merely a formal rite. But if either he does not consult me at all, or is evidently not about to follow my advice, I do not go self-called to such a person to counsel him, nor would I do so by compulsion, even if he were my son. But I would give advice to a slave, and force him, even unwilling, (to follow it.) I should however think it not holy to force my father or mother, unless they were, through disease, afflicted with silliness. But if persons are living an established mode of life, pleasing to themselves, but not to me, I should not, when admonishing them in vain, dislike them, nor yet by flattering, minister to them, and afford them the means of gratifying their desires, which if I were to embrace, I should not wish to live. With the same sentiments respecting a state a prudent man ought to live, and speak out, if it appears to him not to have a good form of government, (and) if he is about not to speak in vain, nor to lose his life by speaking; but never to apply violence to his country on account of a change in the form of government, unless it cannot become the best without the banishment and slaughter of persons; but leading a quiet life, to pray for the good both of himself and of the state.

In this very manner I would advise you (to act); and so did I together with Dion advise Dionysius to live day by day, so that in the first place he might be about to become the master of himself, and acquire faithful friends and associates, in order that he might not suffer what his father did; who, after he had got possession of many and great cities in Sicily, which had been laid waste by the Barbarians, was not able to establish and preserve in each of them forms of government, faithful under his associates, or strangers coming from any part whatever, or brothers, whom he himself had brought up as being younger, and had made them rulers, after being merely private persons, and remarkably rich, after being (very) poor. For among these he could not attach to himself a single one as the sharer of his dominion, although working upon them by persuasion, and teaching, and kindnesses, and alliances; and he was sevenfold worse off than Darius; who, placing a trust in persons not his brothers, nor brought up by him, but in those alone associated with himself in their mastery over the eunuch, divided amongst them seven parts of his dominions, each larger than the whole of Sicily, and made use of them as faithful associates, and attacking neither himself, nor each other; and gave likewise an example of what a lawgiver and a king ought to be. For he established laws, by which he has preserved even now the Persian power; and besides this the Athenians, although they had not colonized themselves many Grecian cities, which had been overturned by the Barbarians, but merely got hold of them, when already inhabited, preserved their empire over them for seventy years, through having persons friendly to them in each of the towns. But Dionysius having through his wisdom brought together the whole of Sicily into one state, yet, through confiding in no one was with difficulty saved. For he was poor in persons friendly and faithful; than which there is no greater sign as regards virtue and vice, than in being destitute or not of men of that kind. I therefore and Dion advised Dionysius, since what he had received from his father had come to him unacquainted with instruction, and unacquainted too with befitting associates, in the first place to proceed in that direction to procure for himself friends, different from his relations, but both his equals in age and in accordance with him respecting virtue. But we particularly advised him to be in accord with himself; for that he was wonderfully deficient in this we asserted, not indeed in such clear terms—for this was not safe—but in hints and contending in our discourses, that in this way every man will preserve both himself and those over whom he is the ruler; but that by not turning himself in this direction he will bring to pass every thing the very reverse. But if, after going on, as we said, and rendering himself prudent and temperate, he peopled the cities of Sicily, that had been made desolate, and bound them together with laws and forms of government, so as to be of one family with himself and an assistance to each other against the Barbarians he would not only double his ancestral dominion, but make it in reality much larger. For if this were done, it would be much more easy to enslave the Carthaginians, than was the slavery effected by them during the reign of Gelon; but not as now on the contrary, his father fixed the tribute he was to carry to the Barbarians.

This is what was said and the advice given to Dionysius by us who were plotting against him, as the reports were circulated on many sides. Such, that after prevailing with Dionysius, they caused him to drive out Dion, and threw myself into a state of terror. But, that I may bring to a close not a few events which occurred in a short time, Dion, departing from Peloponnesus and Athens, admonished Dionysius indeed. Since then (Dion) had liberated and twice restored the town to the citizens, the Syracusans were affected in the same manner towards him, as Dionysius had been, when he endeavoured by educating and bringing him up to make him thus a worthy partner of his power through the whole of life. But (he gave his ear) to those that were calumniating Dion, and saying that he was doing all that he did at that time, while plotting against the absolute power of Dionysius, in order that the one, being lulled in his mind by his attention to instruction, might neglect his kingdom, and commit it to Dion, and the other make it his own by fraud, and cast out Dionysius from his dominions.

These reports being then bruited a second time among the Syracusans prevailed by a victory very absurd and disgraceful to those who were the causes of it. For how it happened it is proper for those to hear, who are calling upon me on the subject of the present affairs.

Being an Athenian, and the associate of Dion, and one who had battled with him against the tyrant, I arrived, that I might produce a peace instead of a war; but while battling against the calumniators I was overcome. But Dionysius, attempting to bribe me by honours and riches, to become on his side a witness and a friend, touching the propriety of his casting out Dion, failed in all of these things happening to him. And Dion afterwards, on returning home from exile, brought with him two Athenian brothers, who had become his friends, not through philosophy, but through that acquaintance, which runs through the generality of friends, and which they formed [513] from paying the rites of hospitality, and from being Mystæ and Epoptæ. Moreover these two, by having brought Dion back, had become his friends, and, from such causes, and the assisting him in his return from exile, his companions. But when, on their arrival in Sicily, they understood that Dion had been exposed by those Siceliotes, who had become free through him, to the calumny of plotting to become a tyrant, they not only betrayed their associate and guest, but became, as it were, the perpetrators of a murder, in that, with weapons in their hands, they stood by to assist the murderers. However, I neither pass by this base and unholy deed, nor do I detail it; for to many others it (has been) a care to hymn it, and it will be so at some future time.

But the charge, which has been alleged respecting the Athenians, how that it was they, who bound this disgrace around the city, I will take away. For I say that he too was an Athenian, who did not betray this very person, when it was in his power to obtain wealth and many other honours. For he did not become a friend through a shop-mate friendship, but through the communion of a liberal education; to which alone he, who is endued with mind, ought to trust, rather than to the alliance of souls and bodies; so that those two were not fit to bring disgrace on the city through having murdered Dion, as being persons of no account at any time. All this has been said for the sake of the advice given to the friends and kindred of Dion.

I give you besides the same counsel, and for the third time address you three in the same words. Do not place Sicily, or any other city, as a slave under persons with despotic power, but under laws; such at least is my dictum. For this is not the better either for the enslaving or the enslaved, or for their [514] children or their children's descendants; but the experiment is altogether a destructive one. For souls, whose habits are little and illiberal, love to seize upon gain of this kind, as knowing nothing of what is good and just for the future and present time, nor of things human and divine. Of this I endeavoured to persuade Dion first, and secondly Dionysius, and now I do you the third. Be persuaded then by me, for the sake of Zeus the third saviour. In the next place look to the case of Dionysius and Dion; the former of whom by not being persuaded is now living not honourably; whereas the latter, by being persuaded, died honourably. For it is a thing altogether correct and honourable for him, who aspires after things the most honourable both for himself and his country, to suffer whatever he may suffer; for not one of us is naturally immortal; nor, if this should happen to any one, would he become happy, as it seems he would to the multitude. For in things inanimate there is nothing either good or evil worthy of mention; but good or ill will happen to each soul, either existing with the body or separated from it. But it is ever requisite to trust really to the sacred accounts of the olden time, which inform us that the soul is immortal, and has judges of its conduct, and suffers the greatest punishments, when it is liberated from the body. Hence it is requisite to think it is a lesser evil to suffer, than to do, the greatest sins and injuries. This, indeed, the man who is fond of money and poor in soul does not hear; and should he hear, he laughs it down, as he imagines, and impudently snatches from all sides whatever he thinks he can, like a wild beast, eat or drink, or can contribute (aught) to the miscalled pleasure of sexual intercourse, at once servile and graceless. (For) being blind, he is not able to see how great an evil, ever united to each act of wrong, follows the never being satisfied with the unholy perpetration of such snatchings; which it is necessary for him, who has acted unjustly, to drag along with himself, both while he is moving about upon the earth, and when he takes under the earth a journey without honour, and thoroughly miserable in every way.

By detailing these and other reasons of the like kind, I was enabled to persuade Dion. And I should have felt most justly against those, who murdered him, an anger, in a certain manner, almost as great as against Dionysius; for both had injured myself and all the rest, so to say, in the highest degree. For the former had destroyed a man, who was willing to make use of justice; while the latter (was) unwilling to make use of it through the whole of his dominions, although possessing the greatest power. In which (dominions) had philosophy and power existed really, as it were in the same (dwelling), they would have set up amongst all men, both Greeks and Barbarians, an opinion not vainly shining, (and) in every respect the true one, that neither a state nor a man can ever be happy, unless by leading a life with prudence in subjection to justice, whether possessing those things themselves, or by being brought up in the habits of holy persons their rulers, or instructed in justice.

This injury did Dionysius inflict. But the rest would have been a trifling wrong, as compared to these. But he, who murdered Dion, did not know that he had done the same deed [516] as Dionysius. For I clearly know, as far as it is possible for one man to speak confidently of another, that if Dion had retained his power, he would never have changed it to any other form of government than to that, by which he first (caused) Syracuse, his own country, after he had delivered it from slavery, to look joyous, and had put it into the garb of freedom; and after this, he would by every contrivance have adorned the citizens with laws both befitting and the best; and he would have been ready to do what followed in due order after this; and have colonized the whole of Sicily, and have freed it from the Barbarians, by expelling some and subduing others, more easily than Hiero did. But if these things had taken place, through a man just, and brave, and temperate, and who was a philosopher, the same opinion of virtue would have been produced amongst the multitude, as would have been amongst all men, so to say; and have saved Dionysius, had he been persuaded by me. But now some dæmon surely, or some evil spirit, falling upon with iniquity and impiety, and, what is the greatest matter, with the audacity of ignorance, in which all evils are rooted, and from which they spring up, and afterwards produce fruit the most bitter to those, who have begotten it, this has a second time subverted and destroyed every [517] thing. However, let us, for the sake of a good augury, keep for the third time a well-omened silence.

I advise therefore you, my friends, to imitate Dion, in the goodwill he felt for his country, and in his temperate mode of living, but for the better. But under what auspices you ought to endeavour to fulfil his wishes, and what they are, you have clearly heard from me. But upon the person, who is among you unable to live according to his country's customs in a Dorian fashion, but adopts the life of the murderers of Dion, and what is followed in Sicily, do not call; nor believe that he will in any thing ever act faithfully and sincerely. But call upon the rest to form a settlement of the whole of Sicily, and introduce both from Sicily itself and all Peloponnesus an equality of laws, and do not fear the Athenians; for men are there, who surpass all others in virtue, and who hate the daring of guest-murderers.

But if these things be done at a later period, and the differences, produced each day by factions, are many and of all kinds and hasten you on, it is requisite surely for every man, to whom a divine fortune has imparted even a small degree of correct thinking, to know that there will be no cessation of evils to those engaged in revolts, until the victors in battle and in the banishment and slaughter of persons shall cease to have a recollection of wrongs, and to turn themselves to the punishment of their opponents; but, having a mastery over themselves, shall lay down laws common to all, and no less acceptable to themselves than to the vanquished party, and compel them to use these laws, by the two-fold necessity of fear and shame; of fear, through their being superior, by showing their strength; and of shame, on the other hand, through their seeming to be superior in the being both willing and able to be (the masters) over pleasures, and the slaves of [518] the laws. For it is not possible otherwise for a state, divided against itself, to cease from ills; but divisions and enmity, and hatred and distrust, are ever wont to arise in states thus arrayed themselves against themselves. It is then ever requisite for those, who have gained the power, when they are desirous of preserving it, to choose from amongst themselves, in preference to the rest, such as they hear are the best; in the first place, old men, who have children and wives at home, and ancestors the most in number and renown, and all possessing a competence. Now for a city of ten thousand persons fifty such will be sufficient. These should be sent for from their home with prayers and the greatest honours possible; and they, who have sent for them, should take an oath, and beg and request them to lay down laws, and give not more to the victors than to the vanquished, but what is equal for, and common to, the whole state; and when the laws have been fixed, all things are in this. For when the victors exhibit themselves more subject to the laws than the vanquished, all things will be full of security and felicity, and there will be an escape from every ill.

But if not, call not upon me or any other to take a part for him, who is not persuaded by the precepts now conveyed. For these are the sisters of what I and Dion did with good intentions attempt to do for Syracuse; although they were, on the second occasion; for the first were those, which were first attempted to be done in conjunction [519] with Dionysius, a common good to all. But a certain fortune, superior to man, scattered them all. Do you then attempt to accomplish all at present more prosperously, with the aid of some kind destiny, and a luck god-sent. And thus much be it said about my advice and letter, and first visit to Dionysius.

But in my second journey and voyage to Sicily, how reasonably and carefully they took place, he, who feels any interest may hear what followed. For the first period of my sojourn in Sicily passed away, as I have stated, before I could advise the relatives and associates of Dion. But subsequently I persuaded Dionysius, as far as I was able, to let me go. But on peace being made—for there had been then a war in Sicily—we both came to an agreement; for Dionysius said that he would send for Dion and myself again, after he had established for himself a state of affairs connected with his government more securely than before; and he thought it proper for Dion to understand that this was not a banishment at that time, but merely a change of residence. And on these conditions I agreed to come.

On peace being made, Dionysius sent for me; but he requested Dion to stop another year; but he thought it proper for myself to come by all means. Dion then exhorted and entreated me to set sail. For a strong report had gone abroad from Sicily, that Dionysius had become again wonderfully eager after philosophy at that moment; and on this account Dion earnestly begged of me not to decline the invitation. But I knew that many such things happen to young men in the case of philosophy. However it seemed to me to be more safe, at least at that time, to bid a long farewell to Dionysius and Dion; and I gave offence to both by answering that I was an old man; and that nothing of what was now being done had taken place according to the agreement. But after this it seems that Archytas had betaken himself to Dionysius; now [520] before my departure having made a hospitable and friendly acquaintance with Archytas, and certain other Tarentines, the guests and friends of Dionysius, I sailed away. There were likewise certain other persons at Syracuse, who had heard some of the doctrines of Dion, and among these some others, filled with wrong notions about philosophy, and who seemed to me to attempt to discourse with Dionysius about things of this kind, as if Dionysius had heard all such matters as I had in my thoughts. But in other respects he was not without natural talent or the power to learn, and had a love of honour in a wonderful degree. Perhaps then the discourse of these men was pleasing to him, and he was manifestly ashamed that he heard nothing from me when I was sojourning there. Hence he came the same time to the longing to hear me more clearly, and at the same time his love of honour urged him on. But on what account he did not hear me during my first sojourn, I have detailed in the account given above.

After I had returned home safe, and refused on his inviting me a second time, as I have just now mentioned, Dionysius appeared to be thoroughly on fire through his love of honour, lest I should seem to some persons to hold him in contempt, and that, as being acquainted with his nature and habits, and mode of living, I was unwilling to be annoyed by going to him. But I am justified in speaking the truth, and in enduring, if any one, on hearing what had occurred, should despise my philosophy, and think that the tyrant possessed a mind. For Dionysius sent to me the third time a trireme for the sake of making easy the voyage. He sent also Archedemus, whom he [521] thought I valued the most of all the associates of Archytas, who were then in Sicily, and others of his (own) acquaintances. And all these told to us the same story, that Dionysius had wonderfully increased in philosophy. He sent too a long letter, well knowing how I was affected towards Dion, and that Dion was desirous I should set sail and come to Syracuse. With a view to all these particulars, therefore, the letter was composed, and at the commencement it said somehow to this effect "Dionysius to Plato." After saying what usually follows, he said nothing previous to this, except that "should you at my persuasion come now to Sicily, in the first place the matters relating to Dion shall be put into a train in the way you may wish yourself; for I know that you wish what is moderate, and I will accede to them; otherwise nothing that relates to the affairs of Dion, nor upon other points, nor as regards himself, will take place." This is what he said. But the rest that was said would be here prolix, and foreign to the purpose. Other letters likewise came to me from Archytas, and others at Tarentum, speaking in high terms of the love of wisdom shown by Dionysius; and that, unless I came now, I should bring into a state of calumny the friendship existing with Dionysius, which had been effected through me, and which was of no little moment to their political affairs.

Such then being the state at that time of the sending for me, some of those from Sicily and Italy dragging me thither, and others at Athens pushing me away plainly by their entreaties, the same reason returned, that I ought not to betray Dion, nor my guests and friends at Tarentum; and it [522] occurred to me, that it was nothing wonderful that a young man, who had heard incorrectly of things worthy of mention, should come with a docile spirit to the love of the best life; and that I ought to prove clearly, in what state the matter stood, and not by any means to betray it, nor to become myself the cause of a disgrace so truly great, if the case was in reality such as reported. Clothing myself then in this reasoning, I departed, fearing much, and prophesying, as it seems, not altogether well. Arriving then the third time, for the saviour this at least I did in reality. For I was again luckily saved. And for this it is meet for me to give thanks to Dionysius, after the deity, because, when many were wishing to destroy me, he prevented them, and gave up to pity some portion of my affairs. When therefore I arrived, I thought I ought first to obtain some proof whether Dionysius was in reality touched by philosophy, as by a fire, or whether this great report had come to Athens in vain. Now there is a certain method of making an experiment upon matters of this kind, by no means ignoble, but truly adapted to tyrants, and especially to such as are full of incorrect notions; which, as soon as I arrived, I perceived was very much the case with Dionysius. To such it is requisite to show what (philosophy) is, and of what kind, and through how great deeds how great a labour it demands. For he who hears this, if he is truly a lover of wisdom, and related to it, and worthy of it, as being a divine person, thinks he has heard of some wonderful road, and that he ought forthwith to betake himself to it, and that life is not to be endured by him, who acts otherwise. After this he does not, putting both himself and his leader on the stretch, give up the road, until he puts a finish upon all things, or obtains a power so as not to be unable to conduct himself without a person to show the road. [523] In this way and with these thoughts does such a person live, acting (correctly) in whatever transactions he may be engaged; but before all things perpetually keeping close to philosophy, and (making use of) that food for the day, which may especially render him quick to learn, and of a good memory, and able to reason in himself, by abstaining from wine; and by which he becomes the hater of a practice contrary to this.

But they, who are not lovers of wisdom in reality, but have a coating of colour in their opinions, like those, whose bodies are sunburnt, when they perceive how many things are to be learnt, and how great is the labour, and what temperance in daily food is requisite for that thing, they deem it too difficult and beyond their powers, and become unable to attend to it at all. But some of them persuade themselves that they have sufficiently heard the whole, and want no further exertions. This kind of experiment is clear and the most safe, when employed in the case of those living luxuriously and unable to endure labour, through the person throwing the blame not upon the guide but on himself, as being unable to attend to all that is requisite for the matter in hand.

In this way was, what has been now stated, mentioned to Dionysius. But neither did I detail them all, nor did Dionysius require it. For many things, and of the greatest moment, he pretended to possess sufficiently himself through the incorrect notions he had heard from others. And I hear that he afterwards wrote about what he had then heard, as if he were composing what was his own art, when there was nothing of his own, as I hear. However, of this I know nothing. But I know that certain others have written about the same things, but who they are not they themselves. [524]

Thus much however I can say about all, who either have writ-

ten, or shall write, and state that they know about what things I am
occupied, whether they have heard from myself or others, or have
discovered themselves, that it is not possible for them to know any
thing according to my opinions upon the matter; for there is not,
and never will be, any composition of mine about them. For a
matter of that kind cannot be expressed by words, like other things
to be learnt; but by a long intercourse with the subject and living
with it a light is kindled on a sudden, as if from a leaping fire, and
being engendered in the soul, feeds itself upon itself. Thus much I
know, however, that what has been written or said by me, has been
said in the best manner; and moreover that what has been written
badly, does not pain me in the least.

But if it had appeared to me that such matters could be written
or spoken of sufficiently before the masses, what could have been
done by us more beautiful in life than to impart a great benefit to
mankind, and to bring nature to light before all? I think, however,
that the attempt in favour of such being promulgated, would not be
beneficial except to a few, who are able with a little showing to make
discoveries for themselves. But of the rest, some it will fill not
correctly with a contempt by no means in reason, and others with a
lofty and vain hope, as if they had learnt something solemn. And it
has now come into my mind to say something further still. For
perhaps by what I am about to say a portion of what has been said
will become more clear. For a certain true account is the antagonist
of him, who dares to write any thing whatever about matters of this
kind; and which, although it has been stated by me frequently
before, seems it must be stated at present likewise.

There are three things belonging to each of those, through
which it is necessary for science to be produced. But the fourth is
science itself. And as to the fifth, it is requisite to establish that which
is known and true. Of these one is its name; the second its definition; the third its resemblance; the fourth its science. Now if you are
desirous of understanding what has been just now asserted
respecting one example, take it, and imagine thus respecting all. A
circle is called something, to which there is the name we have just
mentioned. Its definition is the second thing, composed of nouns

and verbs. For that, which is every where equally distant from the extremes to the middle, would be the definition of that, to which the name is of a round, and a circumference, and a circle. But the third is the circle, painted or blotted out, and made by a turner's wheel, or destroyed. By none of which accidents is the circle itself, of which all these properties are predicated, affected, as being of a different nature. But the fourth is science and intellect, and a correct opinion about them. And the whole of this again must be laid down as one thing, which exists neither in voice, nor in a corporeal figure, but is in the soul; by which circumstance it is manifest, that there is something different from the nature itself of the circle, and the three previously mentioned. But among the number of these, intellect, by its relation and similitude, approaches the nearest to the fifth; while the rest are more remote. The same is the case with respect to a thing straight, and circular, and with figure, and with colour, and of a thing good, and beautiful, and just, and of every body, both fashioned by the hand, and produced according to nature, and of fire, and water, and all things of that kind, and of every animal, and of the habit in souls, and of all actions and passions. For unless a person does, after a certain manner, understand of these things all the four, he will never perfectly participate in the science relating to the fifth. Moreover these (four) no less endeavour to show forth the quality, as respects each thing, than the being of each, through the want of power in words. On this account, no one possessing a mind will ever dare to place under the same view, and this [526] too never to be changed, the objects, which are perceived by the mind, and those, that are represented by figures, which is the case with those four.

And this again, what has just now been said, it is requisite to learn. Every circle described by its doings, or fashioned by a turner's wheel, is full of that, which is contrary to the fifth; for it every where touches upon the straight line. But we assert that the circle in the abstract has neither more nor less in itself of a contrary nature; and we assert too, that there is no fixed name for anything; for there is nothing to prevent things, that are now called round, from being called straight, and those straight, round; nor will there be any less stability in them, when they are changed and called by a contrary name. The same assertion is likewise true of a definition, that, since it is composed of nouns and verbs, there is nothing stable in a sufficiently stable manner. And there is an infinity of reasons respecting each of the four, that it is uncertain. But what is of the greatest moment is, that since there are, as I have stated a little before, two things, being and quality, when the soul seeks to know, not the quality of a thing, but [527] what it is, unless each of these four previously sought for by the soul through reason and effect, and at last turns out correctly discussed by the senses, through all things that are said and shown, it fills every man, so to say, with all doubt and uncertainty.

In such cases then as through a depraved education we are not accustomed to seek the truth, but the image of it, which is placed before us, is sufficient (for us to touch upon), we do not become ridiculous to each other, the interrogated to the interrogating; but we are able to bandy about those four, and to examine them. But in such cases as we compel a person to exhibit that fifth, any one of those, who are able to reply, and to overthrow, is the superior, and causes him, who is explaining (this fifth) either by speech, or writing, or answers, to appear to the multitude of his hearers entirely ignorant of the things, about which he attempts either to write or speak, persons being sometimes ignorant, that it is not the soul of the writer or speaker that is confuted, but the nature of each of the four (spoken of), when it is existing improperly. But the procession through all these, while changing its place towards each upwards and downwards, scarcely at length generates the knowledge of a thing existing naturally well in a person existing naturally well. But when it exists naturally [528] ill, as exists naturally the habit of the soul of the multitude, with respect to learning, and to what are called morals, and these are depraved, not even Lynceus himself can cause such as these to see. And in one word, neither docility in learning nor memory will cause (a person to do so), who is not germane to the matter; for they are not originally inherent in foreign habits; so that neither they, who are not naturally close to, and allied with, what is just, and the other things that are beautiful, but are docile and of a good memory, some with respect to some things, and others to others, nor they, who are allied, but are indocile and of a bad memory, will ever learn, as far as is possible, the truth relating to virtue and vice. For it is necessary to learn these, and at the same time the falsehood and truth of the whole of being, with all exertion and much time, as I stated at the commencement. But after each of these have been rubbed together, names and definitions, and the sense of seeing, and (the other) senses, and have been tried by tests in a kindly spirit, and by questions and answers without a feeling of envy, there has with difficulty shone forth an intellectual perception respecting each, and a mind putting itself on the stretch, as far as it is possible for human power to do so.

On this account, let every careful man be very far from writing about things truly worthy of care, lest at some time, by writing amongst men, he throw (himself) into envy and [529] difficulties. But, in one word, it is requisite to know from hence, when any one sees the writings of another, either of a legislator upon laws, or of any person whatever upon other subjects, that these are not those, on which he has been the most careful, if he is himself a careful person; but that the objects of his pursuit are situated some where in a country the most beautiful. But if the subjects, on which he has been the most careful, are committed to writing, then not the gods but men themselves have their own intellect destroyed.

Now he, who follows this story and digression, will understand correctly whether Dionysius has written any thing of the highest and first kind respecting nature, or any other person inferior or superior to him; since, according to my reasoning he has neither heard or learnt any thing sound about what he has written; for he would have venerated them equally with myself, nor have dared to cast them forth into a state unfitting and unbecoming; nor has he written about them for the sake of remembering them; since there is no fear that any one will ever forget them, if he has once comprehended them by the soul; for of all things they lie in the smallest compass. But (perhaps he did so) for the sake of base ambition, considering them as his own, or as sharing in a kind of instruction, of which he was unworthy, and loving the renown arising from such a participation.

If however this occurred to Dionysius after one meeting, the fact may be so. But let Zeus, says the Theban, know how it occurred. For I went through these matters, as I have said, only once; and never afterwards at all. In the next [530] place, he, who is interested in discovering what occurred relating to those matters, and how it occurred, ought to consider through what reason it was we did not go through them a second and a third time and oftener; whether it was that Dionysius, having heard them only once, thought he knew them, and did know them, sufficiently? or that he discovered them himself, or had learnt them previously from others, or that what had been said was trifling? or thirdly, that they were not according to his standard, but greater; and that thus he would not be able to live, if he paid any regard to prudence and virtue? For if (it be said that he considered) the matters frivolous, he will oppose many witnesses, who assert the contrary, and who are much more competent to judge about things of this kind than Dionysius; but if, that he discovered or learnt them, and that they are worthily suited for the instruction of a liberal soul, how should he, not being a wondrous man himself, have so readily dishonoured the leader and the lord in these matters?

And how he did dishonour him, I will relate. After an interval of no long time, although he had previously permitted Dion to possess and enjoy his property, he did not permit his guardians to send it to Peloponnesus, as if he had entirely forgotten his letter; for (he said) it was not Dion, but Dion's son, of whom, as being his own nephew, he was according to law the guardian. Such were the transactions of that time that took place up to this period. And from these occurrences I clearly saw the desire Dionysius had for philosophy; and it was lawful for me to be indignant, whether I wished it or not. For it was already summer at that time, and ships were sailing out. But it seemed I ought not to be more offended with Dionysius than with myself, and with those, who compelled me to come the third time to the strait about Scylla, [531]

"And dread Charybdis measure still again." [*Odyss.* xii, 428] and to tell Dionysius, that it was impossible for me to stay with him, while Dion was treated so dirtily. But he soothed me, and begged me to stay, thinking it would not be well for him should I be so swift a messenger of such doings; but unable to persuade me, he said he would prepare the means of sending me away. However, I determined to go on board and sail amongst the vessels outward bound, being enraged, and thinking I ought to suffer every thing, if he should attempt to stop me, as I had been injured, although I had plainly done no injury. But on seeing that I had no desire at all to stay, he devised a plan of this kind, for delaying my sailing away. On the day after this had taken place, he plausibly addresses me. From myself and you, said he, let Dion, and the affairs of Dion, be removed out of the way, for the sake of our (not) being frequently at variance about them. For I will, said he, thus act on your account, to Dion. I think it right for him to take away his property and to reside in Peloponnesus, not as an exile, but as one, who may come hither, when it shall seem good to him, to me, and to you who are his friends; and this shall be, if he forms no plot against myself; and you, and your relations, and his here shall be his sureties; and let him give you a guarantee; and let the property, which he takes away, be deposited in Peloponnesus and at Athens, with those you shall think fit; and let Dion enjoy the use of it, but not the power to take it away without your consent; for I have not any very great trust in him that, if he can use the property, he will be just towards myself; for it will not be trifling. But I have greater confidence in you and yours. See, therefore, if this is agreeable to you, and remain on these terms for this year, and then depart to your well-doing, taking with you the property; and well I know, that Dion will be greatly indebted to you for having managed matters in this way on his behalf.

On hearing this speech I felt indignant; but still I said I [532] would take counsel of myself until the following day on these points, and communicate my resolves. This was our compact at that time. I hereupon, being all alone, and very confused, took counsel of myself. And this consideration first presented itself as taking the lead in my designs. What, if Dionysius intends to do nothing that he says, but on my departure both he and many others of his friends should write in a plausible manner to Dion, what he has now said to me, that Dionysius indeed was willing, but I unwilling, for him to do what he urged me, and that I entirely neglected his concerns; and moreover should Dionysius be unwilling to send me away, and himself give no orders to any master of a vessel (to take me), and easily signify to all men, that I was sailing away without his consent, what sailor would be willing to take me on board, while I was hastening from the dwelling of Dionysius? For in addition to other evils, I dwelt in the garden which surrounds the dwelling, from whence the porter would not be willing to let me out, unless an order were sent from Dionysius. And should I remain a year, I could indeed send an account of these doings to Dion, and in what state I was, and what I was doing. But should Dionysius do aught of what he says, my conduct would be not entirely ridiculous; for perhaps the property of Dion, if one rightly values it, is not less than a hundred talents. But if what is now looming should, as is likely, take place, I shall be at a loss how to conduct myself. At the same time it is perhaps necessary for me to labour for a year longer, and to endeavour to prove the designs of Dionysius by his deeds.

Having thus determined with myself, I told Dionysius on the following day that I had made up my mind to stay. I hold it right however, said I, for you not to consider me as the master of Dion, and that you should, together with myself, send letters to inform him of the determination, and to ask him whether he was satisfied? and if not, whether he wished for [533] and demanded any thing else? and to send word as soon as possible; but that you should do nothing new in his affairs. This was said (by me), and this agreement did we make nearly in the manner just now detailed.

After this the vessels sailed, and it was no longer possible for me to depart; when Dionysius, while speaking, remembered that the half of Dion's property ought to remain with his son, and that the other half should be sent to Dion; and he said he would sell it, and after it had been sold, deliver one half to myself to send to Dion, and leave the other half for his son; for that this would be the most equitable arrangement. Astonished at the statement, I thought it would be very ridiculous to say any thing further. I told him however, that we ought to wait for the letter from Dion, and again send him an account of these matters. But Dionysius immediately after this did, in a very bold manner, sell the whole of Dion's property at what time, and in what manner and to whomsoever he pleased; nor did he say any thing whatever about it to myself; and in like manner I said nothing to him about the affairs of Dion; for I thought I should be able to do nothing more in the matter.

Thus far was assistance given by myself to philosophy and my friends. But after this, I and Dionysius were so living, that I, like a bird, was (always) looking out, and longing to fly away; while he was devising in what manner he might frighten me off, and give up none of the property of Dion. We gave out however through the whole of Sicily, that we were friends forsooth.

Dionysius had attempted to reduce the pay of the veteran mercenaries now to a lower rate than according to the custom of his father; and the soldiers, being enraged, collected together in a body, and declared they would not permit it. [534] Dionysius therefore endeavoured to force them, by closing the gates of the Acropolis; but the soldiers immediately rushed to the walls, raising a kind of barbarous cry and warlike pæaean; at which Dionysius being terrified, conceded all demands, and even more to those of the light-shield-bearers, who had been collected together. But a report was quickly spread, that Heracleides was the cause of this disturbance. On hearing which, Heracleides took himself out of the way and disappeared, while Dionysius endeavoured to lay hold of him; but being in a difficulty, he sent for Theodotes to come to the garden, in which I happened to be then walking. Now of the rest of their discourse I neither knew nor heard; but what Theodotes said in my presence to Dionysius, I both know and remember. For, said he, Plato, I am persuading Dionysius here, that if I am able to bring Heracleides hither to a conference respecting the charges now laid against him, and if it does not seem good (to Dionysius) for him to dwell in Sicily, I think it is proper for him to take his wife and son, and sail to Peloponnesus, and reside there, doing no injury at all to Dionysius, and enjoying his own property. I have therefore sent to him already, and I will now send to him again. But whether he hearkens to my first or second application, I deem it right to request of Dionysius, that if any one falls in with Heracleides, either in the country or here, no ill shall happen to him, but that he shall be removed from the country, until Dionysius shall decide upon something else. To this, said he, do you accede? addressing Dionysius. He answered, I do accede; nor shall he suffer any ill, contrary to what has now been stated, should he make his appearance at your house.

However, on the evening of the following day, Eurybius and Theodotes came to me in great haste and wonderfully alarmed; and Theodotes said to me, Plato, you were present yesterday at the compact which Dionysius made with me and you respecting Heracleides? To which I replied, How not? But now, says he, the soldiers with light shields are running all round seeking to lay hold of Heracleides; and it appears almost that he is some where here. Follow us then, by all means, to Dionysius. We went therefore and came to him; and they indeed stood silent and in tears, but I said, These persons, Dionysius, are afraid lest you should do something of a novel kind to Heracleides, contrary to the compact made yesterday; for it seems to me, that he has returned and is clearly some where here. And he, on hearing this, burnt with rage, and assumed all kinds of colours such as a person in anger does. But Theodotes falling at his feet, and laying hold of his hand, burst into tears, and implored him not to do any such thing. Then I, taking up the discourse, consoled him and said, Cheer up, Theodotes; for Dionysius will not dare to act contrary to the compact made yesterday. But he looking at me, and in a very tyrannic manner, With you, says he, I made no compact, either great or small. By the gods, said I, you (did agree not to do) what this man now requests you not to do. After saying this, I turned from him and went out.

After this Dionysius endeavoured to hunt down Heracleides. Theodotes, however, sent messengers to him, and exhorted him to fly. But Dionysius sent Tisias and the soldiers with light shields, and ordered them to pursue him. Heracleides, however, as it is said, anticipated them, and escaped in the small part of a day into the dominions of the Carthaginians. Hereupon the old plot for his not giving up the property of Dion seemed to Dionysius to offer a plau-

sible pretext of enmity against myself. And in the first place he sent
me from the Acropolis, framing an excuse, that it was requisite for
the women to perform some ten-day sacrifice in the gardens where I
resided. He therefore ordered me to remain out during that period
with Archidemus. While I was there, Theodotes sent for me, and felt
very indignant respecting the transactions of that time, and found
fault with Dionysius; who, hearing that I had been with Theodotes,
made this another pretext, and the sister to the former, for enmity
against me, and sent a person to ask me, whether I had really been
with Theodotes on his sending for me? and I readily replied, I had.
The [536] party therefore said, Dionysius has ordered me to tell
you, that you are acting by no means correctly in always making
much of Dion and the friends of Dion. This is what was said; and
after this Dionysius never again sent for me to his residence; as it
was now clear that I was the friend of Theodotes and Heracleides,
and his enemy; and he no longer considered me well affected
towards him, because the property of Dion had been consumed
entirely.

After this I dwelt out of the Acropolis among the mercenary
soldiers; but others, Athenians, and some likewise my fellow-citizens,
who were in the service of Dionysius, came and told me that I had
been calumniated by the light-shield soldiers, and that certain
persons had threatened to kill me, if they could lay hold of me. I
devised therefore the following plan for my preservation. I sent to
Archytas, and other friends at Tarentum, telling them in what state I
happened to be; and they, making some pretext of an embassy to
the city, sent a ship of thirty oars, and Lamiscus, one of my friends;
who, on his arrival, made a request to Dionysius on my behalf,
saying that I wished to depart, and begged of him not to act otherwise. And he consented, and sent me away after providing me with
means for the voyage. However, I neither asked for the property of
Dion, nor did any one give it me.

On reaching Peloponnesus at the Olympic games, I met with
Dion, who was a spectator there, and I told him what had
happened. And he, calling Jupiter to witness, immediately declared
to me and my relations and friends, that he would prepare to

revenge himself upon Dionysius, both for his having deceived me, his guest—for thus he spoke and thought—and for his own unjust expulsion and banishment. On hearing this, I advised him to call upon his friends, if they were willing. But as for myself, I said, you together with others had by force caused me in some manner to share in the food, and the hearth, and the sacred rites of Dionysius; who perhaps has thought, in consequence of many calumniating [537] me, that I was plotting in conjunction with you against him and his tyranny, and yet he did not put me to death, but treated me with respect. Besides I am of an age to take a part with scarcely any one in war; but I would be a common friend to you all, if at any time in want of a friendly feeling towards each other you should wish to do any good; but if you are desirous (of doing) evil, call upon others. This did I say through a feeling of disgust to my wandering about Sicily, and adverse fortune in it.

By not obeying and being not persuaded by the reasonings (urged) by myself, they have been themselves the cause of all the evils that have at present happened to them; of which nothing, humanly speaking, would have occurred, had Dionysius given Dion his own property, or had been perfectly reconciled to him. For I could easily have restrained Dion from both by my will and power. But now they have rushed against each other, and filled all things with evils. And yet Dion had the same wish, which I would say both myself and any other moderate person ought to have, who should consider, touching his own power, and that of his friends, and of his own city, how, by doing a benefit when in power, things of the greatest moment would be in the greatest honour. But this will be, not if a person enrich himself and his friends and city, by laying plots and bringing together conspirators, when he is poor and has no command over himself, through his yielding to cowardice, as [538] regards pleasures, and subsequently by destroying those, who possess property, and, calling them enemies, scatters the wealth of such persons, and exhorts his fellow-doers and friends (so to act), that no one shall, by saying that he is poor, bring a charge against him. After the same manner, he who benefits his city, will be honoured by it, in consequence of distributing by voting the property of a few among the many; or when any one being the president of a great city, and one ruling over many lesser cities, unjustly distributes to his own city the property of the lesser. For in this way, neither Dion, nor any other person, will ever voluntarily proceed to power, pernicious to himself and family for all time, but to a form of government and the establishment of laws, the most just and best, and effected through the fewest deaths and banishments.

This conduct did Dion lately adopt, by choosing to suffer rather than to do unholy deeds, yet taking care lest he should suffer; still, however, did he stumble, after he had arrived at the very point of being superior to his foes. Nor did he suffer any thing to be wondered at. For a man holy, temperate, and prudent, will never be deceived entirely respecting unholy things, respecting the soul of such. But it would perhaps be not wonderful, should he suffer the suffering of a good pilot, from whom a storm about to be has not entirely lain hid; but from whom the violence unusually great and unexpected of tempests may have lain hid, and, having lain hid, have by their force overwhelmed him. The same thing upon a small scale caused Dion to stumble. For they, who tripped [539] him up did not lie hid from him, as being wicked men; but what a depth of ignorance, and of the rest of depravity, and greediness insatiable they possessed, this did lie hid; and stumbling on this point, he lies (dead), and Sicily wraps in sorrow infinite.

What therefore I advise you to do, after the facts just now detailed, has been nearly told, and let them be told. But it appeared to me necessary to show, why I undertook the second journey to Sicily, and, as it were; of somewhat a compulsory kind, on account of the absurdity and irrationality attached to the transactions. If then what has been now said has appeared to any one to be more reasonable, and it seems to any one that the excuses for what have occurred are sufficient, what has been now said will have been (said) moderately and sufficiently (well).

Printed in the USA
CPSIA information can be obtained
at www.ICGtesting.com
LVHW090840161023
761116LV00061B/619